Photography, Trace, and Trauma

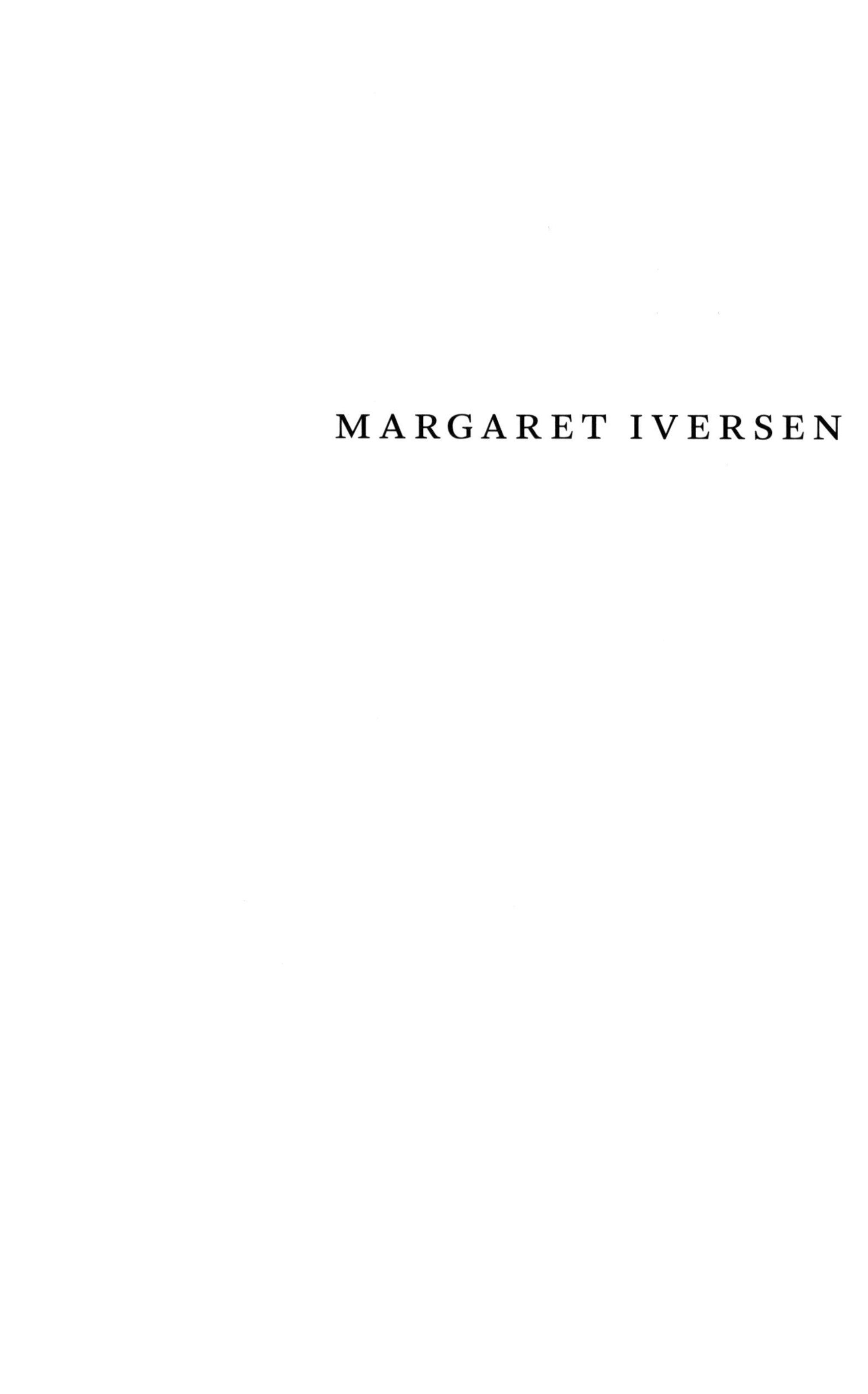

MARGARET IVERSEN

Photography

Trace and Trauma

THE UNIVERSITY OF CHICAGO PRESS   CHICAGO AND LONDON

The University of Chicago Press, Chicago 60637
The University of Chicago Press, Ltd., London
© 2017 by The University of Chicago
All rights reserved. No part of this book may be used
or reproduced in any manner whatsoever without
written permission, except in the case of brief
quotations in critical articles and reviews. For more
information, contact the University of Chicago Press,
1427 E. 60th St., Chicago, IL 60637.
Published 2017.
Printed in the United States of America

26 25 24 23 22   2 3 4 5

ISBN-13: 978-0-226-37002-6 (cloth)
ISBN-13: 978-0-226-37016-3 (paper)
ISBN-13: 978-0-226-37033-0 (e-book)
DOI: 10.7208/chicago/9780226370330.001.0001

Library of Congress Cataloging-in-Publication Data
Names: Iversen, Margaret, author.
Title: Photography, trace, and trauma / Margaret
Iversen.
Description: Chicago ; London : The University
of Chicago Press, 2017. | Includes bibliographical
references and index.
Identifiers: LCCN 2016034779 |
ISBN 9780226370026 (cloth : alk. paper) |
ISBN 9780226370163 (pbk. : alk. paper) |
ISBN 9780226370330 (e-book)
Subjects: LCSH: Photography—Social aspects.
Classification: LCC TR183 .I947 2017 | DDC 770—
dc23 LC record available at https://lccn.loc.gov
/2016034779

⊗ This paper meets the requirements of ANSI/NISO
Z39.48-1992 (Permanence of Paper).

I am learning to see. I don't know why
it is, but everything enters me more
deeply and doesn't stop where it once
used to. I have an interior that I never
knew of. Everything passes into me
now. I don't know what happens there.

Contents

Acknowledgments

Looking back, I realize that the germ for this book was planted years ago in an article I wrote for an anthology called *The New Art History* (1986). My brief contribution, "Saussure v. Peirce: Models for a Semiotics of Visual Art," went against the grain of the trend for "reading pictures" inspired by Ferdinand de Saussure's linguistic model of semiology. Instead, it favored C. S. Peirce's more generous multiple typology, which introduced the concept of the indexical sign. Rereading the article, I see just how decisive was the influence of two figures on my thinking, namely Peter Wollen, author of *Signs and Meaning in the Cinema* (1969), and Mary Kelly, who at that time had completed *Post-Partum Document* (1973–79) and was working on *Interim*. Also important, though more remotely, was Rosalind Krauss's two-part essay for *October*, "Notes on the Index" (1977). Yet, despite this fertile ground, "the book on the index" was deferred until now. Instead, I wrote about contemporary art, psychoanalysis, and art historical methodology. This research led me to the belated realization that all my concerns could be grouped around the terms photography, trace, and trauma. This book is an unpacking of my initial thoughts about this constellation of terms, first set down in an article on *Camera Lucida* and Jacques Lacan, "What Is a Photograph?" (1994), and reprinted in my *Beyond Pleasure: Freud, Lacan, Barthes* (2007).

The award of a major grant from the British Arts and Humanities Research Council for a three-year project called "Aesthetics after Photography" (2007–10) made it possible to pursue these thoughts intensively. The project was codirected by Diarmuid Costello, a philosopher with a genuine understanding of the visual arts. I am grateful for his support and critical acumen, and that of our research fellows, Wolfgang Brückle and Dawn Wilson. The grant spurred on my research, but it had always been generously supported by the institution where I have happily spent my entire academic career, the

University of Essex. My colleagues in the Department of Art History and beyond were always willing to offer their expertise, particularly those neighboring my field of study, Dawn Ades, Neil Cox, and Marina Warner. Too numerous to mention individually are the many graduate students who brought much fresh thinking to this topic over the course of the book's long gestation. Beyond Essex, colleagues who have been important to me as friends and as models of brilliant critical writing are Parveen Adams, Jo Applin, Claire Bishop, David Campany, Mark Cousins, Briony Fer, Tamar Garb, Mark Godfrey, Ed Krčma, Stephen Melville, Michael Newman, and Mignon Nixon.

Many of the artists whose work I discuss contributed by kindly giving me permission to reproduce their work, but some have been instrumental in forming my ideas. This is especially true of Mary Kelly and Susan Morris. Zoe Leonard helpfully sent me unpublished material and made comments on my draft chapter. Chapters 3 and 5, which appeared first in journals, benefited greatly from the editors at *Critical Inquiry* and *Tate Papers*. I also wish to thank my excellent editors at University of Chicago Press, Susan Bielstein, James Toftness, and Joel Score, as well as the thoughtful anonymous readers.

One supportive colleague at Essex whom I did not mention above, Jules Lubbock, is also my husband. I dedicate this book to him.

Exposure 1

Photography as a medium is often associated with the psychic effects of trauma. The automaticity of the process, the wide-open camera lens, and the light sensitivity of film all lend themselves to this association. Just as photography, to some extent, bypasses artistic intention and convention, so also the traumatic event bypasses consciousness. Both involve an indelible impression of something generated outside. This book is an exploration of the idea of photography as an analogue of trauma. It also considers art in other media, especially those sculptural forms, like direct casts, that can readily be understood as presenting or simulating a trace or residue of a traumatic event. This book weaves together two strands of thought—semiotic theories of the indexical sign or trace, especially those that pertain to photography, and psychoanalytic theories of individual and collective trauma. This textual material makes it possible for me to make more explicit the concerns of several artists whose practice engages with notions of trauma in the form of material traces. In this introductory chapter, I provide some background, both theoretical and art historical, to this body of thought and develop the concept of "exposure" as a term that combines both psychic and photographic connotations. An introduction to the semiotics of the index is provided in chapter 2.

Trace and Trauma

In his brief but suggestive essay "A Note upon the 'Mystic Writing Pad'" (1925), Sigmund Freud proposed an analogy between a child's toy, a "Wunderblock," and his model of the mind, especially as regards its capacity for both receiving and retaining impressions.[1] The toy, commonly known in English as a magic slate, consists of a wax tablet covered with a delicate piece of waxed paper that adheres to it and a transparent sheet of celluloid or plastic. One draws on the slate using a stylus, pressing on the sheet of plastic and making indentations in the wax below, which appear as dark traces. When the sheets of plastic and paper are lifted from the surface of the wax tablet, the marks disappear and the slate can then receive fresh impressions. The wax, however, retains all of the previous marks in a jumbled palimpsest. In Freud's analogy, the clear plastic sheet and paper represent the faculties of perception and consciousness with their protective psychic shield against stimuli; the retentive wax below represents memory and the unconscious. The analogy neatly accommodates in one system the two key mental functions of receptivity and retention, consciousness and the unconscious: the magic slate combines the notebook's permanent retention of marks and the chalk slate's renewable receptivity to them. Yet elsewhere Freud declared that "becoming conscious and leaving behind a memory-trace are processes incompatible with each other within one and the same system," for "*consciousness arises instead of a memory-trace.*" While consciousness must be permanently on erase, its contents expiring quickly to make way for new impressions, memory traces are "often most powerful and most enduring when the process which left them behind was one that never entered consciousness."[2] Freud understood that a great deal that is perceived is not consciously registered. Some of these mental contents are traumatic impressions, mainly formed in infancy and childhood; since they are not consciously registered, they are not integrated into experience until, perhaps, much later. This thought led Freud to propose a more high-tech apparatus as an analogy for mental functioning: the camera has the capacity to capture something unexperienced, which comes to light only later, when the film is developed.[3] Walter Benjamin made the same connection when he remarked that "it is through the camera that we first discover the optical unconscious, just as we discover the instinctual unconscious through psychoanalysis."[4]

Freud's analogy of the mystic writing pad, although somewhat crude, lends itself especially well to our aim of formulating an aesthetics or poetics of the trace and trauma, for the writing pad is itself a sort of medium of depiction. Especially suggestive is the idea of the soft, vulnerable stuff of the tablet that is so receptive and permanently retentive. As we shall see, understanding the waxy stuff as a medium implies an attitude to art-making that is the very antithesis of an approach that involves active formulation. The commonly held view of the work of art as the paradigm case of a mind-formulated artifact, wholly porous to the intentions of its maker, is here challenged by a view that understands it as constituted by an encounter with the world. The Mexican artist Gabriel Orozco is one prominent contemporary artist who is interested in figuring this kind of creative receptivity. This is particularly evident in his piece *Yielding Stone* (1992), a ball of soft, gray plasticine that he rolled through the streets gathering dust, fragments, and impressions made by whatever it encountered (plate 1). Benjamin Buchloh saw this as an example of "transforming a surface into a purely passive receptacle of merely accidental pictorial and indexical marks."[5] Plasticine, Orozco observed, "is hardly ever used for the definitive version of a work. . . . Its malleability and vulnerability make it unsuitable for permanent forms in a finished piece."[6] Like the waxy stuff of the magic slate, the child's toy that Freud compared to the contents of memory and the unconscious, it is a material that retains the traces of impressions. But Orozco's *Yielding Stone* has nothing comparable to the mystic writing pad's protective celluloid layer. Rather, its touch-sensitive surface is "accidented" all over and remains vulnerable to pokes, kicks, and gravity even when it is displayed on the gallery floor. That it is intended as a surrogate self is signaled by Orozco's statement that the ball is the same weight as himself. The dimension of latent trauma is further drawn out by a remark the artist made in an interview about the connection between a vulnerable or receptive attitude and the importance of vessels and containers in his work. I will return to Orozco's work in chapter 5, "Index, Diagram, Graphic Trace."

Freud's understanding of trauma is clearly more complex than the elementary model figured in his "Note upon the 'Mystic Writing Pad.'" In *Beyond the Pleasure Principle* (1920), Freud elaborated the idea that the mind is susceptible to traumatic exposure when powerful stimuli breach its protective shield.[7] It was the recurrent nightmares of shell-shocked soldiers treated by Freud during World War I that forced him to abandon his vision of the mind as dominated by the pleasure principle and his notion of the dream as its playground. After the war, he came to see the connections among the psychical traumas of childhood, those of wartime, and peacetime accidents and disasters.[8] In all cases, trauma involves the unexpected occurrence of an event that the subject is ill prepared for and unable to assimilate. This has the effect of dividing the subject from him or herself. In *Unclaimed Experience*, Cathy Caruth put it this way:

> In trauma there is an incomprehensible outside of the self that has already gone inside without the self's mediation, hence without any relation to the self, and this consequently becomes a threat to any understanding of what a self might be in this context.[9]

Trauma creates a disturbingly ambiguous relation between inside and outside, self and other.

Trauma also disturbs what one normally takes to be the linear temporality of experience. Freud gave the name *Nachträglichkeit*, usually translated as "deferred action," to the curious retrospective temporality of trauma. He discovered that memory traces, specifically unconscious ones from infancy, are revived in later life by some, perhaps anodyne, experience, which is then given disproportionate significance and emotional weight. The initial event, hardly experienced, otherwise lies dormant; it only becomes traumatic retroactively. In the case of accident or war trauma, the event is received in a numbed state and only later reexperienced as nightmare or hallucination. In *Moses and Monotheism*, Freud drew the analogy between photographic and psychic deferred action: the latter may be made "more comprehensible by comparing it with a photographic exposure which can be developed after any interval of time and transformed into a picture."[10] While these temporal displacements cannot be figured by the model of the mind conveyed by the mystic writing pad, it nevertheless functions as a productive metaphor for the psyche's receptivity to and retention of accidental impressions that subtend conscious experience.[11]

We have seen how Freud's account of the retroactive causality of trauma points to the limitations of the mystic writing pad analogy. Neither it nor photography can deal properly with the relation between the indexical trace that initiates trauma and its subsequent symptoms, unconscious elaborations, and repetitions. Traumatic impressions are liable to be dreamed or recollected in analysis in distorted ways. To take one example, the traumatic impression in Freud's case history of the so-called Wolfman was his witnessing in infancy his parents' copulation.[12] But the traumatic disturbance was only triggered years later in a dream of wolves sitting in a tree outside his bedroom window. Because of this disjunction, Freud likened the task of the analyst to that of the archaeologist obliged to construct an artifact out of fragments. What has been forgotten is hinted at in traces that come to light in free association or the transference. Yet Freud also insists that unconscious impressions are in fact preserved whole, like the remains of Pompeii: "Even things that seem completely forgotten are present somehow and somewhere, and have merely been buried and inaccessible to the subject."[13] Freud's model of the unconscious, then, is of traces laid down that are indelible, although they may manifest themselves in displaced, distorted forms. One consequence of my focus on artists who deploy indexical procedures to summon notions of memory or trauma is that this first moment of trauma is emphasized more than its "fictive" elaborations. However, my final chapter, on Thomas Demand, is aimed at addressing the issue of fictive elaborations of trauma, not as symptom, but as a means of assimilating traumatic impressions into experience and memory proper.

Photography

The surrealists were quick to respond to Freud's theorization of trauma. André Breton's conception of "objective chance" is a case in point. By the time he wrote *Nadja* (1928) and *L'amour fou* (1937), Breton had read Freud's *Beyond the Pleasure Principle*, which was translated into French in 1927. In these texts, Breton took up and elaborated Freud's theory of trauma in his formulations of the chance encounter and the lucky find spotted amid the detritus of a flea market. These sorts of occurrence bypass one's consciousness and intentionality. Breton's "modern materialist" definition of chance allied it with the idea of a traumatic encounter: *"Chance is the form making manifest the exterior necessity which traces its path in the human unconscious."*[14] Just as traumatic events bypass the psychic defenses of consciousness, the "protective shield against stimuli," leaving behind an indelible trace, so also does the chance encounter breach that shield and touch an exposed nerve. Breton evoked photography's affinity with trauma by emphasizing its unguarded quality and referring to the camera as a "blind instrument."[15]

As we've seen, the conjunction of the terms chance, trace, and trauma bears closely on photography. This is especially true of photography as imagined in Walter Benjamin's "Little History of Photography" (1931), a text deeply indebted to both *Beyond the Pleasure Principle* and surrealism. In that essay, Benjamin was attentive to photography's ability to record the trace of the trauma. He imagined the camera as an eye wide open, with no protective shield, that is, with no buffer against shock. For example, he wrote of the photographer Karl Dauthendey's self-portrait with his fiancée, who was later to commit suicide, that it fills one with "an irresistible urge to search such a picture for the tiny spark of contingency" left behind by the reality that has "seared" the subject.[16] Although the portrait is formal and posed, Benjamin seeks in the distant gaze of the young women a sign of her future despair. He seems to be offering here an account of photography that is not so much auratic as traumatic.[17]

Photography can be understood, then, as a medium that registers without consciousness of registration. As literary theorist Ann Banfield put it, "What the photograph is sensible of can be outside the ego, a thought unthought, unintended, involuntary and without meaning."[18] The indexicality of the medium is usually credited with making the absent object present, but, as Banfield points out, it also has the effect of absenting the viewing subject as the camera records a world without a subject: "The photograph records the contingency of the subject as such; this is the nature of death in it." It does this "by conjuring away the subject who observes, whether photographer or viewer."[19] Mary Ann Doane has also argued that photography made possible what had previously seemed impossible—the inscription of contingency: "Anything and everything in the order of materiality could be photographed, filmed, or recorded, particularly the unexpected, the rupture in the fabric of existence."[20]

Another writer who has recently reflected on the nature of photographic contingency is the German art historian Peter Geimer. He argues that photographers are only partly aware of what they are doing, and the aesthetic or epistemic value of their pictures often depends precisely on this blind spot. Much about a photograph is calculable, foreseeable, and leaves open the potential for formal intervention. However, there is also a dimension of the unforeseen. A photograph is, in this respect, also an occurrence: something in the image *occurs* or something *falls into* the image.[21]

Although photographic contingency has been viewed as a positive condition of the medium since its earliest beginnings, it has been especially favored within particular art historical movements, including surrealism. The American photographer Moyra Davey, for instance, claims that her own photography and writing are governed by the principle. In her book *Photography and Accident*, she tells of opening John Cage's book *Notations* at random and reading, "I mix chance and choice somewhat scandalously." She continues, "I copy this phrase into a notebook, a perfect encapsulation of my own desire for contingency within a structure. I decide to allow chance elements, the *flânerie*, as it were, of daily life, to find their way into this essay."[22] It also finds its way into her photographs, which depict the most mundane aspects of her daily life, including cluttered desktops, piles of books, and a fridge bristling with clippings. As Geimer remarks, one consequence of the unforeseeable, of accidental coincidences and "useless" information in photography, is that it throws art historical interpretation into disarray, since contingency undermines notions of intentionality and expression.[23]

As is well known, the theme of traumatic photography as sketched by Benjamin was taken up by Roland Barthes in *Camera Lucida: Reflections on Photography* (1980), a book which concerns the connection between the medium of photography and the traumas of separation, loss, and death. In fact, the book is structured around the trauma of the recent death of Barthes's mother, which prompted the search for her authentic photographic image and his reflections on the "essential" nature of the medium. Sometimes Barthes wrote of photography as if he believed it were capable of restoring the lost object, of making the absent present: "A sort of umbilical cord links the body of the photographed thing to my gaze: light, though impalpable, is here a carnal medium, a skin I share with anyone who has been photographed."[24] Given the context of the son's mourning for his mother, the analogy of light as an umbilical cord has unusual resonance. Although Barthes declared that "the photograph is literally an emanation of the referent," he also acknowledged that, like the rays of light from a distant star that reach us only after the star has ceased to exist, the photograph can only attest to the past existence of the object; the photographic declaration, "that-has-been," hovers between presence and absence, now and then. Part of what is traumatic about photography is that it is an indexical trace of someone or something that is no more, or is no longer the same. We are dealing, then, not with presence but with *past* presence, which is to say, the hollowed-out presence of an absence. Another traumatic aspect of the photograph for Barthes is the disturbing detail, or punctum, which is identified with an unintentional, automatic moment of the photograph—the moment when the photographer's attention was elsewhere. The implication is that the accidental point in the photograph is somehow equivalent to the unassimilated traumatic impression. Laura Mulvey put the point most succinctly: "Trauma leaves a mark on the unconscious, a kind of index of the psyche that parallels the photograph's trace of an original event."[25] The possibility, always latent in the medium, of bypassing intention and artistic convention has made photography a favored medium for artists interested in the conjunction of chance, trace, and trauma.

As I have argued elsewhere, *Camera Lucida* is a book deeply indebted to Jacques Lacan's reading of Freud on trauma.[26] At the beginning of the book, Barthes observes that the defining characteristic of photography is its attachment to "the absolute particular, the sovereign Contingency, matte and somehow stupid, the This . . . , in short, what Lacan calls *Tuché*, the Occasion, the Encounter, the Real, in its indefatigable expression."[27] In this passage, Barthes brings together references to Lacan and Breton, both of whom stress the evanescence of the object of desire. The same can be said of Barthes's understanding of the photographic referent; his imagination of the photograph is indexical and traumatic in the senses I have elaborated. Nevertheless, some critics continue to read *Camera Lucida* as though Barthes thought of the photograph as a promise of plenitude regained. Jacques Rancière, for example, suggests that Barthes's theory of photographic "hyper-resemblance," as he calls it, serves only "to expiate the sin of the former mythologist" who once denounced the photographic image as through and through coded and ideological, and now proclaims its "utter self-evidence."[28] Yet I do not think that Barthes's account of photography is susceptible to the criticism that it revives nostalgia for lost immediacy or presence, for only a ghost of referentiality is introduced. As a sort of emblem of the book as whole, the frontispiece of the original edition, a color photograph by Daniel Boudinet, then called *Polaroid*, now called *La chambre claire* (The Light Room; 1979), depicted an empty room in mourning, curtains drawn against the light and drenched in blue (plate 2). Similarly, the art that interests me claims some referential weight and deep significance, but indirectly, belatedly.

The Creaturely Gaze

The writings of Freud, Breton, Benjamin, Lacan, and Barthes are essential reading for any account of the aesthetics of trauma. I would like to add one more name to this list. An illuminating meditation on the connections that link trace, trauma, and photography as a medium can be found in Eric L. Santner's *On Creaturely Life: Rilke, Benjamin, Sebald* (2006).[29] Discussing Rilke's poetry and prose, Santner draws attention to the poet's notion of the creaturely gaze. This is quite different from our ordinary sort of perception, which is reflective, conceptually mediated, articulated and crossed by various purposes that tend to position a subject over against an object. Our consciousness is usually closed in on itself, reflecting readymade representations. The human gaze is normally twisted by the knowledge of death and clouded by memory. For Rilke, animals, children, those near death, or those in love are best placed to look, not at the objects of habitual experience, but into the Open (*das Offene*).[30] This romantic conception was taken up and critiqued by Heidegger and modified by a number of German-Jewish writers including Kafka, Benjamin, and W. G. Sebald.[31] For these writers, creaturely life designates the condition of humans in modernity, that is, the condition of "thrown-ness" into an enigmatic, contingent open where one is exposed to political power and surrounded by the cryptic ruins of defunct forms of life. Moods of boredom and melancholy are attuned to this sort of traumatized, creaturely exposure to the Open. These moods are also associated with insight and creativity; as Benjamin observed, "Boredom is the dream bird that hatches the egg of experience."[32]

Santner's chapter on Sebald bears most closely on the way that creaturely exposure relates to photography. Sebald was a German gentile writer who lived in England and who identified closely with the Jewish intellectual tradition as well as with Holocaust victims and survivors. The degree to which chance and coincidence are important factors in Sebald's narratives is well-known. *Austerlitz* (2001), for example, is a book in the form of a possibly fictional memoir of meetings with a man in search of his past: the key to Austerlitz's past—his entering the ladies' waiting room in Liverpool Street Station a few weeks before it was demolished—is presented as a chance occurrence. That event precipitated the recovered memory of his life prior to being transported, as a child, from Nazi-occupied Czechoslovakia to the safety of Britain, and so unlocked what had long constrained his subsequent life. In this case, it was a lucky break, a happy chance, that opened for him the possibility of change. History and memory were, so to speak, condensed in the architecture.[33] In *Unrecounted*, Sebald wrote, "Because (in principle) things outlast us, they know more about us than we know about them: they carry the experiences they have had with us inside them and are—in fact—the book of our history opened before us," if we are lucky enough, or open enough, to encounter them.[34] There is an obvious Proustian resonance in this idea that memories are locked within material objects; Proust noted of these memory-laden objects that "we have no idea which one it is. And whether we come upon this object before we die, or whether we never encounter it, depends entirely on chance."[35]

Another important feature of Sebald's books is the presence of grainy black-and-white photographs punctuating the text. But to describe them in this way is to diminish their importance, for opaque, old, found photographs or clippings from newspapers were often the starting point for his literary investigations. Sebald closely associated photographs with loss and chance recovery. In an interview, he remarked that old photographs are almost destined to be lost, vanishing in the attic or a box, "and if they do come to light they do so accidentally, you stumble upon them. The way in which these stray pictures cross your path, it has something at once totally coincidental and fateful about it."[36] In addition, photographic indexicality ties the image to the circumstantial, the detail, the purely contingent, and it is these features that connect photography with the creaturely gaze. We encounter that gaze on the opening pages of *Austerlitz*; the narrator is recounting his visit to the Nocturama at the zoo in Antwerp, where he watched a raccoon, "with a serious expression on its face, washing the same piece of apple over and over again, as if it hoped that all this washing . . . would help it to escape the unreal world in which it had arrived, so to speak, through no fault of its own." Several of the "denizens of the Nocturama," he continues, "had strikingly large eyes, and the fixed, inquiring gaze found in certain painters and philosophers who seek to penetrate the darkness which surrounds us purely by means of looking and thinking."[37] The page is filled with photographs of four pairs of eyes, two animal and two human, one of which is Wittgenstein's. This sort of radical exposure to the creaturely condition of the other can also be found in Benjamin's traumatic theory of photography and Barthes's "mad realism."

There are two reasons why photography, or at least a certain understanding of it, is so important in this context. The photograph involves an automatic mechanism, on the one hand, and exposure to what it encounters, on the other. The automatism of the medium connects it with the initial traumatic experience, which is "recorded" without being properly assimilated by the subject. Exposure, itself a photographic term, is tied up with the indexicality of the medium and links photography with the vulnerability of the subject of trauma and corresponding pity for the creatureliness of the other. What follows are accounts of a few works by two artists, Chantal Akerman and Felix Gonzalez-Torres, which I hope will help to clarify what is meant by "exposure" in this dual sense.

Chantal Akerman

The pertinence of the work of Belgian artist and filmmaker Chantal Akerman in this context can be seen in one sequence of her film *News from Home* (1977). She positioned her film camera in a New York subway car opposite the sliding doors. The train arrives at a station where the doors part to reveal

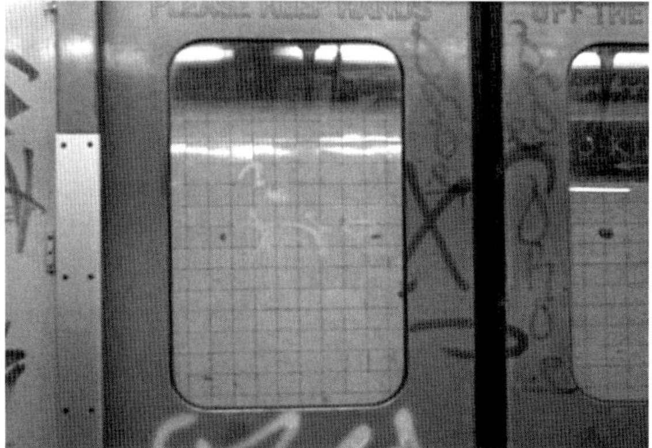

Figure 1 Chantal Akerman, *News from Home*, 1977. Film still.

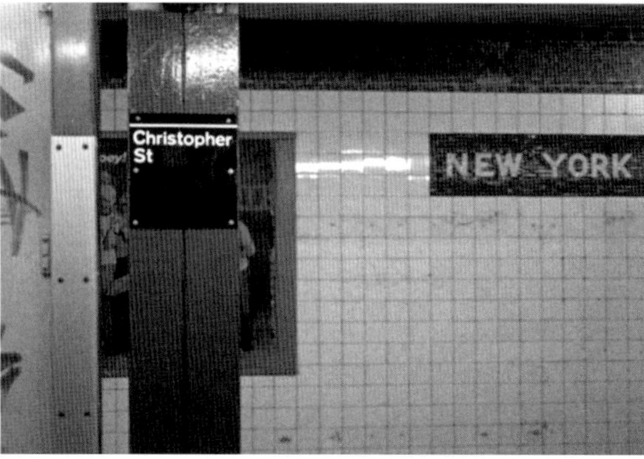

Figure 2 Chantal Akerman, *News from Home*, 1977. Film still.

a chance composition of pillars, posters and people on the platform. The doors slide shut and the process is repeated several times (figs. 1.1 and 1.2). The filmmaker obviously hopes that at each stop the doors will frame a striking composition, but she has no way of controlling the outcome. The train and the camera are on automatic. In fact, Akerman uses the sliding doors as a large, slow camera shutter.

Can Akerman's gaze in *News from Home* be described as creaturely? It was made in the 1970s in New York, where she became acquainted with Yvonne Rainer, Michael Snow, and other experimental filmmakers. A postminimal reading of the film's chance effects brought about by mechanical means might, then, be possible, were it not for the sound track. Apart from street noise and the roar of the train, this consists of a voice-over of Akerman reading letters from her mother in Belgium. Read by the daughter in New York in a neutral, unexpressive tone, the mother's letters speak of her love, her worry, her desire. "I love you"; "I miss you"; "Please write." Some verge on emotional blackmail. The daughter has clearly, with some difficulty, separated herself from home, from the Mother, in order to make her own way in the world as a filmmaker. The trauma, anxiety, and guilt of separation are invoked by Akerman at the level of form. We sense this in the distanced observational posture of the camera and the rigorous serial structure of the film. The repetitive scenes gather a mechanized life of their own. Furthermore, the margins of New York where Akerman films have a ruined, somewhat derelict character that matches her mood. "Now everything is repainted," she remarked in an interview, adding, "unfortunately."[38]

Akerman's relation to her mother is complicated by the fact that her mother, a survivor of the Nazi death camps, is haunted by the death of her own mother in Auschwitz in 1942.[39] This raises the issue of intergenerational trauma.[40] Akerman claims for herself the identity of a Jewish filmmaker, and many of her films deal implicitly with the themes of the Holocaust and diaspora. *D'est* (From the East; 1993), for instance, documents a journey made possible by the collapse of the iron curtain that started in East Germany and ended in Moscow. One of its most affecting scenes is a tracking shot of people waiting for buses in the Moscow winter snow. The camera, mounted on a moving vehicle, slowly scans these cold, creaturely people seemingly worn down by history. There is something implacable about the long, slow tracking shot. "It is always the same thing that reveals itself," Ackerman remarked. "Marches in the snow with packages toward an unknown place, faces and bodies placed side by side."[41] This historical "primal scene" keeps repeating in her work. Griselda Pollock points out that the Eastern European communities Akerman passes through on her journey have been emptied of their Jewish populations. She remarks:

> These modern-day people walking and queuing thus become a reminder, an evocation of other queues, other streams of people passively waiting transport, a different kind of transport, to an unimaginable destination.[42]

These considerations prompt me to return to *News from Home*. Looking back, I now realize that everything in the film is about transit, exile, and isolation. The closing shot is a reversal of the traditional immigrant's first view from a ship approaching the harbor; Akerman's camera is fixed at the back of a ferry as it pulls away from the dock, slowly revealing New York's skyline—its promise, perhaps, also receding. Akerman's films demonstrate that, although the representation of trauma often evinces an apparent lack of affect, as if numbed, this has nothing to do with the so-called postmodern death of affect and more to do with the creaturely gaze.

Felix Gonzalez-Torres

Illness and the pain of losing a loved one render people more vulnerable and exposed, more "creaturely" in the sense I have defined. The work of the Cuban-American artist Felix Gonzalez-Torres was deeply affected by the AIDS crisis and by the loss of his partner to the disease. His work consistently alludes in oblique ways to this context. In 1992, for example, he exhibited, on twenty-four billboards around New York City, a photograph of an unmade double bed with two pillows bearing what appear to be the impressions of a couple's heads (plate 3). *"Untitled"* (1991) is striking because it makes such an intimate domestic scene so public. It is also remarkable for its doubling effect—not only the doubling of identical pillows, but also the doubling of the indexical traces on the pillows by the indexical photographic medium. The all-white image of recent intimacy is soft and inviting, but it takes on a darker shade once we realize that 1991 was the year that Gonzalez-Torres's partner, Ross Laycock, died of AIDS after a long illness. At least retrospectively, then, the piece functions as a memorial, both celebrating their loving relationship and commemorating it. Yet this reading may tie the image too closely to autobiography, for the work also has a distinctly political edge. It is a protest and provocation that intervened in what was at the time a highly charged situation. The intimacy of the image and the publicity of its exhibition were particularly transgressive in the context of the hysterical reaction in the United States to the AIDS epidemic, which provoked fierce conservative attacks on homosexuality. If the work is viewed as a memorial, it is illuminating to observe how it inverts, point by point, the form of medieval tomb sculpture. Those monuments, made of enduring materials like bronze or marble and sheltered in the sacred space of a church, show royal or aristocratic couples lying in effigy side by side, their heads resting on hard pillows. *"Untitled"* seems to evoke these tombs but exchanges their features for the ephemerality, profanity, and democracy of the commercial billboard. Moreover, the couple in Gonzalez-Torres's posters is indicated only negatively, not by statuary but by the impressions left behind on pillows. Viewed now, in retrospect, the emptiness of the bed foretells the artist's own tragic death only five years later, in 1996.

As Nancy Spector has observed, "The concept of the index as a sign contingent on the empirical world—a world that can only be narrated in the past tense—reverberates throughout Gonzalez-Torres's work."[43] She points to other photographs that bear the traces of departed people, doubling the index to convey a sense of past presence. For example, *"Untitled" (Cold Blue Snow)* (1991), a photograph of footprints in the snow, marks an absence that is redoubled by the ephemerality of the traces left behind. The support for the image is a jigsaw puzzle held together in a plastic sheath, underscoring a sense of fragility and impermanence. *"Untitled" (Sand)* (1993–94) is a series of photogravures that also show footprints. Here the fine grain of the sand is doubled by the fine-grained texture of the reproductions. Spector claims that the doubling of the index has the effect of canceling both iterations and so "annulling the existence of any referent beyond themselves."[44] I incline to the view, however, that the doubling only serves to underscore the connotations of the index that tie it to past presence, trauma, and loss.

Gonzalez-Torres was an artist steeped in the writing of Benjamin, Barthes, and Louis Althusser, among others. He was also evidently a reader of Rilke, as he made explicit reference in interviews to the notion of "blood-remembering." This is an idea Rilke introduced in the context of his semi-autobiographical novel *The Notebooks of Malte Laurids Brigge* (1910). In the relevant passage, Rilke reflected that one should write poetry only late in life, when the simple feelings of youth have sedimented into experience and even the memories of those experiences have been forgotten. He concludes:

> For it is not yet the memories themselves. Not till they have turned to blood within us, to glance and gesture, nameless and no longer to be distinguished from ourselves—not till then can it happen that in a most rare hour the first word of a verse arises in their midst and goes forth from them.[45]

Memory, in the deepest sense, is closely related to forgetting. The crucial point for Gonzalez-Torres would seem to be the way Rilke advises against direct expression of emotion or literal autobiography. The image or object of art must have a certain poetic opacity, even to the artist himself. Yet this passage must have especially appealed to him because of the specific things that Rilke says are necessary for the poet to feel, experience, remember, and forget:

> One must be able to think back to roads in unknown regions, to unexpected meetings, and to partings one had long seen coming. . . . One must have memories of many nights of love, none of which was like the others. . . . But one must also have been beside the dying, must have sat beside the dead in the room with the open window and the fitful noises.[46]

Gonzalez-Torres made a series that consists of spills of candy wrapped in colorful cellophane and deposited on the gallery floor, where visitors are free to take a piece or not. One such work, *"Untitled" (Portrait of Ross in L.A.)* (1991), is, like the billboard poster, dedicated to the memory of Ross Laycock, a portrait in his absence. The work has various manifestations, but it does stipulate that its "ideal weight" is 175 pounds, alluding perhaps to Ross's "ideal weight." It is tempting to see in this work Gonzalez-Torres gesturing toward Rilke's idea of blood-memory in the form of a participatory work of art where the work is literally incorporated in the body of the other. The piece might also allude to the impossibility of securing a sense of bodily cohesion; like the effect of trauma, it tends to blur the boundary between inside and outside. Both Gonzalez-Torres and Akerman, I propose, make use of a poetics of exposure to explore the forms of ego-dispersion or absence that accompanies trauma, love, and death.

*

While the art of trauma and memory has attracted considerable artistic and critical attention in recent decades, discussion of the indexical sign or trace as an artistic strategy has been more intermittent. One major contribution to the field is Rosalind Krauss's groundbreaking two-part article "Notes on the Index," published in 1977.[47] As we shall see in the following chapter, her concentration on the "empty" index, called a shifter, means that she did not draw out what connotations or affective resonances attach to the index as trace. Although she described the index as "a trauma of signification," she did not elaborate this in psychoanalytic terms. Two decades later, Hal Foster introduced a psychoanalytic framework in his influential article "Death in America" (1996), in which he proposed an interpretation of Warhol's photo silk screens as both simulacral and as indexically touched by the real.[48] Another important moment in this history was Georges Didi-Huberman's 1997 exhibition at the Centre Pompidou, *L'empreinte*.[49] More recently, Mary Ann Doane made a contribution to the study of Peirce's semiotics in the context of contemporary visual culture with her book *The Emergence of Cinematic Time: Modernity, Contingency, the Archive* (2002).[50]

Coincident with the rise of interest in indexicality has been a surge of interest in analogue photography and cameraless photography as indexical mediums. Focusing on this aspect of the medium goes against the grain of what was the dominant poststructuralist trend in the 1970s and 1980s, which stressed the constructedness of the photographic sign and the disparity between the image and what it represents. It also runs counter to advances in technology. The current revival of interest in analogue photography is no doubt related to the rapid development of digital technologies that render this poststructuralist critique of the image redundant. The rapid proliferation of the virtual, constructed digital image has brought back into focus the issue of indexicality in both practice and theory. Griselda Pollock, who has written extensively on the art of trauma in relation to indexicality, observed:

> While earlier theories of photography sought to dissipate the delusion of photography's unmediated reproduction of the real in order to stress the role of rhetorics of the image and ideological overdetermination of the "truth" effect, faced with the dissolution of the indexical link between photograph and its object . . . , theorists became interested in the politics of indexicality or its absence in contemporary image-making and theory.[51]

In terms of accessibility, dissemination, speed, and efficiency, the benefits of digitization are universally acknowledged, yet, as we have seen, some artists and theorists are acutely sensitive to what is being lost in this great technological revolution. They have responded by using the near-obsolete medium of analogue photography or by adopting forms of sign-making involving a physical imprint or close contact, that is, indexical practices such as direct casting or rubbing. Chapter 3 addresses the poetics of analogue photography in the work of Zoe Leonard and Tacita Dean. Relatively little has been written on the conjunction of trauma and indexicality in mediums other than photography. A brief history of these nonphotographic, indexical artistic techniques and their implications is presented in chapter 4, "Casting, Rubbing, Making Strange."

In chapter 5, "Index, Diagram, Graphic Trace," I consider artistic uses of the graphic trace and argue that it is a hybrid form of representation that has aspects of both the index and the diagram. A graphic trace, such as seismograph, is an indexical diagram: it takes from the index a registration of something unique—the impress of a particular event, while incorporating the diagram's abstraction from what is immediately given in perception. Graphic traces are produced by sensitive recording instruments that detect invisible movements. Étienne-Jules Marey was a pioneer in the development of these devices, and his chronophotographic investigation of the trajectory of animal and human movement was an important precedent for many visual artists.

Alongside a renewed interest in the trace, there has been mounting interest in the subject of trauma, and in the whole domain of affect and the arts. A key factor in this revival was the long-delayed and widespread public reflection and debate about how to commemorate the Holocaust in the form of memorials, works of art, exhibitions, books, and films. Akerman's films, to cite just one example, form a part of this wider context. In chapter 6, I join this debate with a consideration of Didi-Huberman's book *Images in Spite of All: Four Images from Auschwitz* (2008). The book is a defense of a few images that were smuggled out of Auschwitz. While some writers insist that the Holocaust is "unrepresentable," Didi-Huberman argues that these images do manage to represent, in a powerful if fragmentary way, the horror of the death camps. This debate about the representability of atrocity coincided with a critique of poststructuralist theory; Hal Foster has diagnosed the mood as a "dissatisfaction with the textual model of reality—as if the real, repressed in post-structuralist modernism, had returned as traumatic."[52] Roland Barthes, Jean-Francois Lyotard, and Gilles Deleuze have all contributed to this critique. Also important is the influence of feminist and queer theory and politics, both of which privilege affect and the body. In addition, the AIDS epidemic prompted artists to invent new forms of memorialization, as we have seen in the case of Gonzalez-Torres. More recently, the attacks of 9/11 challenged artists to make some kind of appropriate response. The intensity of trauma and its problematic relation to representation have, I believe, made it a challenging subject for artists and curators. It is no wonder that there have also been several significant exhibitions devoted to the theme.[53] The art of trauma has the advantage of referring to events that have personal significance but also involve history, memory, and culture in general, crossing the divide between public and private spheres, the social and the personal. This is a theme explicitly taken up by the German artist Thomas Demand, who, as I argue in the final chapter, chooses traumatic subjects that have had public impact but that also form part of people's personal biographies. His work evokes those invisible traces seared in the mind of the viewer with a view to deepening experience under contemporary cultural conditions.

The conjunction of trace and trauma in the work of many artists carries with it an implicit ethics and aesthetics of attention, receptivity, vulnerability, and affect that I sum up with the term "exposure." Throughout the book, I attempt to identify places where the ethical and photographic senses of exposure merge.[54] As I will demonstrate, at work in both trace and trauma is the notion of some kind of impact that leaves behind an indelible mark, although not necessarily an immediately accessible or unalterable one. One writer on the subject has succinctly summed up the Freudian conception of the trace that informs this book. Catherine Malabou writes about Freud's notion of "the plasticity of psychic life"; this is a phrase he used that "refers to the indestructible nature of the traces that make up the psychic fate of the subject. We know that for Freud no experience is forgotten. The trace is indelible. The trace can be modified, deferred, reformed—but never erased."[55] Briefly put, this book is about the analogies drawn by artists and theorists between this form of psychical trace and material or photographic traces. As we shall see, techniques that involve close physical contact or that short-circuit artistic agency are favored by artists who wish to convey something of the disorienting effect and elusive character of trauma. The following chapter critically reviews a few key texts on the subject of indexicality, focusing particularly on those that bring out its inherent affinity with trauma.

Indexicality 2

A TRAUMA OF SIGNIFICATION

There are a few discussions of indexicality that warrant close attention. First and foremost is the work of the founder of the study of semiotics, the American pragmatist philosopher Charles Sanders Peirce (1839–1914). Unlike his Swiss counterpart Ferdinand de Saussure, whose discipline was theoretical linguistics, Peirce had a background in chemistry, mathematics, and logic. He was employed by the US Coast and Geodetic Survey. This meant that his study of semiotics was not limited to formal systems of communication but included all kinds of manifestation that could be taken for signs, including medical symptoms, shadows, sunflowers, oxidation, and any involuntary trace of an action or condition. As part of a highly complex theory of sign systems, Peirce introduced three main categories—icon, index, and symbol. Following Mary Ann Doane's account, I distinguish between the index as deixis, or pointing, and the index as trace. The person who did most to disseminate Peirce's ideas was the theoretical linguist Roman Jakobson, a Russian who immigrated in the 1920s to Prague and eventually to the United States. He had an abiding interest in avant-garde art and poetry since his youthful involvement with Russian formalist criticism and futurist poetry, so he was inclined to bring poetics to linguistics and aesthetics to the study of signs. His many contributions to semiotics included a development of Peirce's concept of the shifter, a subspecies of the index. The category of the shifter was later taken up by Rosalind Krauss in her important two-part essay, "Notes on the Index: Seventies Art in America" (1977), where she deployed it in her account of Duchamp's work and later art practices. Krauss suggests in passing that the advent of indexical signs in art was symptomatic of "a trauma of signification," a claim I will examine more closely by setting her essay in dialogue with Leo Steinberg's "Other Criteria."

Indexicality

Peirce understood the sign as a tripartite entity binding together the sign, the thing signified, and the cognition or feeling produced in the mind of the interpreter. Although he was not particularly interested in aesthetics, he was unusually attentive to what might be called the affective aspect of signs, that is, how they work upon the interpreter. He described the index as the most "forceful" type of sign: it signifies by establishing an existential or causal link to its referent, either by directing our attention to something or by being physically impressed or affected by it.[1] A pointing finger and the demonstrative pronoun *this* are indexes of the first, directive kind, while a fingerprint is an example of the second type, the index as trace. The crucial difference is that pointing fingers and demonstrative pronouns must be simultaneous with and adjacent to their objects, while the fingerprint is a mark or trace of some past contact. These functions of the index, although different, are not necessarily in tension. Think, for example, of a footprint on a sandy beach, formed by the impression of a foot. It is a classic example of an index as trace, but its status as index would be doubled if it drew attention to something—if for example, it were the footprint on the beach that shattered Robinson Crusoe's belief that his desert island was uninhabited and thus produced a radical shift in his state of consciousness. This kind of disruption is, for Peirce, what chiefly characterizes the index: "The index asserts nothing; it only says 'There!' It takes hold of our eyes, as it were, and forcibly directs them to a particular object, and there it stops."[2] Since any sudden change of perception is to some extent shocking, every index carries with it a potential shock. On this account, then, the index has an inherently traumatic power.

The icon, in Peirce's typology, is a sign that signifies by resembling or by sharing some quality with its object. For example, a footprint resembles the underside of a human foot, and we recognize this shared property as part of our interpretation of it as a hybrid sign, part icon and part index. Yet an index need not share any qualities of its object: for example, blue litmus paper turns red when exposed to acid, but acid is not red. As this case also exemplifies, however, the index is a sign that is actually modified by it object. This is one reason Peirce regarded it as particularly forceful. The final type of sign, the symbol, is the least compelling; it refers to its object through habit or convention. Examples include phonetic linguistic signs, Arabic numerals, and color-coded traffic lights. "A symbol, in itself," Peirce declared, "is a mere dream; it does not show what it is talking about. It needs to be connected with its object. For that purpose, an index is indispensible."[3] Neither icon nor symbol has the imperative character of the index, which, on the one hand, draws our attention to something in the world and, on the other, is physically connected to it.[4]

In "The Indexical and the Concept of Medium Specificity," Mary Ann Doane draws attention to this underlying tension in Peirce's account of the index, between the "purest index"—like the demonstrative pronoun *this* or *that*, which picks out a particular object here and now, perhaps with the help of a pointing finger—and the index as trace.[5] Doane, whose main area of expertise is film theory, is no doubt sensitive to this tension because the distinction bears on a difference in temporality. The directing of attention to an object, what Doane calls "deixis," happens in the present moment and in the presence of the object, or at least the sensible experience of it. The index as trace is produced or caused by contact with an object (the footprint in the sand) and indicates past presence. As Doane observes, unlike pure deixis, "the trace does not evaporate in the moment of its production, but remains as the witness to an anteriority."[6] Doane explores other aspects of the difference between these two types of index, which I will refer to as deixis and trace. She notes that the index as deixis, such as the pointing finger, "implies an emptiness, a hollowness that can only be filled in specific, contingent, always mutating situations."[7] The trace, in contrast, marks the past presence of a particular thing and often, as in the photograph, displays an excess of detail. In this "dialectic of the empty and the full," the present and the past, there is a curious echo of the operation of Freud's mystic writing pad, its top layer always ready to receive new inscriptions, while the bottom one is permanently marked by past traces. We find the possibility of detachability and reassignment, on the one hand, and intimacy and particularity, on the other. This paradox of indexicality is further explored in chapter 4, on casting and rubbing.

In the late 1960s and 1970s, theorists critical of a purely structuralist model of linguistics gravitated toward the work of Roman Jakobson. Although he was associated with structural linguistics, he discovered the semiotics of Peirce in the early 1950s and wrote articles that advanced his theories. Jakobson absorbed Peirce's often excessively complicated system, expressed his ideas in more accessible terms, and disseminated them to a wider audience. He particularly drew on Peirce to critique the conception of language as a system of wholly arbitrary, conventional signs. While Peirce agreed that language is predominantly conventional—in his terms, "symbolic"—he also explored the indexical and iconic components of language. In several key essays, Jakobson attended to properties of language that are neglected within a purely structuralist model. In "Quest for the Essence of Language" (1965), for example, he posed the question of the nonarbitrary or motivated aspects of language and identified numerous examples of iconicity in language.[8] Of particular interest in the context of visual art is one subspecies of the icon, the diagram, which displays logical relations by means of spatial relations. We will return to this topic in chapter 5, "Index, Diagram, Graphic

Trace." Writing of the indexical properties of language, Jakobson noted, with Peirce, that although the pronoun *I* is a symbol, it cannot represent its object without being in some existential relation to it. I, like other pronouns, shifts its meaning according to who is speaking, which is why this category of sign is called a shifter. The shifter is "empty" in the sense that it directs our attention to something but does not name or describe it. Roland Barthes had read Jakobson and referred to the photograph in terms that make its role as shifter explicit: "The photograph is never anything but an antiphon of 'Look,' 'See,' 'Here it is'; it points a finger at a certain *vis-à-vis*, and cannot escape this pure deictic language."[9] By simply framing and focusing on something, the photo acts as a "pure" index, yet its photochemical or photoelectronic properties also make it an indexical trace. The latter aspect is stressed in Barthes's notion of photography's traumatic "that-has-been."

The investigation of the indexical properties of language was taken up by the French philosopher Jean-Francois Lyotard, whose book *Discourse, Figure* (1971) begins with a phenomenological description of the very different experiences of reading and seeing. Lyotard observes that a text occupies a flat space and that the marks on the page, "transparent signifiers of meaning," are not especially attended to. In the sphere of discourse, "it is as if humans had become two-dimensional beings, with nothing to feel," but instead "groped along gaps in the network."[10] The phenomenology of the visual world, in contrast, is complex and multidimensional and includes my body in a surrounding space. It is this space, what he calls the figural, that is marginalized in our discourse-dominated culture. In order to counter this, one must begin by indicating the insufficiency of discourse—its dependence on a world outside the self-contained system of language. To this end, Lyotard argues that language is not only signification (a signifier calling up a signified) but also *designation*. Calling on Peirce and Jakobson to make his case, he states that pointing words, such as *here, now, I, you,* or *this,* do not gain their meaning solely from their position in a closed system. Language gestures outside itself "to the sensory field in which speaker and listener co-exist." Through reference, then, language encounters "the depth of the visible."[11] Commenting on Lyotard's sense of the indexical aspect of language, David Rodowick writes:

> Indexicality means that discourse in shot through with the visible: the *enoncé* must point beyond its borders to objects positioned in space with respect to it. It is plunged into a gestural space that surrounds it, and it is riddled from within by deictic holes whose function is to indicate positionality in space (here/there) and in time (now/then).

The index recruits the body in space and time and introduces "the intractable opacity of the visible."[12]

The indexical aspects of visual representation have not been so positively valued among theorists of photography and film, who have tended to think of the index as tied to the aesthetics of realism. This is based on a misunderstanding. According to Peirce's typology, it is the icon that signifies by virtue of resemblance, and so photography is classed as a hybrid type of sign—part index, part icon.[13] Strictly speaking, the index guarantees only existence, not resemblance. In his influential essay "Ontology of the Photograph," André Bazin exaggerates the bond between indexical image and object to the point of identification, yet he also makes a crucial point: "No matter how fuzzy, distorted, or discolored, no matter how lacking in documentary value the image may be, it shares, by virtue of the process of its becoming, the being of the model of which it is the reproduction; it *is* the model."[14] The slippage in this passage from fuzzy image to identity is clearly a case of hyperbole. Nevertheless, Bazin's remark highlights the fact that the index, like the symbol, is a nonmimetic sign—a point that I think has not been sufficiently registered. Although an index may resemble its object, say, in the case of a death mask, it is the way the death mask is fabricated, by first forming a mold directly from the face, that makes it indexical and so quite different in character from a purely iconic painted or sculpted portrait. Our relation to a life or death mask is colored by the knowledge of how it was produced. These same considerations inflect our reception of photographs. For some, this impersonal, automatic form of image-making disqualifies both the cast and the photograph as proper works of art. Yet, during the twentieth century, such processes came to be valued by artists precisely because, by restricting the agency of the artist, they cut through artistic conventions and opened the work of art onto a contingent world.[15] This is precisely what is at stake in Rosalind Krauss's contribution to the discussion of indexicality and art.

More Notes on the Index

The central claim of Krauss's "Notes on the Index: Seventies Art in America" is that the apparent plurality of practices characteristic of 1970s art masks a deeper affinity that has to do with the widespread use of indexical procedures, whether photographic or not. She isolates one particular type of index, the shifter, observing that this is a category of language that can be filled by any number of referents only because it is empty. Words such as *I, you, here,* or *there* change their referent according to the context or who is speaking. Each is a shifter—empty and open until filled by something outside it. While these pronouns are clearly conventional, arbitrary signs, and so symbols in Peirce's sense, the way their meaning depends on the copresence of an object outside the language system gives them the hybrid character of indexical symbols.[16] As we shall see, significant implications follow from Krauss's stress on the shifter—an index of the purely deictic kind.

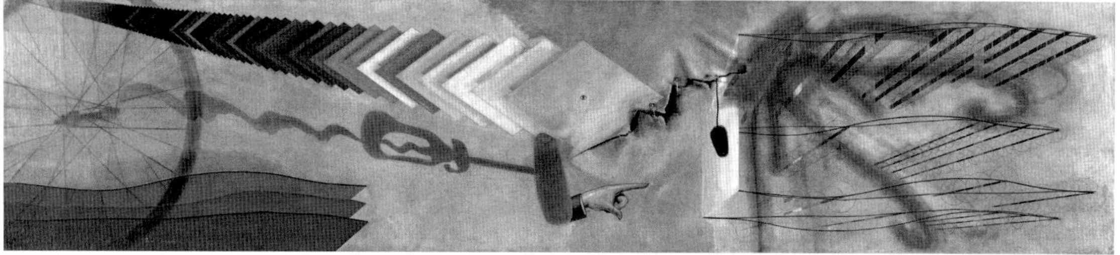

Figure 3 Marcel Duchamp, *Tu m'*, 1918. Oil on canvas, with bottlebrush, safety pins, and bolt. 69.8 × 303 cm (27½ × 119⁵⁄₁₆ inches). Yale University Art Gallery, New Haven. Gift of the Estate of Katherine S. Dreier. © Succession Marcel Duchamp/ADAGP, Paris/DACS, London, 2015.

Part 1 of "Notes" concerns the prehistory of contemporary artists' interest in indexicality. In her discussion of Duchamp's *Tu m'* (1918; fig. 3), a work she describes as a virtual "panorama of the index," Krauss observes that Duchamp apparently signaled his interest in indexicality by giving his painting a title consisting of two shifters, "you" and an abbreviated form of "me."[17] As if to announce the importance of this sign-function, a naive sign-painter's depiction of a hand with a pointing finger takes center stage. Furthermore, the ten-foot expanse of the canvas is filled with what look like distorted shadows cast by readymades, formed by projecting images of them on the canvas and tracing them with a lead pencil. Yet shadows, and Duchamp's tracings of them, are traces, not shifters. Presumably, Krauss includes them because they point to something that was outside the frame and so direct the viewer's attention to the original context of its making.[18] Krauss also discusses the work of Duchamp's friend and frequent collaborator, the American photographer Man Ray, and here she understands the index as trace. Man Ray's attraction to the index was most clearly manifested in his experiments with cameraless photography. The Rayograph, his name for the photogram, is an exemplary case of a type of photography that takes advantage of the indexical, more than the iconic, aspect of the medium. While all photography is indexical, the Rayograph, as Krauss observes "forces the issue of the photograph's existence as an index."[19] The images that result from putting objects directly onto light-sensitive paper are described as the "ghostly traces of departed objects." Man Ray himself put it beautifully when he called the Rayograph "a residue of an experience . . . recalling the event more or less clearly, like the undisturbed ashes of an object consumed by flames."[20] Although Krauss refers to Man Ray's photograms as "ghostly traces," this is not the aspect of them that really concerns her. What is crucial about the Rayograph and photography in general is that its physical genesis seems "to short-circuit or disallow those processes of schematization or symbolic intervention that operate within the graphic representation of most paintings." The photograph, like other indexical signs, "could be called sub- or pre-symbolic, ceding the language of art back to the imposition of things."[21] The index as trace emerges here as a kind of deliberate regression aimed at undoing the traditional conventions of painting. This regression, Krauss suggests, mimes an autistic or aphasic withdrawal from language.

The inarticulate trace and the empty index both undo artistic convention. For Krauss, then, the index "heralds a disruption in the autonomy of the sign. A meaninglessness surrounds it which can only be filled in by the addition of a text."[22] One consequence of the repression of traditional pictorial conventions is that the symbolic tends to return in the form of notes, accompanying texts, captions. And so we find, accompanying Duchamp's work, a compensatory hypertrophy of detailed, if puzzling, notebooks. The altered relation between sign and meaning manifested in Duchamp's practice amounts, claims Krauss, to "a trauma of signification," brought on by the rise of abstraction, on the one hand, and photography, on the other.[23] "Trauma" is used here metaphorically to describe what was, for some artists in the early twentieth century, an artistic crisis or impasse. This disturbance or trauma in the field of artistic conventions is what precipitated Duchamp's "autistic" artistic practice.

In part 2 of her essay, Krauss argues that Duchamp's deployment of the indexical sign set an important historical precedent for 1970s artists. In particular she draws attention to work that is quasi-photographic in the sense that it takes indexicality as its model. Some work mimes photography's "imposition of things," invoking "sheer physical presence" as a way of evading "the more highly articulated languages of aesthetic conventions."[24] Its regressive aspect involves a "reduction of the sign to a trace." The works under consideration were all shown in 1976 at the inaugural exhibition of the exhibition space P.S. 1, in Long Island City, Queens, New York. The show, called *Rooms*, consisted of interventions by seventy-eight artists in the fabric of the dilapidated former public school building.[25] Gordon Matta-Clark's *Doors, Floors, Doors* involved the removal of sections of ceiling and floor boards on three floors to create a vertical shaft; Michelle Stuart made rubbings of sections of the crumbling wall and displayed the results on the opposite side of the corridor; Lucio Pozzi made two-colored painted panels that replicated abrupt color changes on the walls to which they were affixed. This last example is particularly striking since it clearly represents a shift away from an internal, deductive logic of abstraction, exemplified by Frank Stella's shaped canvases, toward a quasi-indexical practice where the canvas has, so to speak, absorbed the given configuration of colors on the wall behind it, like a chameleon: the autonomy of the work is deliberately compromised. In this exhibition, Krauss concluded, "paintings are understood . . . as shifters, empty signs (like the word *this*) that are filled with meaning only when physically juxtaposed with an external referent, or object."[26] In other words, a work's character as a shifter renders it site-dependent. In each of the cases listed above, an intervention was made in the fabric of the building that was inseparable from it.

Krauss's emphasis on the meaningless trace and the empty shifter in her analysis of the exhibits at P.S. 1 foregrounds the works' here-and-nowness, their sheer physical presence. She makes little reference to the trace as "witness to an anteriority," and consequently the ambivalence at the heart of the index, which I sketched at the outset of this chapter, is lost.[27] The index as trace is characterized by its being a mode of mark-making that has the paradoxical quality of being a trace of (past) presence, that is, a presence invaded by absence and loss. This poignant contradiction is precisely why Barthes found the shadowy figures in old photographs wounding; in looking at them one is suspended between a deictic present-tense "that" and the past-tense "has been." Apparently alluding to this ambivalence, Anna Lovatt recently observed of one of the artists exhibited at P.S. 1 that "the imprint functions throughout [Michelle] Stuart's practice as a means of thematizing location and dislocation, plenitude and loss."[28] Indeed, the title of her piece at P.S. 1, *East/West Wall Memory Relocated* (1976), suggests that Stuart intended her rubbing to evoke the past-tense temporality of the trace and the space of memory.

Although it is not spelled out, it seems clear that a certain position regarding the state of art after modernism lies behind Krauss's particular appropriation of Peirce's tripartite division of signs. While the inarticulate or empty index and the symbolic or linguistic register are given prominence in the analysis of Duchamp and the 1970s artists she considers, the third type of sign in Peirce's typology, the icon, features only as a missing term. It is missing, I suspect, because that term is most closely associated with what is traditionally understood as pictorial art. Krauss's promotion of the art of the index, with its dependence on its spatiotemporal context, is aimed squarely at Michael Fried's critique of minimal art for being too objectlike, that is, for lacking the autonomous pictorial character of modernist painting. Krauss championed art practices that offered alternatives to this model of pictorial art, and this overriding concern explains why she was interested in the linguistic character of cubism, on the one hand, and the subsymbolic index, on the other: both can be mobilized in artistic strategies for evading pictorial conventions. The indexicality of 1970s art signaled, for her, the imminent demise of the pictorial paradigm still at home in modernist painting.

I have stressed the way in which indexical strategies partially bypass the agency of the author, opening up the work to contingency. They are caught up in the accidental, unintentional, traumatic—in short, they are closely associated with exposure. We have seen that, for Peirce, the index is the type of sign most closely associated with shock, reality, contingency, and chance. It forces our attention. It is the one type of sign that is actually affected by its object. As Mary Ann Doane puts it, "The concept of the index . . . seems to acknowledge the invasion of the semiotic system by the real."[29] While Krauss's appeal to the site-dependence of the shifter gestured in this direction, she confined its significance to the sphere of art, that is, to a formal means of subverting artistic convention and autonomy.

Flatbed

Krauss's essay, which makes reference to Peirce, Jakobson, and Barthes, was a highly original contribution to art criticism. It bears comparison with Leo Steinberg's equally original and influential essay "Other Criteria" (1972). They were aimed at the same target, Greenbergian formalism, and each outlined an alternative history of twentieth-century art that privileges Duchamp. Yet Steinberg's contribution leads in a quite different direction. In "Other Criteria," he proposes that Duchamp's *Large Glass* and *Tu m'* were key sources for what he postulates as a midcentury shift from a vertical pictorial to a horizontal "flatbed" conception of the picture plane.[30] This new work, he wrote, "is no longer the analogue of a world perceived from an upright position, but a matrix of information conveniently placed in a vertical situation." The artist who did most to develop this new conception of the picture plane was Robert Rauschenberg who, after decades of abstraction's dominance, "let the world in again." He did not let in the natural world, however, but rather a mash-up of urban stimuli. Rauschenberg effectively exchanged the model of painting as a view through a window for a model of painting as a "receptor surface on which objects are scattered, on which data is entered, on which information may be received, printed, impressed—whether coherently or in confusion."[31] Surfaces mentioned include tabletops, studio floors, charts, and bulletin boards. All these examples are solid objects, but what is remarkable about Steinberg's account, given that it was written in the early 1970s, is how penetrated it is by the language of information technology. For Steinberg, the surface of Rauschenberg's combines of the 1950s stands in for mental processes in contact with a technological and mediatized world:

> dump, reservoir, switching center, abundant with concrete references freely associated as in an internal monologue—the outward symbol of the mind as a running transformer of the external world, constantly ingesting incoming unprocessed data to be mapped in an overcharged field.[32]

This material, he continues, is organized so as to "maintain a symbolic continuum of litter, workbench, and data-ingesting mind." Steinberg senses that information is often imperfectly registered: the pictures include the "waste and detritus of communication—like a radio transmission with interference; noise and meaning on the same wavelength." The images render "the ceaseless inflow of urban message, stimulus, and impediment."[33]

Steinberg is clearly describing here a "trauma of signification," but one that is rather different from that referred to by Krauss. Freud had a word for it—*Reizüberflutung*, a flooding of the mind with an excess of stimulation—and Walter Benjamin adapted the concept to characterize life under modern capitalism.[34] Rauschenberg's complex canvases, which picture the mind under the conditions of modernity, feature indexical traces that bypass intention—they are "received, printed, impressed," as Steinberg says. He cites Duchamp's *Tu m'* as setting a precedent for this understanding of art as a receptive surface wide open to the contingencies of urban life and mass media, to everyday traumas and world-historical events experienced secondhand through various media channels.[35] The flatbed is equivalent to a mind exposed to shocks with no protective shield, or, to shift the metaphor, it is a more dynamic version of the receptive and retentive surface of a magic slate. As Steinberg put it, Rauschenberg's picture plane is "a consciousness immersed in the brain of the city."[36]

Curiously, two years prior to "Notes on the Index," Krauss wrote a piece on Rauschenberg that was deeply indebted to Steinberg. In "Rauschenberg and the Materialized Image" (1974), she cites his 1972 article "Reflections on the State of Criticism," the first published version of "Other Criteria."[37] In her essay, Krauss stresses two things about the appearance of Rauschenberg's work from the mid-1950s. First, she notes the materiality of the stuff, "like so much clutter and debris," that he suspended within the pictorial matrix. This has the effect of turning the image into something that must be scrutinized and deciphered over time. She also observes how he levels the diverse components of the image so that each possesses an equal degree of density and opacity. This feature, Krauss contends, makes the images resemble "the space of memory," that is, a space where having seen a reproduction in a magazine can have the same weight as having met a friend on the street. Yet here memory is figured, not as a private internal space, but as something external and collective—"a collection of facts . . . each of which leaves its imprint as it burrows into and forms experience."[38] Krauss's emphasis on the materiality and externality of Rauschenberg's imagery is, I believe, her way of capturing the undigested, traumatic character of experience in modernity. In this essay, in contrast to "Notes on the Index," found objects and indexical imprints connote the trauma of signification precipitated by the conditions of modern life.

Dust Breeding

Tu m' set one sort of precedent for Rauschenberg and other artists who would open their art to the world of urban information overload. *Dust Breeding*, a collaborative work by Duchamp and Man Ray, set a rather different, albeit related, one (fig. 4). In 1920, Duchamp asked Man Ray to photograph the bottom half of what was to become his great work *The Bride Stripped Bare by Her Bachelors, Even*, otherwise known as the *Large Glass*. The *Glass* had been resting horizontally near an open window in Duchamp's New York studio, collecting dust for some months. Man Ray set up his camera, opened the shutter, and the two went out to lunch. After about an hour, they returned and Man Ray closed the shutter. The anecdote is remarkable for several reasons, including the departure of the artists and the lengthy exposure, during which the slow fall of dust through the window onto the glass was doubled by the slow fall of light through the shutter onto the film. This doubling invites us

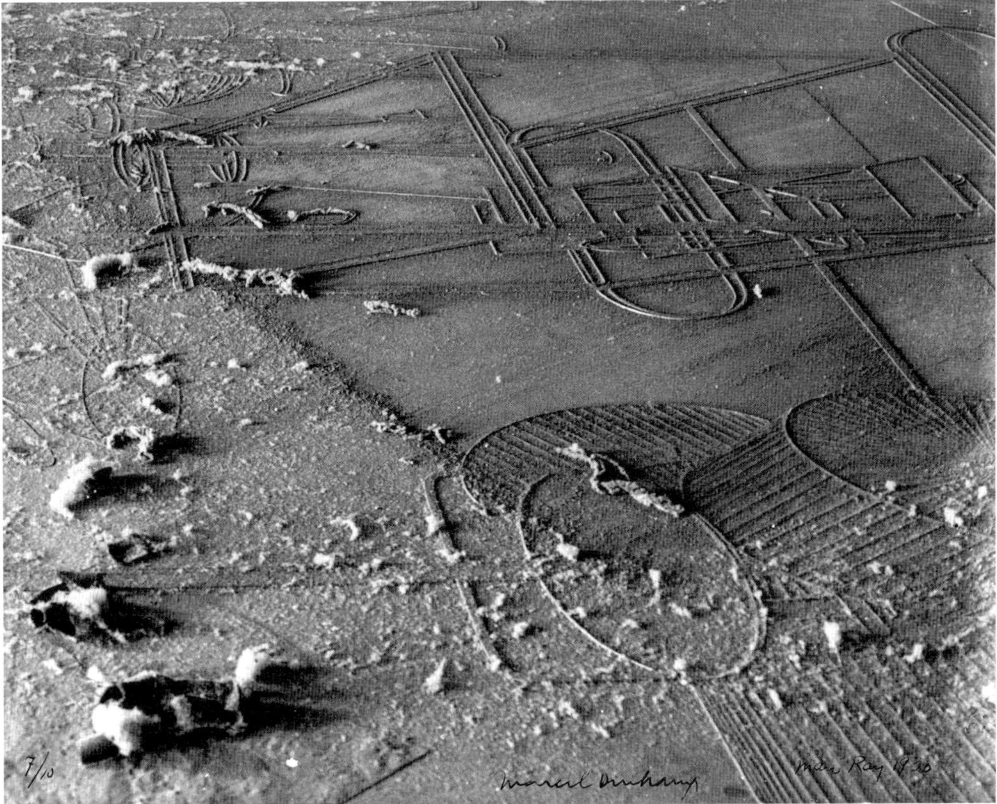

Figure 4 Man Ray, *Dust Breeding*, 1920 (printed ca. 1967). Gelatin-silver print. 23.9 × 30.4 cm. © Succession Marcel Duchamp/ADAGP, Paris/DACS, London, 2015. © Man Ray Trust/ADAGP, Paris/DACS, London, 2015. Image © The Metropolitan Museum of Art/Art Resource/Scala, Florence.

to imagine the film as a photographic flatbed, that is, as a receptive, neutral surface open to whatever befalls it.[39] Certain connotations gather around the falling dust: the index of the passage of time, the accumulation of debris or waste as artistic procedure, the powdery entropic chaos of dust itself. As we shall see, the traumatic associations of dust and lint have been explored by many writers and artists.[40]

If everything in *Dust Breeding* happens in slow motion, Ed Ruscha's collaborative book *Royal Road Test* (1967) is a high-speed version of it. The latter involved throwing a typewriter from the window of a speeding car, then taking snapshots of the resulting field of debris; many of the overhead shots resemble *Dust Breeding*. Conversely, the cropped photograph of the dusty, horizontal *Large Glass* suggests an aerial view of a desert landscape. In fact, it was published in Breton's journal *Littérature* in 1922 with a caption, part of which reads, "view taken from an airplane by Man Ray."[41] The fragments of a mechanical apparatus strewn across the desert landscape in *Royal Road Test* suggest not so much a view from an airplane as the debris of a plane crash. The implicit violence of Ruscha's appropriation of *Dust Breeding* is repeated by Gerhard Richter, who in 2000 made a piece called *14 Feb. 45*. It is a print based on an aerial photograph taken from a US aircraft during the bombing of Cologne, the city Richter has made his home. It shows the moment of impact of a bomb exploding a bridge over the Rhine, but the landscape is pockmarked all over. The photograph is described in Richter's catalogue raisonné as a "photograph behind glass."[42] The glass, the gray tones of the image, the network of roads and the puffs of smoke, clouds, and shadows, all recall the lower half of the Duchamp's *Large Glass* in progress, with its applied wire network of lines and its coating of dust and debris.[43] The French photographer Sophie Ristelhueber also paid tribute to *Dust Breeding* with her aerial and close-up photographs of the terrain of Kuwait (*Fait*, 1992). Taken six months after the end of the first Gulf War, they show traces of debris, craters, and tank tracks left in the desert sand.[44]

The foregoing examples again call up connotations of dust as trace of the passage of time, associated with death, destruction, decay, and transience. This cluster also surrounds dust in W. G. Sebald's remarkable literary account, in *The Immigrants*, of an artist called Max Ferber in the English version but Aurach in the original German. Sebald based the figure of Ferber on Frank Auerbach, a British artist whose parents died in the Holocaust and who was rescued by the *Kindertransport*. The tale's narrator stumbles upon Ferber in a ruined, formerly Jewish quarter of Manchester. In a dusty studio, he finds the artist spreading paint thickly on a canvas and then scratching it off. Hardened deposits of paint cover the floor, and Ferber tells the narrator that he has come to love this debris. "He felt closer to dust, than to light,

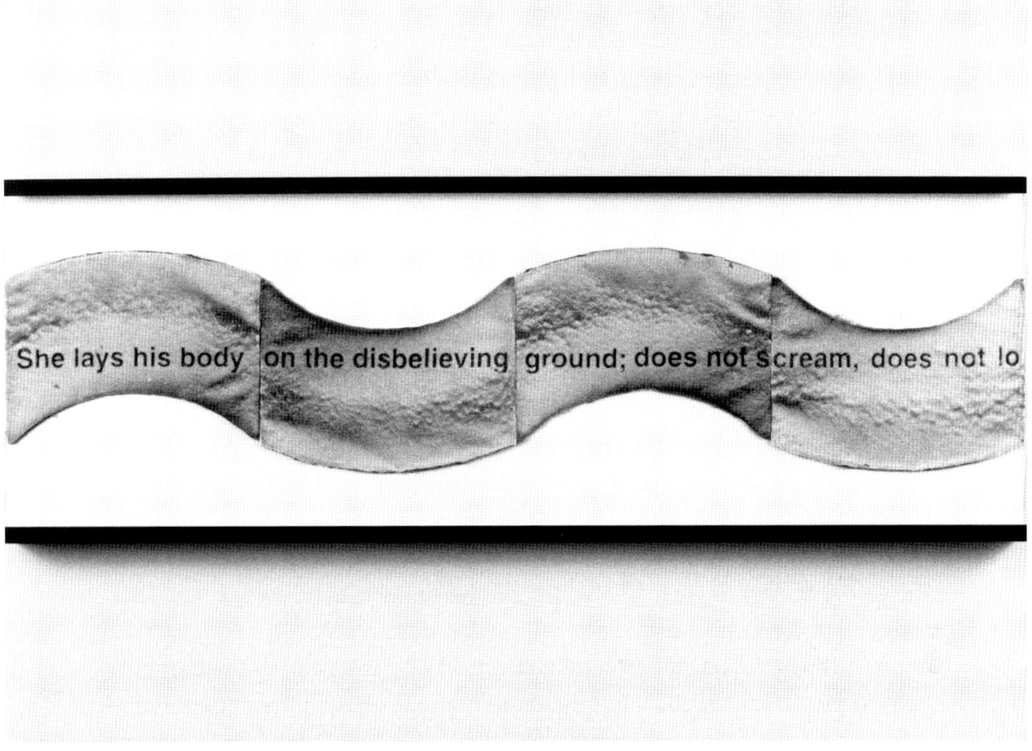

Figure 5 Mary Kelly, *The Ballad of Kastriot Rexhepi* (detail), 2001. Compressed dryer lint, 49 framed panels. Each 17 × 48 × 2 inches; overall length, 206 feet. Courtesy of the artist.

air or water."[45] Eric Santner observes in his discussion of these passages that Sebald's sense of dust is of matter reduced almost to nothing.[46]

These same connotations cluster around Mary Kelly's lint works. Since the turn of the century, much of her work has concerned the subject of war and global atrocities. One such work, *Mea Culpa* (1999), is a large-scale installation. The curious gray swags that festoon the walls of the gallery like mourning crêpe turn out on closer inspection to be arcs of compacted lint carefully harvested, intact, from the filter of her clothes dryer and framed behind Perspex. One moves around the room reading on the repeating modules terse stories of torture and atrocity that have been heard before the International War Crimes Tribunal. Kelly followed this up with *The Ballad of Kastriot Rexhepi* (2001), a more ambitious installation also made of lint modules, this time arranged as a continuous sine wave (fig. 5). Wrapping the room in a band two hundred feet long, the piece recounts the story of an infant left for dead by his grieving mother amid the internecine strife that engulfed the former Yugoslavia in the 1990s. The boy is found alive and adopted by Serbs, then lost again, and finally reunited with his Albanian parents. It was one of many stories of civilian suffering transmitted through the mass media but in danger of being lost; rescued and retold in poetic form by Kelly, it became emblematic of the entire war, especially as it was lived by women. The wave, which metaphorically tracks the pared-down narrative, also evokes a continuous keening sound, which is realized when the exhibition of the work is accompanied by the performance of a piece, composed for the purpose by Michael Nyman, for mezzo-soprano and string quartet.

In effect, Kelly turned her tumble dryer into a primitive printmaking device, forming intaglio letters in light lint and then filling them in with a dusting of dark lint. Fragments of news reports, horrific images of distant disasters, are transmitted into our homes as we go about our daily lives, doing the laundry. We suffer long-distance, mediatized traumatic effects that blur public and private, domestic and global spaces. Griselda Pollock succinctly refers to this condition and Kelly's response to it as "virtual trauma and indexical witness."[47] The materiality of lint residue suggests some soft and vulnerable substance where the traumatic information is filtered and inscribed. Kelly's use of lint is a form of abstract photography that filters out figurative elements and leaves, as she says, "the emotional or affective residue of the event."[48] Kelly explained to me that, around 1973, she gave up photography and began exploring aniconic indexical processes. She realized "the insufficiency of the iconic to register affect." The power of the index, she said, has to do with its closeness to its object, while the iconic image, even a photographic one, always involves some form of articulation and artistic convention, and these in turn imply distance and rationalization.[49]

Although there are no photographs in *Mea Culpa* or *Ballad*, they nonetheless invoke photography's two-sided cultural significance—its digitized ubiquity in the total information world and its precious residue, like dust or ashes, of a "that-has-been."[50] Of course, the lint is not a literal index of traumatic witnessing; it is only a trace or residue of the clothes in the dryer. However, I want to suggest that it functions as an "analogical index." What Kelly has done is to set up an analogical relation between the clothes buffeted in the machine and the residual lint, on the one hand, and the reports of atrocities and the psychic trace of the trauma, on the other. Kelly's work attempts to give mediatized, virtual news stories the texture of the real.

Another artist who has drawn on the connotations that attach to dust and lint is Gabriel Orozco. *Lintels* (2001) is made of compressed lint collected from dryers in a public laundromat in New York City (fig. 6). These fragile "skins," arranged as if on clotheslines stretched high across the gallery space, are composed not only of dirt, dust, and fluff from fabric, but also of hair and tiny flakes of skin. Their delicacy suggests something of the precariousness of human life, and this impression is confirmed when we learn that the lint

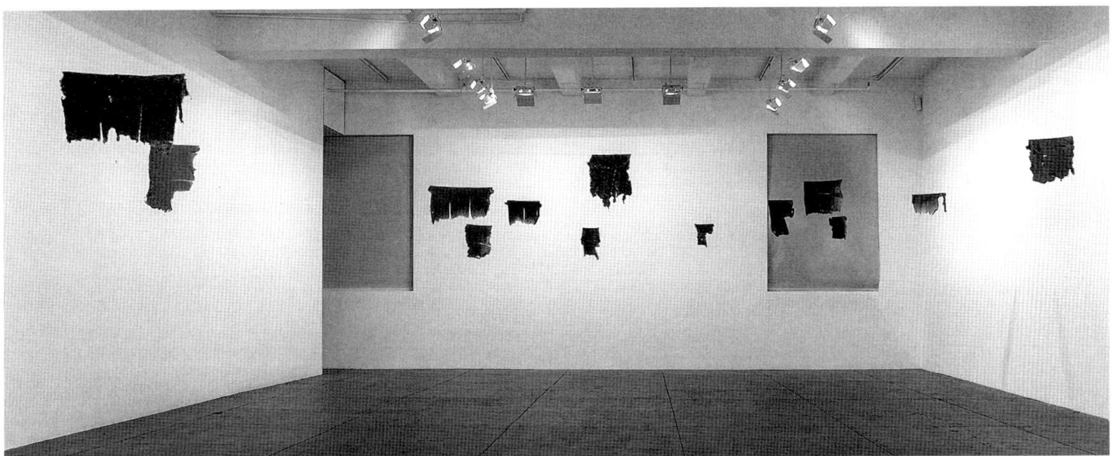

Figure 6 Gabriel Orozco, *Lintels*, 2000. Dryer lint. Dimensions variable. Installation view at Marian Goodman Gallery, New York.

was harvested in New York City and exhibited there in 2001, two months after 9/11. With their lint works, both Kelly and Orozco propose an apparatus as a model of experience and memory that is quite different from Freud's mystic writing pad. The violent motion of the tumble dryer figures the turbulence and traumas of modernity, while the lint figures the real as remainder, residue, the trace of the trauma. Duchamp's *Dust Breeding* anticipated a kind of soft flatbed and inspired a series of works, both photographic and non-photographic, that take up the traumatic connotations that attach to matter reduced to almost nothing.

According to Krauss, artists in the 1970s were attracted to shifters and other indexical signs as means of subverting the autonomy of the work of art. The meaninglessness of the trace and emptiness of the shifter forces it to adhere to its surrounding context for signification. This opening up and turning outward is not altogether dissimilar to Steinberg's flatbed picture plane, which aimed "to let the world in again." However, as we have seen, there is a major difference in the critics' understanding of the significance of this radical receptivity. In "Notes on the Index," Krauss understands indexical procedures as part of a formal strategy leveled at a particular conception of autonomous art. For Steinberg, the indexical flatbed is instead a response to social and technological changes that have deeply affected the way our minds process or, indeed, fail to process, impressions. These changes, in turn, demand new formal means. Branden Joseph underscores this point, noting that "unlike too many facile acclamations of postmodernity that followed, Steinberg's article continues to indicate the complex social stakes in transformations of artistic significance."[51] As Steinberg himself wrote, the change in the picture's orientation "is no more than a symptom of changes which go far beyond questions of picture planes, or of painting as such."[52] In the following chapter, I consider how the rapid rise of digitization in all spheres of life, including art, has prompted some artists to mine the resources of analogue photography as an indexical medium.

Analogue 3

Leo Steinberg's plea in the early 1970s for an art that "let the world in again" was a way of countering the then-dominant New York School of abstract art. The contemporary artists he championed, Jasper Johns and Robert Rauschenberg, turned for inspiration to strategies familiar to the avant-gardes of the 1920s. This included a renewed interest in photography, which, apart from a few interesting experiments in abstraction, could not but let the world in. It is only in recent decades that the essentially receptive, indexical character of photography has been challenged. Digital technologies have vastly increased the photographer's power to manipulate the image, calling into question its difference from depiction in other media, such as painting and drawing. So it is only now, with the rise of digitization and the near obsolescence of traditional photographic technology, that we are becoming fully aware of the distinctive character of analogue photography. This late appreciation of the analogue—the owl of Minerva taking wing as night falls—has prompted artists to mine the medium for its specificity. Indeed, one could argue that analogue photography has only recently become a medium in the fullest sense of the term, for it is only when artists refuse to switch over to digital photographic technologies that the question of what constitutes analogue photography as a medium is self-consciously posed. While the benefits of digitization in terms of accessibility, dissemination, speed, and efficiency are universally acknowledged, some people are beginning to reflect on what is being lost. This chapter does not attempt an ontological inquiry into the essential nature of the analogue; rather, it is an effort to articulate something about analogue photography as an artistic medium for contemporary artists by paying close attention to the meaning and stakes of analogue photography for particular artists. Instead of attempting a general survey, I want to consider the work of just two artists, Zoe Leonard and Tacita Dean, both of whose work is concerned with what is being lost. As Leonard put the case succinctly:

> New technology is usually pitched to us as an improvement. But progress is always an exchange. We gain something, we give something else up. I'm interested in looking at some of what we are losing.[1]

Tellingly, both artists have produced exhibitions of their work simply called *Analogue*. Leonard gave the title to a large project she did between 1998 and 2009 consisting of 412 gelatin-silver and C-prints of local shop fronts in lower Manhattan and poor market stalls around the world.[2] Dean used the title for a 2006 retrospective exhibition of her films, photographs, and drawings.

Debates about the difference between digital and analogue photographic art practices often turn on the issue of agency and automatism.[3] For the past few decades, several celebrated artists have been producing large-scale photographic images in which artistic intention through digital manipulation is foregrounded. In the work of Jeff Wall or Andreas Gursky, for example, the process involves a kind of painting or collage with pixels; emphasis is placed on the carefully controlled synthesis and composition of multiple images to form the final picture.[4] Both Leonard and Dean, by contrast, are resistant to manipulation. Instead, openness to chance and the medium's indexicality are aspects of the analogue valued in their work. Of course, artists using analogue film do exercise considerable agency, in selecting camera and film, framing, focusing, and setting aperture size, length of exposure, and so on, as well as myriad choices throughout the printing process. Yet, for the artists I consider, these forms of intervention do not essentially compromise the analogue's photochemical continuity with the world. The analogue remains defined as a relatively continuous form of inscription involving physical contact. From this point of view, the photogram, produced by contact between an object and light-sensitive paper, only makes explicit what it implicit in all analogue photography. Conversely, digital photography's translation of light into an arbitrary electronic code arguably interrupts that continuity prior to the effects of digital editing. The difference between a photograph and computerized image synthesis, so-called born-digital imagery, is being eroded.[5]

These reflections on the distinction between analogue and digital photography inevitably raise the thorny question of whether digitization has compromised the authority of the photographic document. Those who argue the case are likely to underestimate the extent to which the analogue document is naturally distorted and intentionally manipulated.[6] They also tend to neglect the fact that digital photography provides journalists, astronomers, and doctors, among others, with accurate information about the objects or states of affairs that were the images' origin. Both technologies are, in fact, causally bound up with their objects and susceptible to manipulation. From this practical point of view, there is no substantive difference between the two.[7] From an artistic point of view, however, I argue that there is an important difference. While the truth value of photography is a much-debated and intriguing topic, it is not the focus of my interest in the analogue; my concerns are aesthetic rather than ontological or epistemological. My theme is the impact of the new technology on artistic practice. Digital photography has had inescapable consequences, not only for those artists who have adopted it, but also for those who have not. It is too early to say whether digital photography constitutes a new medium or if, as with the introduction of color film, it is a modification of an old one. In any case, it is possible to point to important shifts in practice that have occurred. The interface of photographic technology with the computer and the availability of large-scale digital printing have revolutionized photographic art in the last thirty years. In response, artists working with analogue film have tended to emphasize the virtues or specific character of predigital technologies. Since digital cameras are designed to mimic the functions of analogue ones, amateur photographers are probably unaware of much difference in the images they produce. Artists, however, are interested in the very specific character of their medium and so are likely to seize on a technical difference and amplify it. An example of this trend can be seen in digital photographic art where low-resolution pictures are enlarged in order to make the pixel grid visible.[8] Meanwhile, certain contemporary analogue photographers, such as Hiroshi Sugimoto, are reviving earlier printing techniques to achieve effects like the incomparable velvety blacks and luminous whites of gelatin-silver prints.

As we shall see, in response to digitization, both Leonard and Dean have found ways of making the character of their medium salient. They adopt a receptive attitude and welcome chance effects. They aim to make the material, tactile quality of the medium palpable. Both artists are drawn to objects that bear the indexical marks of weather, age, and use—discovering an elective affinity between these things and the way they imagine their medium. An analogue record of an object bearing traces of wear or age doubles the indexicality of the image, making the image a trace of a trace, and thereby drawing attention to an aspect of the medium within the image. For example, both Leonard and Dean have made series of photographs of misshapen trees. As in these series, their work often focuses on the damaged texture of the world, for it is precisely this texture that is compromised by the digitally enhanced environment characteristic of commercial digital photography. In short, they associate analogue photography with a kind of attentive *exposure* to things in the world marked by chance, age, and accident. This idea of exposure, in both its photographic and ethical senses, informs my understanding of the work of Leonard and Dean. In the introductory chapter, I offered a brief exposition of the poetics of exposure as formulated in Eric Santner's *On Creaturely Life*.[9] This account of Leonard and Dean develops this idea to argue that their attitude to the world and to the medium is best summed up by the term "exposure." That argument is prefaced, however, by a brief detour through Thierry de Duve's phenomenological description of two different sorts of photographic practice.

In "Time Exposure and Snapshot: The Photograph as Paradox" (1978), de Duve describes two sorts of photography. Couched in terms of a technical difference, his typology offers a way of rethinking photography as a medium with two faces. For de Duve, time-exposure photography emphasizes the light sensitivity and indexicality of a medium that is attuned to objects. The instantaneous snapshot, in contrast, tries to capture events. De Duve aims to expand his analysis of photography beyond a purely semiotic reading to include "the affective and phenomenological involvement of the unconscious with the external world, rather than its linguistic structure."[10] Accordingly, he aligns the snapshot with trauma and the time exposure with mourning. He reasons that the snapshot isolates a single point in time and space and this prevents description or narration; one is rendered "momentarily aphasic" in a way that is analogous to the breakdown of symbolization characteristic of trauma. In addition, the temporality of the snapshot is always one of a missed encounter—too late to change what is about to happen, too early to see what transpires. The stillness and chiaroscuro of a time-exposure photograph, on the contrary, allow for an extended duration of viewing and reverie. As a substitutive object, moreover, it facilitates the work of mourning. One can, of course, cite counterexamples to de Duve's typology (the blurred long exposure of a football player in action; the snapshot portrait with hair and clothes disheveled by a sudden gust of wind), but the effect of these images lies precisely in their going against the grain of the type normally associated with the genre.

The original publication of de Duve's essay preceded Roland Barthes's *Camera Lucida* by two years. It is unclear if Barthes knew it, but in effect he adapted the phenomenological character of de Duve's snapshot—the traumatic "here and formerly"—in such a way that it came to characterize photography in general, but more particularly time-exposure portrait photography, examples of which form the bulk of Barthes's illustrations. Barthes's revision seems to me entirely justified, for an athlete caught in midjump, de Duve's prime example of the snapshot, has none of the pathos of an old portrait photograph. Further, de Duve's characterization of the snapshot resembles Freud's and Benjamin's accounts of how consciousness *defends against* trauma.[11] The ballistic art of film, with its jump cuts and montage effects, is conceived by Benjamin as a means of adapting to modern life, of learning to screen potentially harmful impressions and so preventing harmful effects. Charles Baudelaire, Benjamin's exemplary poet of the shock-experiences of crowds, technology, and gambling, compared the work of the poet or artist to a fencer parrying blows. Baudelaire's poetry, wrote Benjamin, "exposes the isolated experience in all its nakedness."[12] In short, what de Duve refers to as trauma is here consciousness as it screens and parries the shocks of contemporary life.[13] Traumatic experience, conversely, is defined by Freud as having such an overwhelming or ungraspable character that it slips past those defenses to form a reserve of unconscious memory traces, psychical scars that can only be retrieved involuntarily.[14] It is important for my argument to maintain this distinction between the shock effect of the snapshot and the traumatic effect of time-exposure photography. Time exposure is presented here as an alternative model of experience to the snapshot's defensive parrying of blows; it implies a receptivity or vulnerability or exposure to whatever is encountered.

What is fundamentally at issue here is an analogy between the subject of trauma, who is marked by the sight of something that leaves an indelible trace on the psyche, and the wide-open camera lens and light-sensitive medium that records on film a trace of whatever happens. Bypassing the "protective shield against stimuli," traumatic events leave behind an indelible trace.[15] The work of art as the paradigm case of a mind-formulated artifact wholly porous to the intentions of its maker is thus challenged by an alternative practice that contrives ways to capture the unpredictability of our encounter with the world. Agency is involved in setting up the apparatus and in judging the outcome; between these moments, chance is allowed to intervene. While this bracketing of intentionality is a choice, the material that emerges is outside the artist's control. To put the case another way, the fact that an artist intentionally courts chance does not make everything that emerges from that process intentional, unless one claims that retrospective acceptance of chance occurrences confers intentionality—but that seems to me to stretch the concept of intention to its breaking point.

Zoe Leonard

In *Analogue*, her major series of photographs of shop fronts, Zoe Leonard makes apparent the analogue character of her medium (plate 4). For example, she leaves the black surround of the film with the brand name, Kodak or Fuji, clearly visible. She usually hangs the prints under glass with no frame or mat. Their familiar square format, eleven inches square, recalls pictures taken by classic analogue film cameras, like the old Rolleiflex she in fact used. Individual prints are of modest size, although the full installation of all 412 prints, as seen at Documenta XII in 2007, is monumental in scale. The impetus for the project, which involved a decade of work and thousands of pictures, arose from the fact that her neighborhood in the Lower East Side of Manhattan (and later, in Brooklyn) was undergoing rapid gentrification. The old linoleum store and local butcher were making way for new clothing boutiques and bars. It was only at this point, when "the layered, frayed and quirky beauty" of her neighborhood was on the point of disappearing, that she realized how much she loved and depended on it.[16] Although *Analogue* moves out from Leonard's neighborhood, following the movement of unwanted clothes and multinational brand logos from New York to market stalls in Mexico City, Havana, Kampala, Ramallah, cities in Eastern Europe, and elsewhere, the photographer's relation to the things she documents always remains close-up, personal, and small-scale.

Leonard's project, then, in some way resembles Eugène Atget's documentation of old Paris around 1900, which was also subject to ongoing demolition. There are clear allusions to Atget, for example, in the fascination with shop windows, the attention paid to lowly and overlooked quarters, the avoidance of people, and the organization of the photographs into thematic chapters. The book version of *Analogue* contains an essay by Leonard called "A Continuous Signal" (one definition of the word analogue) that is made up entirely of quotations from other writers and has a section devoted to Atget. There are also clear allusions to Walker Evans, who in 1958 published a set of color photos of shop fronts in *Fortune* magazine, together with a statement about the wonders of shop-front displays in New York: "What is as dependably entertaining as a really enthusiastic arrangement of plumbers' tools?" he asks.[17] The examples of Atget and Evans seem to have offered Leonard a way of reconciling the photographic document and art by using the photograph to frame the strange beauty of the ordinary and overlooked.

Shop fronts are Leonard's version of the surrealists' flea market, where, in a receptive frame of mind, one might chance upon something personally revelatory. Leonard photographs of found arrangements of objects and the story they tell are both personal and political. Her photographs are like formally uniform boxes to store the large found objects she encounters in her walks through the streets. The camera becomes a receptacle and the author a receiver. In "The Author as Receiver," Kaja Silverman discusses the fundamentally receptive character of photography and film, as well as the ethics of this position.[18] Other contemporary artists have commented on the significance of vessels and containers in their work as signaling a receptive attitude. For example, commenting on a readymade piece, Gabriel Orozco remarked, "The shoe box is an empty space that holds things. I am interested in the idea of making myself—as an artist and an individual—above all a receptacle." He sums up by saying that "the ideas of the void, of the container and of vulnerability have been important in all my work. I also work a lot with the accident." Orozco makes the links, crucial for my argument, between art practice, receptivity, and chance.[19]

Leonard's sensibility is both informed by and in tension with the formal rigor of minimalism. This ambivalent relation is made very apparent in an installation from 2003. The work, *1961*, consists of forty-one secondhand suitcases in subtle gradations of blue, arranged in a row spanning the length of the room. Leonard has referred to the work as autobiographical; the title is her birth year and the number of suitcases her age at the time the work was made. Personal identity is here turned into a series of spatial compartments, repositories of emotions, thoughts, and memories. There is an analogy to be drawn, then, between the suitcases and her photography, as both relate to what she has called "the impossible task of remembering."[20] The repeated modules recall Donald Judd's installations, but the status of the suitcases as found objects attracts a host of associations—transportation, migration, leaving home, anxiety, and so on. As Leonard has observed, "We use things to communicate complex ideas, feelings; it is a dense, compact, potent language, the language of the found object."[21] And, of course, suitcases are receptacles—closed and private. For Leonard, they evoke the idea of life as a journey: "A trip feels like a metaphor for life. It has a beginning, a middle and an end; it is a combination of choice and chance, of intention and surprise."[22] For Leonard and, as we shall see, for Dean, the journey represents a paradoxical intention to abandon oneself to chance, to launch oneself into the unknown.

Although Leonard takes great care with choice of materials, framing, and printing process, I think it is fair to say that, for her, photography is mainly an art of noticing, recording, and editing. In an interview, she once remarked, "I think my work is less about creating and more about observing."[23] This restriction of authorial agency allows her to be more open to the element of chance. One particularly good example of this strategy can be seen in the series *tree + bag* (2000), which simply records random arrangements of plastic bags caught up in the branches of bare trees. Leonard made another series, *Detail (tree and fence)* (1998–99), of trees in her neighborhood that were struggling in the urban environment yet surviving, albeit in misshapen forms (fig. 7). She commented:

> I was amazed by the way these trees grew in spite of their enclosures—bursting out of them or absorbing them. The pictures in the tree series synthesize my thoughts about struggle. People can't help but anthropomorphize. I immediately identify with the tree.[24]

I find these to be quite painful images that speak of the deforming effects of power and confinement. A sense of vulnerability is powerfully conveyed by the way the flesh of the trees is impressed by the rigid forms of iron bars or a chain-link fence. Yet Leonard is insistent that the living flesh of the trees should be seen as resisting and overcoming those impediments. The trees,

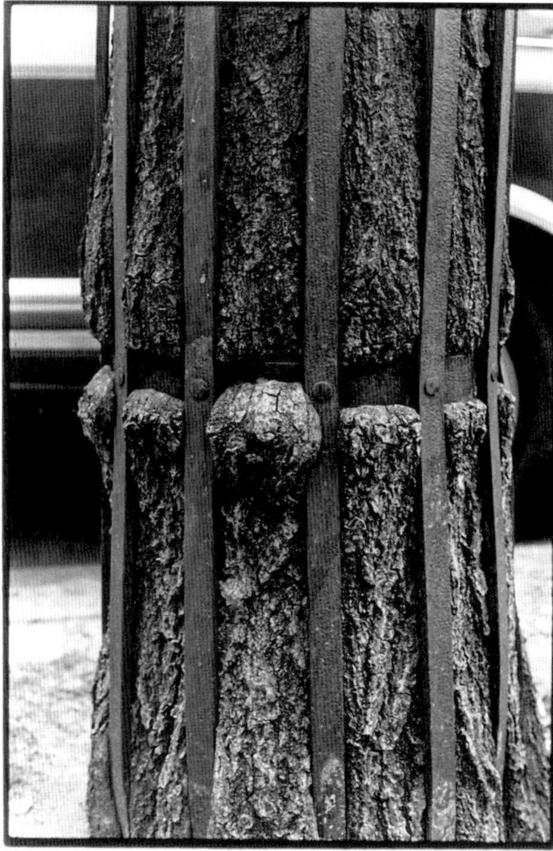

Figure 7 Zoe Leonard, *Detail (tree and fence)*, 1998–99. Gelatin-silver print. 30.5 × 21.6 cm. Courtesy of the artist.

she says, are "growing through and around these fences, so there is evidence of them as living, growing, adapting organisms."[25] For her, they are found, everyday emblems of struggles for survival in inhospitable conditions.

Strange Fruit (1992–97) is a remarkable installation that consists of around three hundred skins of various fruits, each one emptied and then carefully stitched, snapped, or zipped back together (fig. 8). They are scattered on the floor of the gallery, as if fallen from trees. The piece is a work of mourning for all Leonard's friends who had died from AIDS in the years before effective drugs were available. The act of stitching together the empty skins suggests this vain effort might be reparation, restoration. It shows "a desire to make whole, to hold onto the form of something or someone," even after they are gone. For her, this desire to preserve is also bound up with art-making, with photography. While this desire is acknowledged, so too is the impossibility of keeping anything in perpetuity. "This work takes the material of the still life and reworks it. It borrows from the language of *vanitas* pictures and suggests that the artwork cannot preserve the person or the memory any more than the artwork can be preserved."[26] The skins, although owned by a museum, are slowly turning to dust. This piece, more than any other, brings to the fore the theme of the pain of separation. But I think it can act as a lens through which to view her work as driven not by nostalgia but by separation, loss, and desire. What becomes very clear with this work is how deeply the AIDS epidemic affected Leonard. It decimated the community around her, and the lack of public mourning for its victims made it harder to bear. The deserted streets of New York in *Analogue* refer to this traumatic emptying out, as well as to the closure of familiar neighborhood shops.[27]

I have discussed two sculptural installations in my account of Leonard because I think her understanding of photography, with its emphasis on the object represented, is close to sculpture.[28] We recall that de Duve associated slow optics with the sort of photograph that frames a lost or absent object, contrasting it with the snapshot, which tries to capture an event. The paradigm of the first sort is the funerary portrait, that of the second, the abrupt

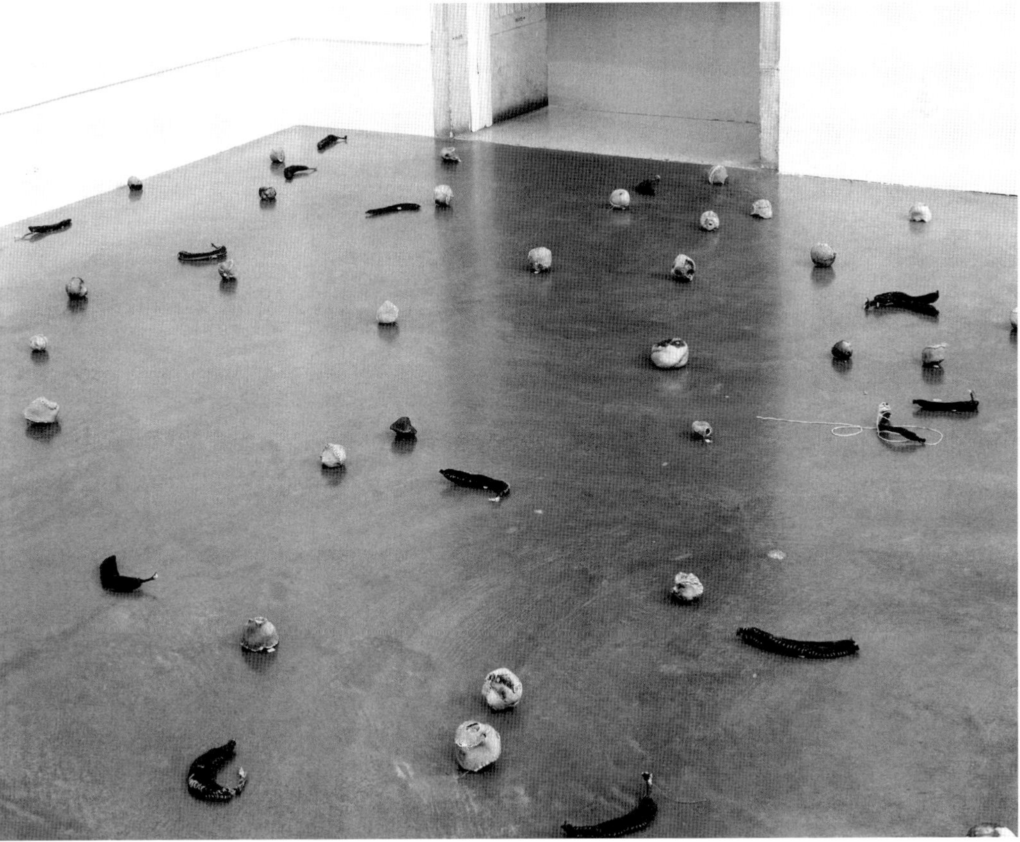

Figure 8 Zoe Leonard, *Strange Fruit*, 1992–97. 297 orange, banana, grapefruit, and lemon skins, thread, buttons, zippers, needles, wax, sinew, string, snaps, and hooks; installed on the floor. Dimensions variable. Collection of Philadelphia Museum of Art. Photo: Adam Reich, Zoe Leonard. Courtesy of Paula Cooper Gallery, New York.

and aggressive press photo. What this implies is that the modality of slow optics is spatial rather than temporal and tied to the object rather than the event. Time exposure, in other words, is more attuned to sculpture than is the prefilmic snapshot. This was also Walter Benjamin's view; describing a photographic portrait of Friedrich Schelling, he ascribes to the lengthy exposure time the emergence of the very tactile creases in the philosopher's face and in the folds in his coat. Schelling grew into his coat and face in the same way that his image grew into the light-sensitive plate. As Benjamin notes, "During the considerable period of the exposure, the subject (as it were) grew into the picture, in the strongest contrast with the appearances in a snapshot." This allowed him "to focus his life in the moment rather than hurrying on past it."[29] Yet if this sort of photography is allied to sculpture, it is the sort of sculpture that is lined with absence, like Leonard's hollowed-out fruit skins or suitcases.

Tacita Dean

I hope that the constellation of linked concepts including loss, trauma, the chance encounter with the found object, and what I am calling the time-exposure style of analogue photography is beginning to emerge. Without wishing to diminish the distinctive achievements of the two artists under consideration here, I now want to see if this same constellation might prove helpful in thinking about the work of Tacita Dean. I detect a similar sensibility at work; for example, her film *Pie* (2003) is a more pastoral version of Leonard's *tree + bag* series (fig. 9). Shot out of the back window of her house in Berlin, the film shows a tree and the random comings and goings of magpies.

Dean is even more outspoken than Leonard in her stand against the digitization of everything. In the introduction to the catalogue for the retrospective exhibition *Analogue*, she declares that analogue is a description "of everything I hold dear." It refers, she points out, to a vast range of things, from the movement of hands on a watch to writing and drawing. "Analogue implies a continuous signal—a continuum and a line, whereas digital constitutes what is broken up, or rather, broken down, into millions of numbers." While the convenience of digital media is wonderful, she confesses, "For me, it just does not have the means to create poetry; it neither breathes nor wobbles, but tidies up our society, correcting it and then leaves no trace." It is not "born of the physical world." We are being "frogmarched," she declares, into a digital future, "without a backward turn, without a sigh or a nod to what we are losing."[30] I can't help hearing in this last phrase an echo of the tragic myth of Orpheus, who descends into the underworld to rescue his dead wife but, leading her back to safety, anxiously turns around and in so doing loses her again. Dean's posture as an artist is just this turning around out of fear

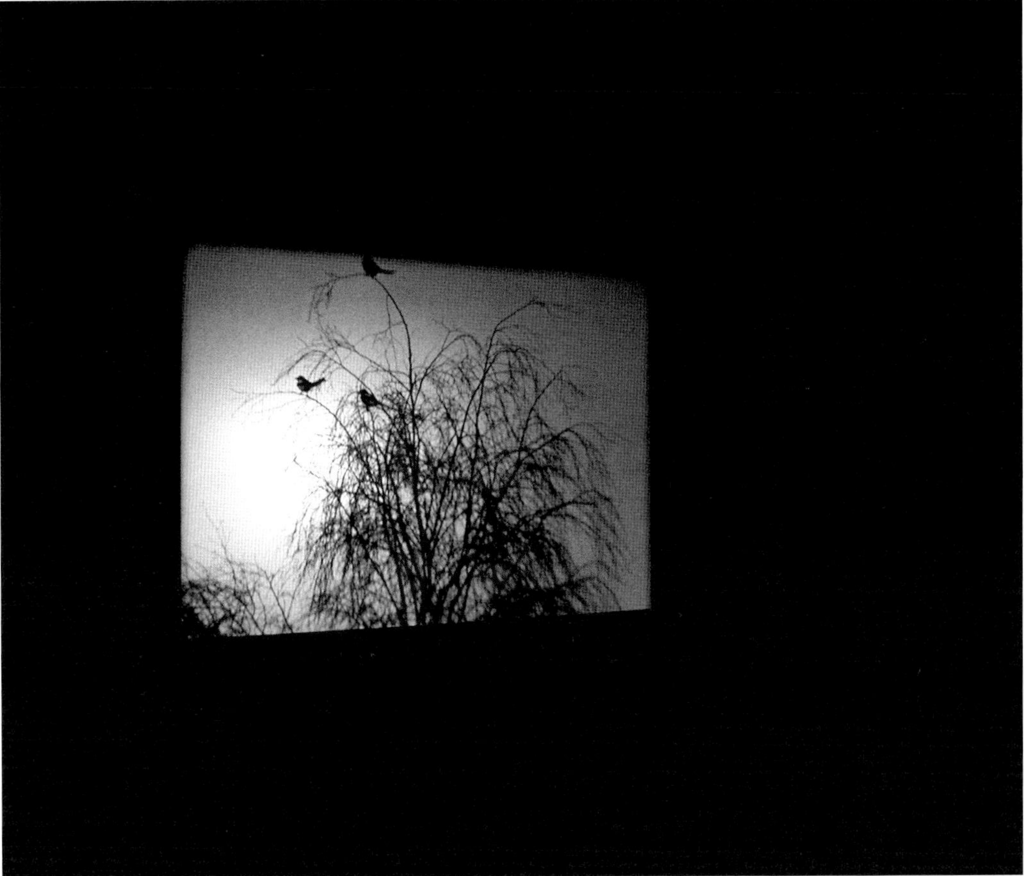

Figure 9 Tacita Dean, *Pie*, 2003. 16 mm color film, optical sound. 7 minutes. Installation view at Marian Goodman Gallery, New York, 2003. Courtesy of the artist and Marian Goodman Gallery and Frith Street Gallery, London.

and love. As a sort of elegy for analogue film, Dean made a film of a French Kodak factory in operation shortly before it was to cease producing celluloid film stock (*Kodak*, 2006). I will confine my attention to those moments in her work when her conjoined interest in chance and analogue film is most apparent. In an email correspondence with me she confirmed her sense of the link between chance and the analogue: "A decline in one will invariably mean a decline in the other and our lives would be greatly impoverished for it."[31] For all the excellent secondary literature on her work, this connection has not been adequately addressed.[32]

Although she is mainly a filmmaker, Dean does use still photography—often in the form of found photographs. She is a *habitué* of the flea market, a collector of the discarded with an eye for old postcards and family snaps—"a junk junkie," she jokes. This sort of collecting is a matter of chance and luck—and Dean loves to court chance. She explicitly connects her collecting activity with the surrealist chance encounter: "I concur with André Breton when he spoke of the objective chance process being about external circumstances acting in response to unspoken desires and demands of the human psyche. I want to be in a position to allow the unforeseeable to happen."[33] She started collecting old photographs in the mid-1990s, but this activity was given a focus only when she was commissioned to make a book for the art press Steidl. The result, *Floh* (fig. 10), has been commented on at length by Mark Godfrey.[34] The 163 amateur photographs included in the book were found in flea markets around the world and reproduced without comment. Dean has stated that this wordlessness is intentional: "I want them to keep the silence of the flea market, the silence they had when I found them, the silence of the lost object."[35] Another prominent feature of the photographs in *Floh* is the plethora of mistakes. The quasi-accidental nature of photography can be seen, perhaps especially, in the hands of amateurs, and even more so in those prints that end up in flea market bins. The photos are a regular inventory of technical errors—odd framing, poor focus, over- and underexposure, camera shake, and blurred subjects in motion, to name but a few. In some cases, one might surmise that the shutter was released accidently. The photographs themselves have also been subject to accidents and wear and tear, bearing fingerprints, scratches, and other marks. It is as though the nature of the medium were being explored by illustrating everything that can go wrong with it. The realization gradually dawns on one that these sorts of accidents don't occur anymore, because modern digital cameras take the guesswork out of making pictures and bad ones are instantly deleted. Furthermore, many people view their photographs only on computers so never have a physical, paper form that could eventually wash up in a flea market. This change reflects the tidying up of our world that Dean finds so impoverishing. The book thus preserves a hundred-year history of a certain kind of photography that was wide open to chance. Some of the results are enigmatic, others hilariously funny, and some incomparably beautiful.

The title *Floh* is the German for "flea," as in flea market, but it also refers to the flow of photographs detached from their moorings, cast adrift on a sea of discarded things. This sort of flow connects with the recurrent theme of the sea in Dean's work—a theme that has long been linked with Fortuna, goddess of luck or chance, who is often represented holding a billowing sail. Dean's large chalk drawings on blackboards of storm-tossed ships are a good example of how she uses her medium analogically in order to evoke the subject: "Because of the flux, the drawing and the erasure, the whole process is so like the nature and the movement of the sea."[36] In a brief prose piece, "And He Fell into the Sea," Dean pays homage to a work by another artist—Bas Jan Ader's final and unfinished performance, *In Search of the Miraculous II* (1975).[37] She has written about Ader's and Donald Crowhurst's unsuccessful

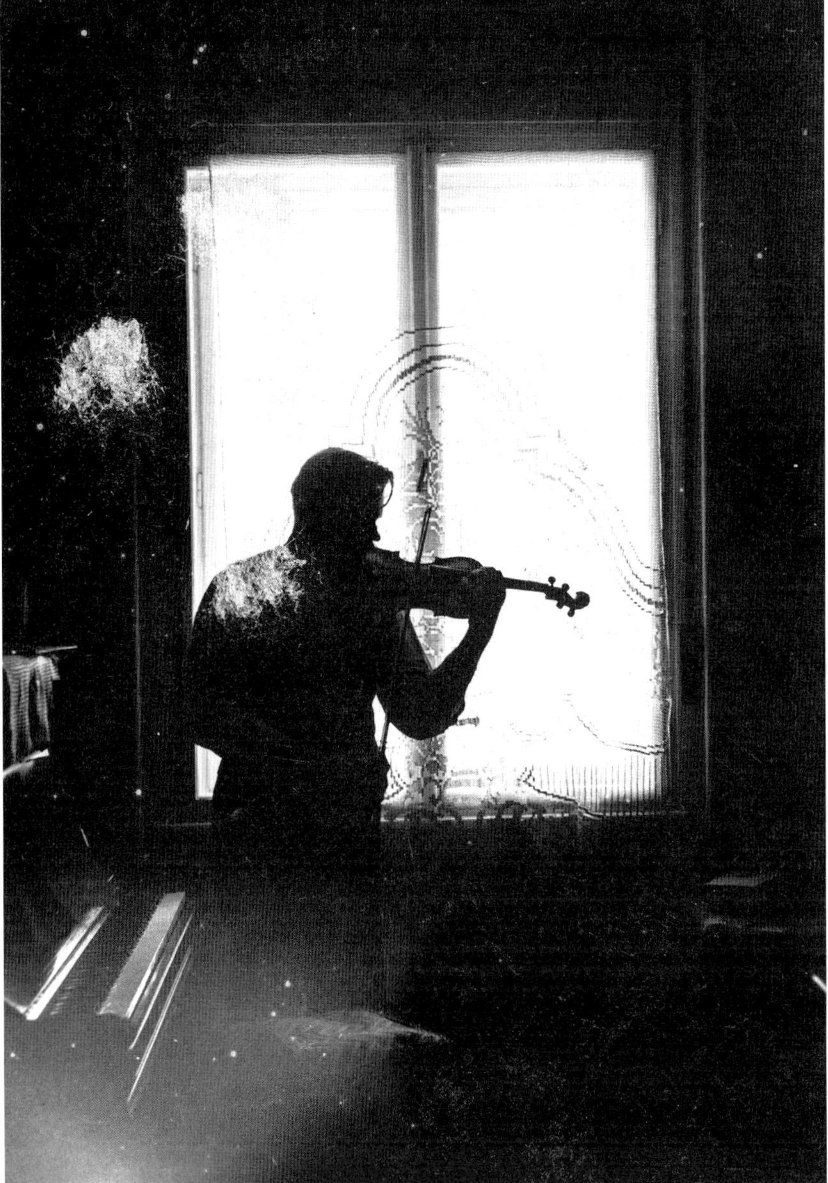

Figure 10 Tacita Dean, one of 163 color plates from *FLOH*, an artist's book made in collaboration with Martyn Ridgewell (Göttingen: Steidl, 2001). 176 pages; 29.7 × 24 cm; hardcover with linen cloth. Courtesy of the artist and Marian Goodman Gallery and Frith Street Gallery, London.

one-man sea voyages, both of which ended in death—which is, sadly, one possible consequence of giving oneself up to contingency, although not the only one. Michael Newman's contribution to Dean's collection of writings, *Seven Books*, bears closely on this issue. In his essay, "Salvage," he discusses Dean's use of the journey as a topos traditionally understood as a metaphor for human life. He notes that Dean added a subtitle to her film *Disappearance at Sea II* (1997)—*Voyage de guérison* (Voyage of Healing).[38] In a short prose piece accompanying the film, Dean wrote of the myth of Tristan, who, poisoned and beyond help, "surrendered himself to the sea and departed on a voyage of healing." He "floated on a small boat with no oars, nor sail nor rudder," hoping to drift to some magical island where he would be cured. Floating alone in the boat for seven days and seven nights, wounded and weary, he finally finds the healing of Isolde.[39] Dean adumbrates here the connections to be found among the sea, the journey of life, and the idea of confiding oneself to chance or giving oneself over to contingency as a way of opening up new possibilities in both life and art.

The strong thematic link in Dean's work between the sea voyage and chance is clear, but the question that concerns me is how this bears on her use of photography as a medium. A scene in *Disappearance at Sea II* shows the beam of light from a lighthouse panning across the dark sea. This shot creates an effect similar to a film technique called the blind pan, a term that refers to the camera's sweep across a field of vision without focal point or object. Although it is not about the sea, her film *Fernsehturm* (2001) is similar in this respect (plate 5). The film is a forty-four minute view of the interior of the revolving restaurant at the top of a television tower in former East Berlin. The movement is similar to a very slow 360-degree pan with a film camera, except in this case the camera is fixed while the restaurant slowly turns, bringing diners into view, during which time the earth itself turns and night falls. Dean was surprised to find how much it looked like the prow of a ship moving through the sea.[40] Interestingly, Dean made a series of photogravures called *Blind Pan* (2004) that show what appears to be high, blasted moorland spread sequentially over five large frames, across which are inscribed stage directions for the self-blinded and lame Oedipus and his daughter Antigone making their way through the wilderness into exile.[41] Haltingly moving forward, blind, with no definite aim, open to what happens—they are at sea on dry land. Dean attaches an ethical value to the blind pan, which, along with the long take with a fixed camera, is the cinematic version of what I've been referring to as time-exposure photography. Commenting on her free-associative curatorial project for Camden Arts Centre, *An Aside*, Dean offered a remark that clearly has wider implications: "Nothing can be more frightening than not knowing where you are going, but nothing can be more satisfying than finding you've arrived somewhere without any clear idea of the route. . . . I have at least been faithful to the blindness with which I set out."[42]

The blind pan in this context is a metaphor; in practice, Dean does not generally use pans or zooms. As she remarked in an interview, "I like the static shot that allows for things to happen in the frame. . . . It is just allowing the space and time for whatever to happen, and that comes very much from the nature of film. . . . I tend to hold the frame until my film runs out."[43] That Dean's films border on still photography and that her favored format is wide-screen is also relevant. The viewer, close to the wide screen in a gallery space, is free to pan across the image. In this context she remarks, "I have always thought that art works best when it is open to this subjectivity, when it is not bound by too much direction and intent."[44] The work itself must be consigned to the contingencies of its reception.

Analogue photography and film as media of contemporary art after digitization have become associated with a longer tradition of photography and writing on photography in which the camera eye is imagined as staring unguarded into an enigmatic Open. Within this tradition, openness, together with the automatism of the camera and the indexicality of analogue film, result in a kind of photography that is marked by contingency and seared by reality. As Dean so eloquently put it, analogue photography is "the imprint of light on emulsion, the alchemy of circumstance and chemistry"—a conception of the medium that I have elaborated in terms of the idea of exposure.[45]

Casting, Rubbing, Making Strange   4

One of the most celebrated archaeological finds from ancient Pompeii is a plaster cast of a dog (fig. 11). The mold was formed by compacted volcanic ash that rained down on the city when Vesuvius erupted on August 24, AD 79. The site was excavated centuries later, beginning in the late eighteenth century, but a satisfactory technique of casting was not developed until 1874. The ash was fine-grained, so some of the cast figures are highly detailed. The story about the dog has it that, during the eruption, the shopkeeper fled, leaving his guard dog chained to a post. The position of the dog is eloquent of its suffocation, struggle, and pain, but it is the telltale sign of what was a studded collar around its neck that makes the creature's plight so pitiable. The dog is seemingly caught in the moment of its agonizing death—its singularity is bodied forth, and this is what makes it so fascinating. Yet casting is a method, not just of representation by contact, but also for the production of replicas, the manufacture of multiples, industrial mass production.

There is a tension inherent in the process of casting between the impression of a unique thing and the mass-produced commodity. As a consequence, our reception of the products of casting also has a double valence. On the one hand, the cast is prized as an indexical imprint of an individual person or thing—like the death or life mask of a historical figure, such as Rembrandt or Napoleon—and may even acquire a cultic value, like a fragment of the true cross. The value people attach to these casts is not, however, matched by a high estimation of their artistic value. As Georges Didi-Huberman argues, casting does away with the traditional criteria of being a work of art, including idea, design, invention, style, and even imitation. In casting it is enough to duplicate the referent by contact without making the optical effort of imitation. It is thus indifferent to any notion of style. There is no artistic work, no craft; it's a simple mold, a mechanically reproducible impress of the world.[1]

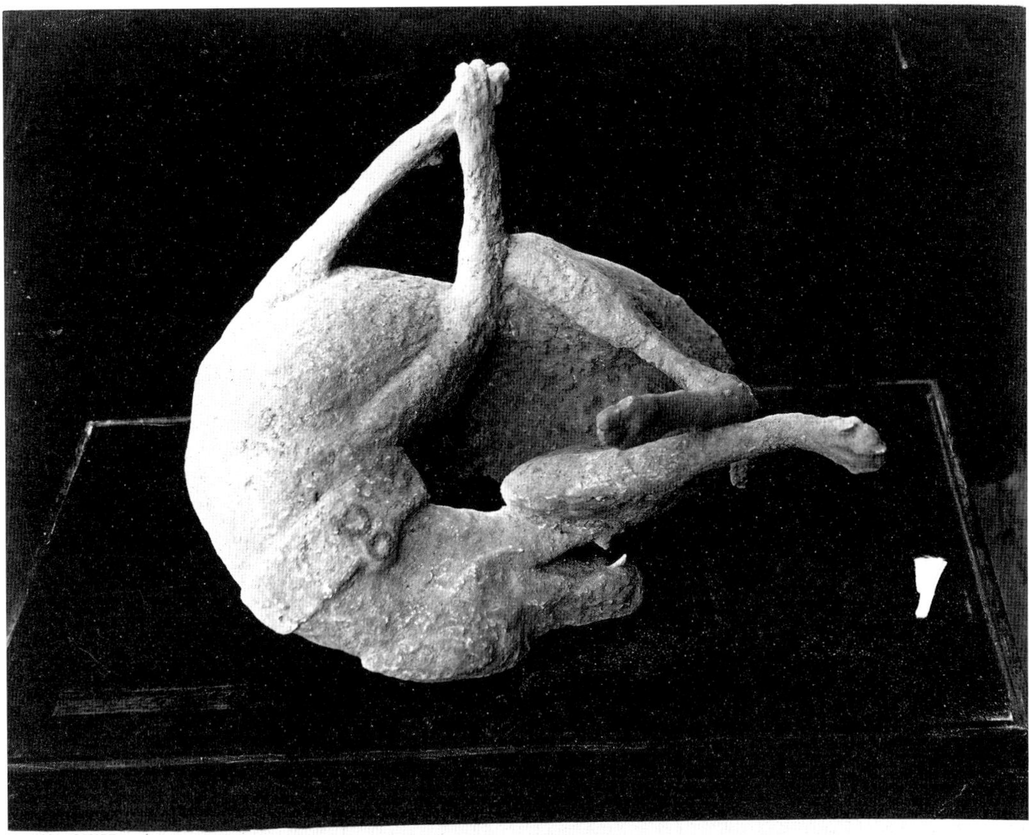

Figure 11 Giorgio Sommer, *Cast of a Dog Killed by the Eruption of Mount Vesuvius, Pompeii,* ca. 1874. Albumen silver print. 19.5 × 25.2 cm (7¹¹⁄₁₆ × 9¹⁵⁄₁₆ inches). J. Paul Getty Museum, Los Angeles.

From plaster-cast replicas of antique statuary to sentimental keepsakes, like bronze casts of babies' booties, the cast is considered subartistic. Of course, it is precisely this extra-artistic status that has made it so attractive to contemporary artists. This chapter considers works of art that engage with the processes of casting and rubbing in order to bring out the ambivalences at the heart of our desire for the authentic trace.

Modeling, Carving, Casting

Like photography, casting involves a moment of proximity, intimate contact with something, but at the same time, because the negative can be recycled or the mold recast, what it produces is easily reproduced. Unlike the two major forms of sculpture, which, according to the English Kleinian art critic Adrian Stokes, are carving and modeling, casting is a lowly art of reproduction. Long associated with the manufacture of artifacts, casting continues to be regarded as subartistic even in the case of prestigious monuments, where the artist fashions a clay model and sends it away to a specialist foundry to be cast in metal. It would seem that casting, from the point of view of art, is too intimate, too close, too real, and, at the same time, too far away, a mere copy, a mass-produced simulacrum. In other words, it shares the ambivalent character of the index.

This fundamental ambivalence lies behind the peculiar psychodynamics of casting. I invoked Stokes just now, for it was his psychoanalytically informed analysis of sculpture that I found most helpful in formulating my thoughts on this topic. In his book about fifteenth-century Italian sculpture, *Stones of Rimini* (1934), Stokes distinguished between two fundamental ways in which artists work their materials. From a psychodynamic point of view, modeling and carving represent two very different sorts of engagement. Steeped in a modernist aesthetic, Stokes emphatically favored the carvers, who, he claimed, have a feeling for their medium, such as limestone, and value the resistance it offers. Modelers, by contrast, tend to impose on the yielding stuff of clay a preconceived design or fantasy. For modelers, plastic material has no "rights" of its own. It is formless mud used, very likely, to make a model for casting in bronze or brass. The treatment of the material may be free, but only in the sense that it is unrestricted by so deep an imaginative communion with the significance of the material itself. The modeler realizes his design using clay in an additive process. Unlike the carver, "he does not envisage the conception as enclosed in his raw material." Modeling, Stokes continues, can produce "the perfect embodiment of conception: whereas, in the process of carving, conception is all the time adjusted to the life that the sculptor feels beneath his tool."[2]

Perhaps perversely, Stokes offers as examples of these techniques a relief by Agostino di Duccio, *Virgin and Child with Five Angels* (ca. 1455), and one by Donatello, *The Dead Christ Tended by Angels* (ca. 1520), both of which are actually carvings. His point is that only Agostino's carving technique allows the character of the limestone to shine forth. Donatello's relief, although realized in carved stone, is an example of the modeler's organization of masses; its undeniable effect upon the viewer is carried by the finely modeled torso of Christ and the rhythm of light and shade. Agostino's carving conception is entirely different:

> Work of this intensely spatial kind recalls a panorama contemplated in an equal light by which objects of different dimensions and textures, of different beauty and of different emotional appeal, whatever their distance, are seen with more or less the same distinctness, so that one senses the uniform dominion of an uninterrupted space.[3]

The use of carefully juxtaposed surfaces that enliven the stone is key to Agostino's carving technique. To illustrate this, Stokes points to the rounded shoulder of the child against the angel's cheek, noting how "face and shoulder give each other shape." In contrast, "One obtains in the Donatello none of the sense of surface making surface to flower." The surfaces in the Donatello are riven by the optical effects of deep shadow; in Agostino's relief, things are allowed to stand.[4]

The explicit psychodynamic implications of these sorts of observation were formulated only in Stokes's later writing, that is, after his extended analysis with Melanie Klein (1929–36, 1938–46). He then made it clear that while modeling represents for him what Klein called the "paranoid-schizoid" position, where there is no boundary between self and other, carvers take up a more mature, "depressive" position, since they attribute some reality to the otherness of the block of stone, acknowledge its integrity, and discover forms in its flinty resistance. In his later writings, Stokes presented Klein's account of infantile development in terms we now recognize as informing his sculptural categories: "The infant's first relationships are with part-objects only, that is to say with objects that are not felt in their own nature to be foreign and altogether separate from himself."[5] The resistant stuff worked on by the carver, by contrast, has a self-sufficiency or separateness; it is not entirely controllable. Klein described the primitive, paranoid-schizoid position as fraught with intense love, greed, anxiety, and aggression; it involves splitting the breast and other part-objects into good and bad, fantasizing a blissful merger with one and rage and fear of persecution in relation to the other. She imagined a constant traffic of dangerous objects defensively projected outward and loved objects introjected. Yet there is also emotional suffering associated with the depressive state, including the pain of acknowledging the separateness of the loved other, mourning its loss, and feeling guilt for prior fantasized attacks on the body of the mother who sometimes frustrated the child's desire. All this prompts efforts to make some reparation—to repair, in fantasy, the damage done. On Klein's account, melancholy seems to be the price paid for our psychic integrity. But if all goes well, there are also feelings of loving and being loved that enable one to withstand the gale of these passions. It is in this context that we should read Stokes's otherwise enigmatic remark: "An impersonal weathered surface is precious to us, a record of our past that cannot signal through a precise semaphore."[6] One senses in Stokes's prose that his art writing is not just the "application" of psychoanalytic theory but an articulation of his encounter with the work through his experience and knowledge of psychoanalysis. As he observed, "If we are to understand a visual art, we ourselves must cherish some fantasy of the material that stimulated the artist, and ourselves feel some emotional reason why his imagination chose . . . to employ one material rather than another."[7]

At times, Stokes seemed to lump casting together with modeling; for instance, he wrote critically of Le Corbusier's cast-concrete, plastic architectural forms.[8] Casting is comparable to modeling in that the material used is liquid or viscous, and offers no resistance of its own. Writing about wax modeling and casting, Didi-Huberman noted the "submissiveness" of a material that is capable of registering every detail. Modeling in wax, one finds that the material registers even one's fingerprints. "Wax, in the matter of resemblance, goes too far."[9] He says this, not to disparage hyperreal Renaissance ex-votos made of wax, but rather to throw a spanner in art historical narratives. Yet, if casting has something in common with modeling, it is arguably closer to carving, as the form to be cast is found outside of the self; it is not a product of the artist's masterly projection of form or "calligraphic omnipotence."[10] Stokes thought that in modern art, the values of carving were preserved in the objective givenness of the readymade scraps that make up a collage, or in collage-type sculpture such as Picasso's or David Smith's. He speculated that such is the hallucinatory, fragmentary nature of contemporary experience that things seem to lose their materiality. Art proposes an alternative model of experience with the cult of the found object and a kind of "reverence for the mere presence of things."[11] Casting is often a matter of reproducing found objects or, like the archaeologists at Pompeii, of filling *found spaces* in order to reveal in positive form the shape of the void. In either case, it involves, not a modernist sensitivity to the specificity and materiality of the medium, but rather attention to the world of things.

We shall see that both the form of attention and the things attended to are of rather special kinds. As suggested by my archaeological starting point, another salient feature of direct casting is that it often involves making a trace of something that is assumed to be ephemeral, inaccessible, or outmoded; casting is closely connected with the anticipation of loss or absence. It is an act of preservation. If casting has a psychic mood, then, it is neither expressionist self-projection, nor "modernist" restraint and respect for the character of the medium. Rather, it seems to involve the ambivalence characteristic of melancholy, of being caught between acknowledgment of loss and refusal to mourn, that is, to give up the object.

JASPER JOHNS

It is strange that more has not been written about Jasper Johns's use of casting as a procedure. After he was discharged from the army, his first works of art involved making life masks of friends' faces or, in the case of *Target with Plaster Casts* (1955), casts of body parts. Even when he seemed to be using

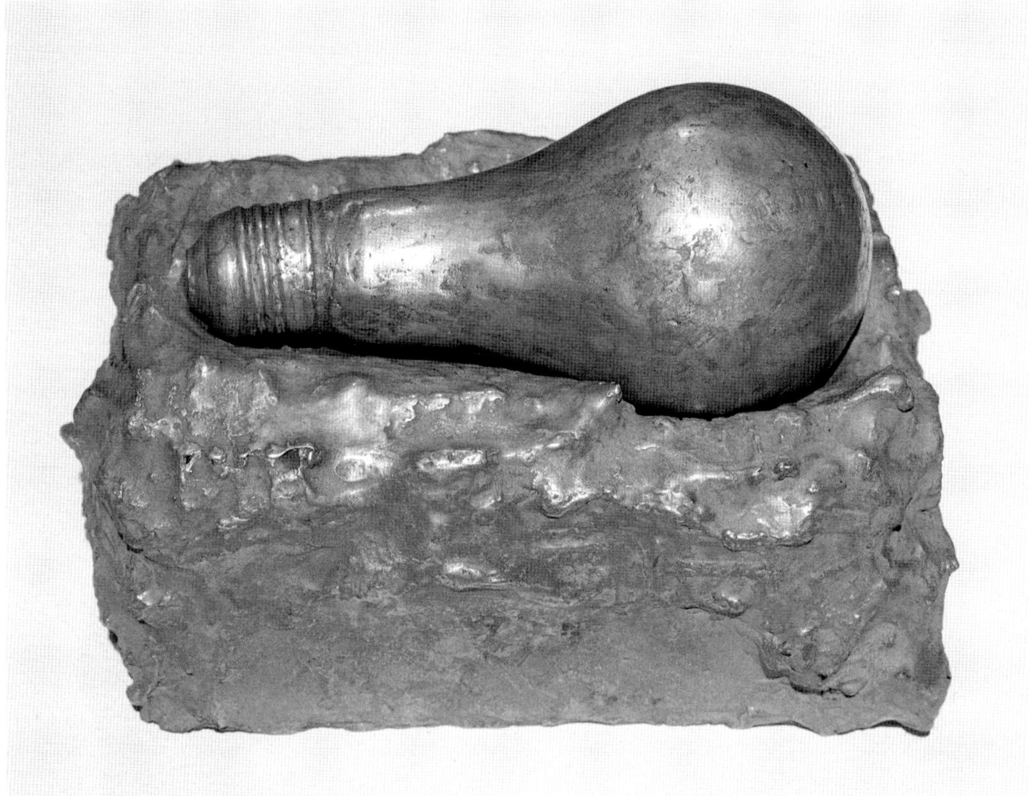

Figure 12 Jasper Johns, *Light Bulb I*, 1958. Sculp-metal. Collection of Museum of Contemporary Art, San Diego. Gift of Mrs. Jack M. Farris, 2005. © Jasper Johns/VAGA, New York/DACS, London 2015. Photo: Pablo Mason.

the casting technique to create multiples, it turns out that he was not. In *Target with Four Faces* (1955), the four casts are made from the lower half of the same person's face, but they are unique and register subtly different expressions. Johns placed these body casts in wooden boxes—maybe because they are not in the round, but also perhaps because the use of boxes, especially when fitted with hinged lids, suggests an aim of safekeeping or, at least, storage. Johns wanted to make three-dimensional casts of some ordinary objects and, as he said in an interview, "in a flash" came up with the idea of doing flashlights and lightbulbs.[12] It is unclear why he chose just these items. Obviously both are sources of illumination, or were once, and so their presentation as dysfunctional objects in a sculptural still life is an intimation of mortality. The first object Johns made in 1958, *Light Bulb I*, probably involved pressing soft sculp-metal into a mold. The bulb form sits atop a roughly modeled brick covered in the same dull material (fig. 12). The first flashlight he made is not really a cast; it is a real flashlight covered in sculp-metal, but he later made several cast examples (fig. 13). A couple of the light-

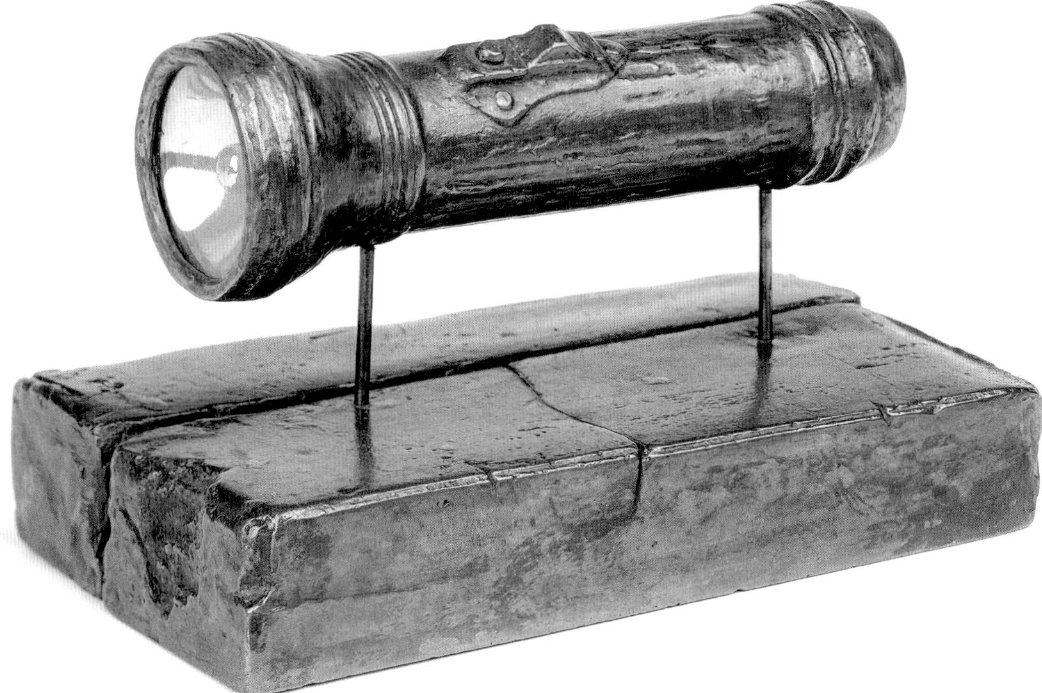

Figure 13 Jasper Johns, *Flashlight*, 1960. Bronze, glass. 4⅝ × 7¾ × 4¼ inches. Collection of Walker Art Center, Minneapolis. Gift of Judy and Kenneth Dayton, 1998. © Jasper Johns/ VAGA, New York/DACS, London 2015.

bulbs and flashlights are not fully distinguished from their bases and seem to be emerging from the earth. Like archaeological finds, they appear partially unearthed. Others, perched on stands, look like relics from an abandoned museum. The dull sheen of the sculp-metal or matte plaster finish gives the things the look of petrified artifacts from a lost civilization. Obdurate and enigmatic, they conjure proleptic visions of future fossils. One early commentator, the artist Fairfield Porter, writing in 1964, remarked on this: "They are as deathly as the castings made from the holes in lava and ash at Herculaneum and Pompeii."[13] Perhaps Leo Steinberg was suggesting something similar when he wrote of Johns's early sculptures that they evoke a thing's "deceleration" as they no longer participate in the mass-produced "outpouring of industry." They suggest "the possibility of an object's lone self-existence," and so they also "intimate our own absence."[14] Referring to his uncanny and anxious encounter with Johns's *Target with Four Faces* and other early paintings, Steinberg wrote:

> In the end, these pictures by Jasper Johns come to impress me as a dead city might—but a dead city of terrible familiarity. Only objects are left— man-made signs which, in the absence of men, have become objects. And Johns has anticipated their dereliction.

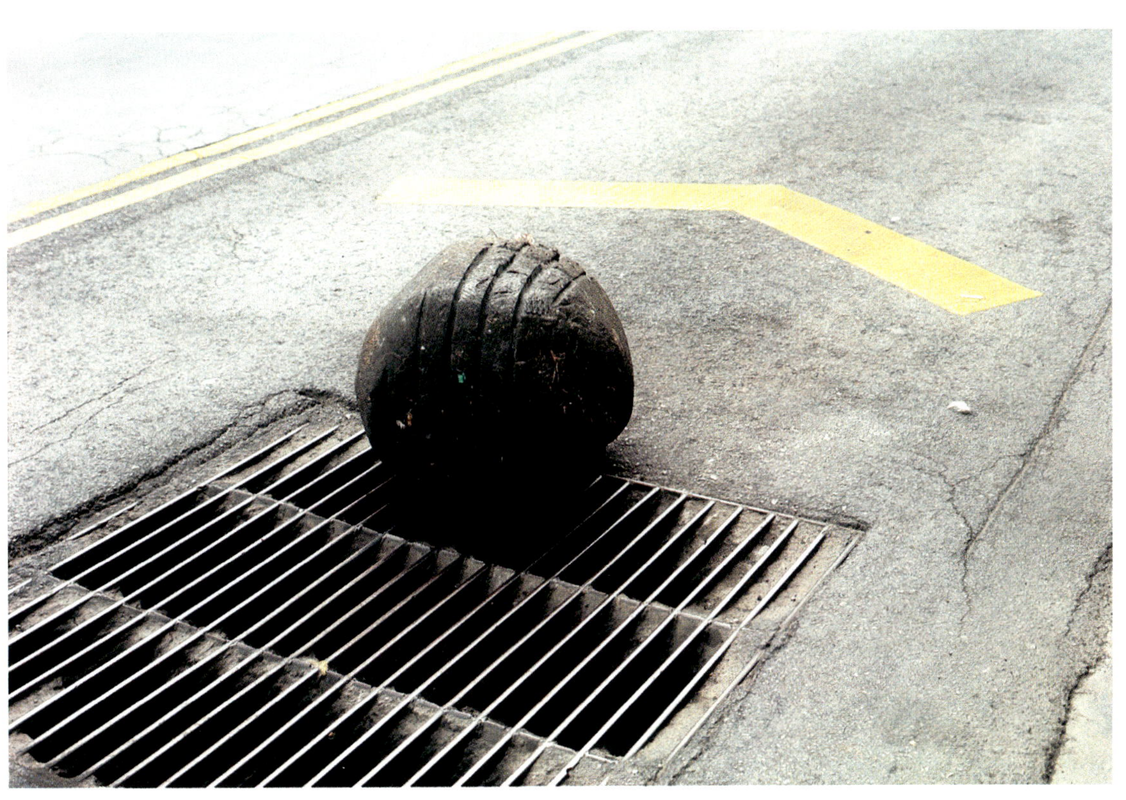

Plate 1 Gabriel Orozco, *Yielding Stone*, 1992. Plasticine. Approx. 36 × 43 × 43 cm (14 × 17 × 17 inches). Courtesy of the artist and Marian Goodman Gallery.

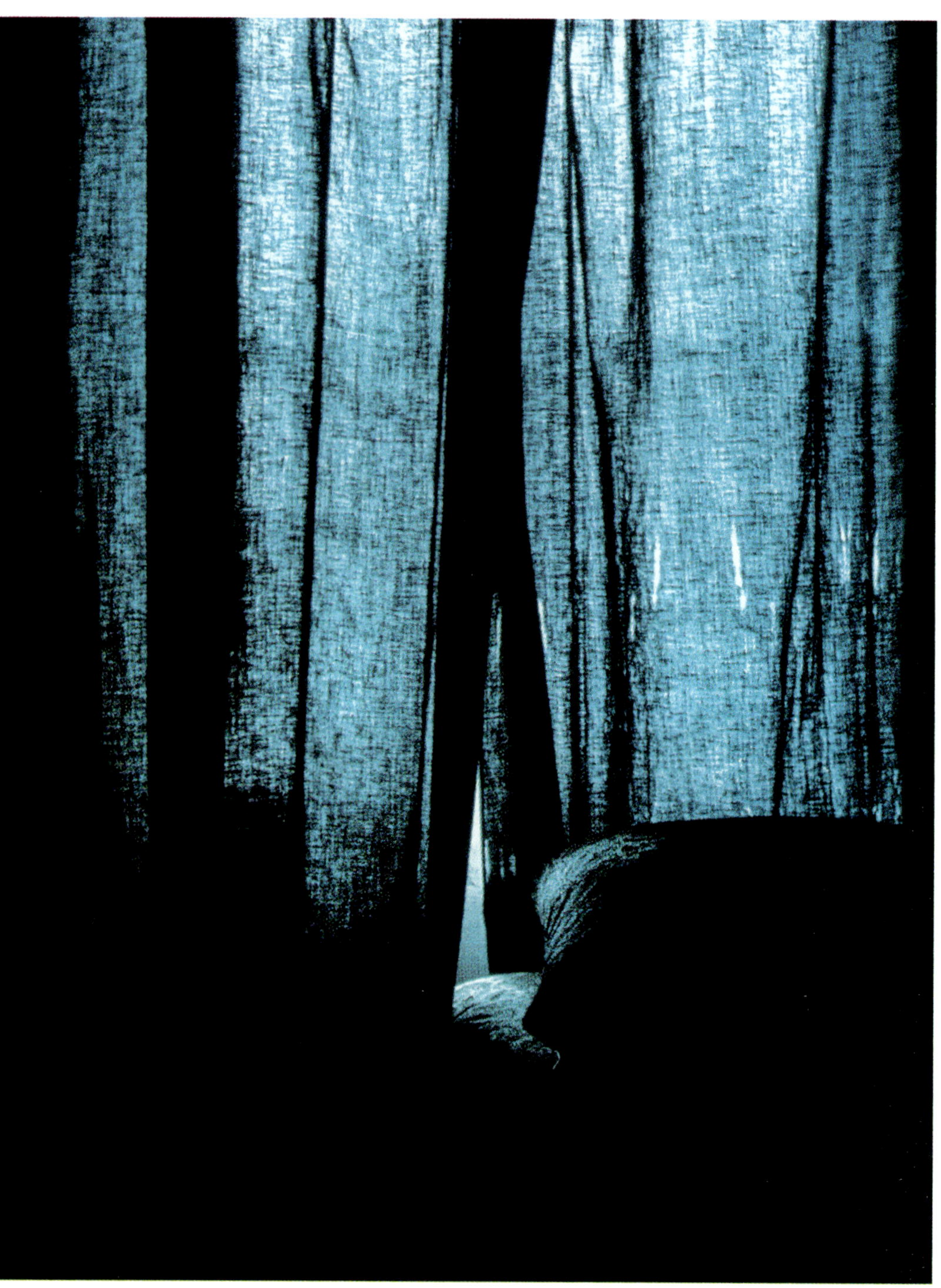

Plate 2 Daniel Boudinet, *La chambre claire* (The Light Room), 1979. © Ministère de la Culture—Médiathèque du Patrimoine, Dist. RMN-Grand Palais/Daniel Boudinet.

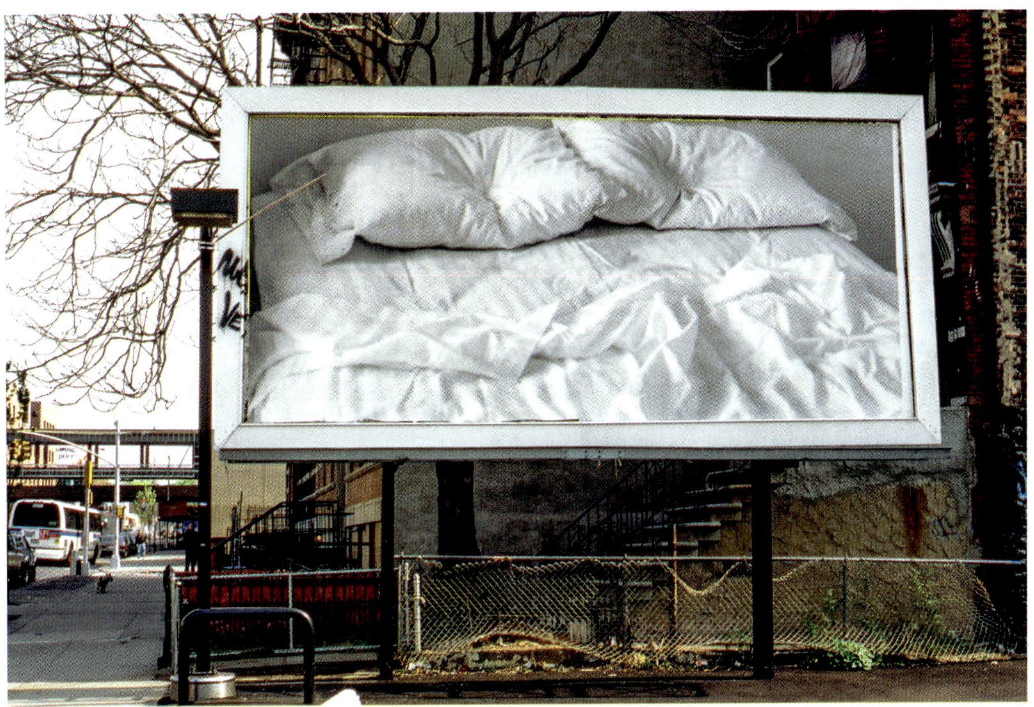

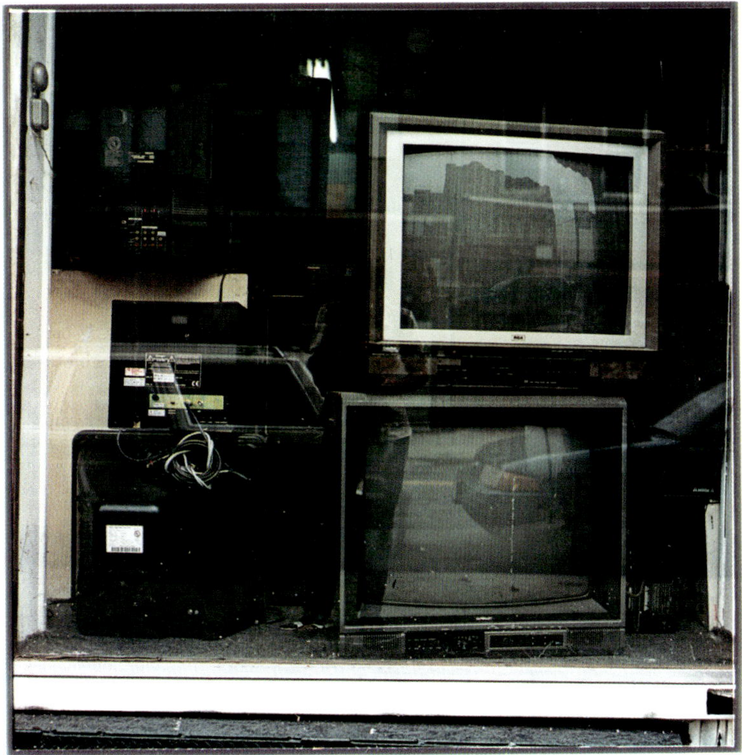

Plate 3 Felix Gonzalez-Torres, *"Untitled,"* 1991. Billboard. Dimensions variable. Installation view from *Projects 34: Felix Gonzalez-Torres*, Museum of Modern Art (MoMA), New York, May 16–June 30, 1992. Billboard location: 2511 Third Avenue/East 137th Street, Bronx. © The Felix Gonzalez-Torres Foundation. Courtesy of Andrea Rosen Gallery, New York.

Plate 4 Zoe Leonard, *Analogue* (detail), 1998–2009. 412 C-prints and gelatin-silver prints. Each 28 × 28 cm. Courtesy of the artist and Galerie Gisela Capitain, Cologne, and Hauser and Wirth, New York.

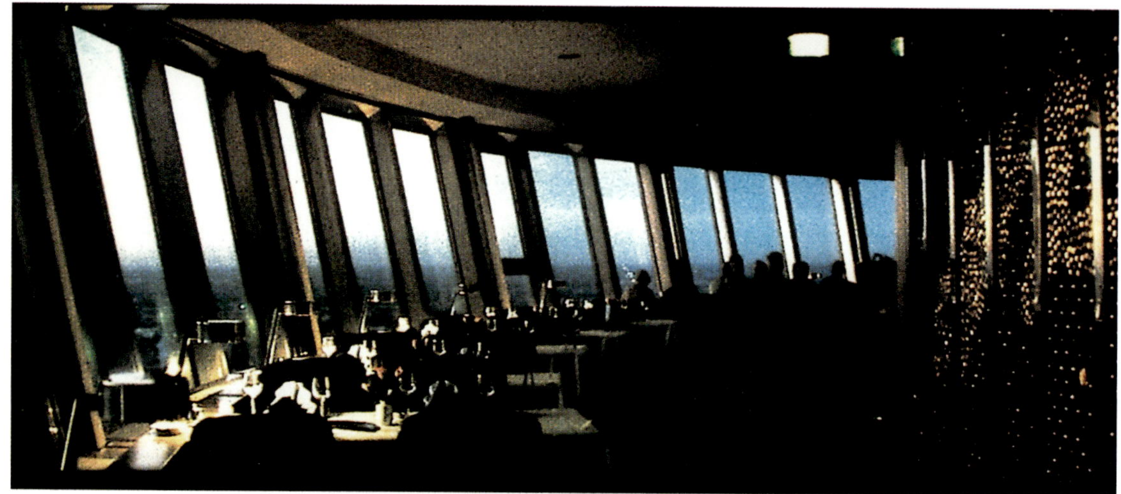

Plate 5 Tacita Dean, *Fernsehturm*, 2001. 16 mm color anamorphic film, optical sound. 44 minutes. Courtesy of the artist and Marian Goodman Gallery and Frith Street Gallery, London.

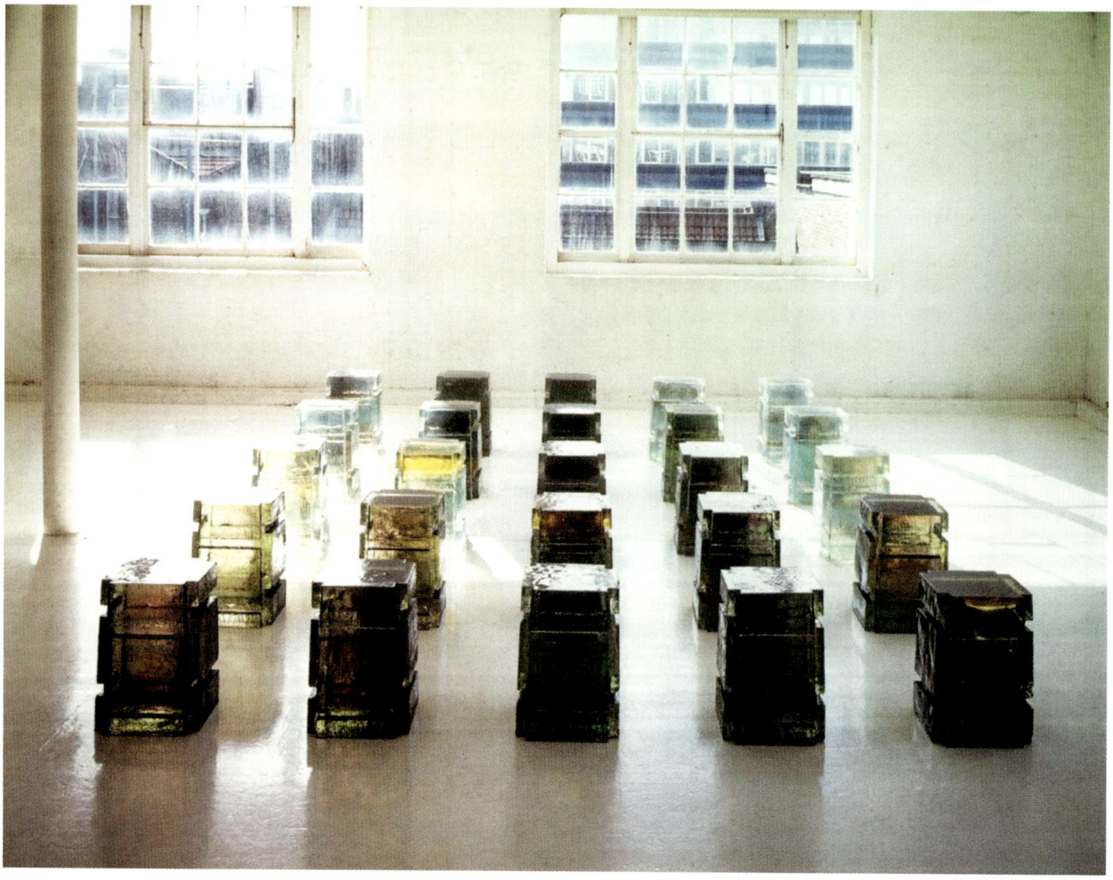

Plate 6 Rachel Whiteread, *Untitled (Twenty-Five Spaces)*, 1994. Resin (25 units). Dimensions variable. © Rachel Whiteread. Courtesy of Gagosian Gallery.

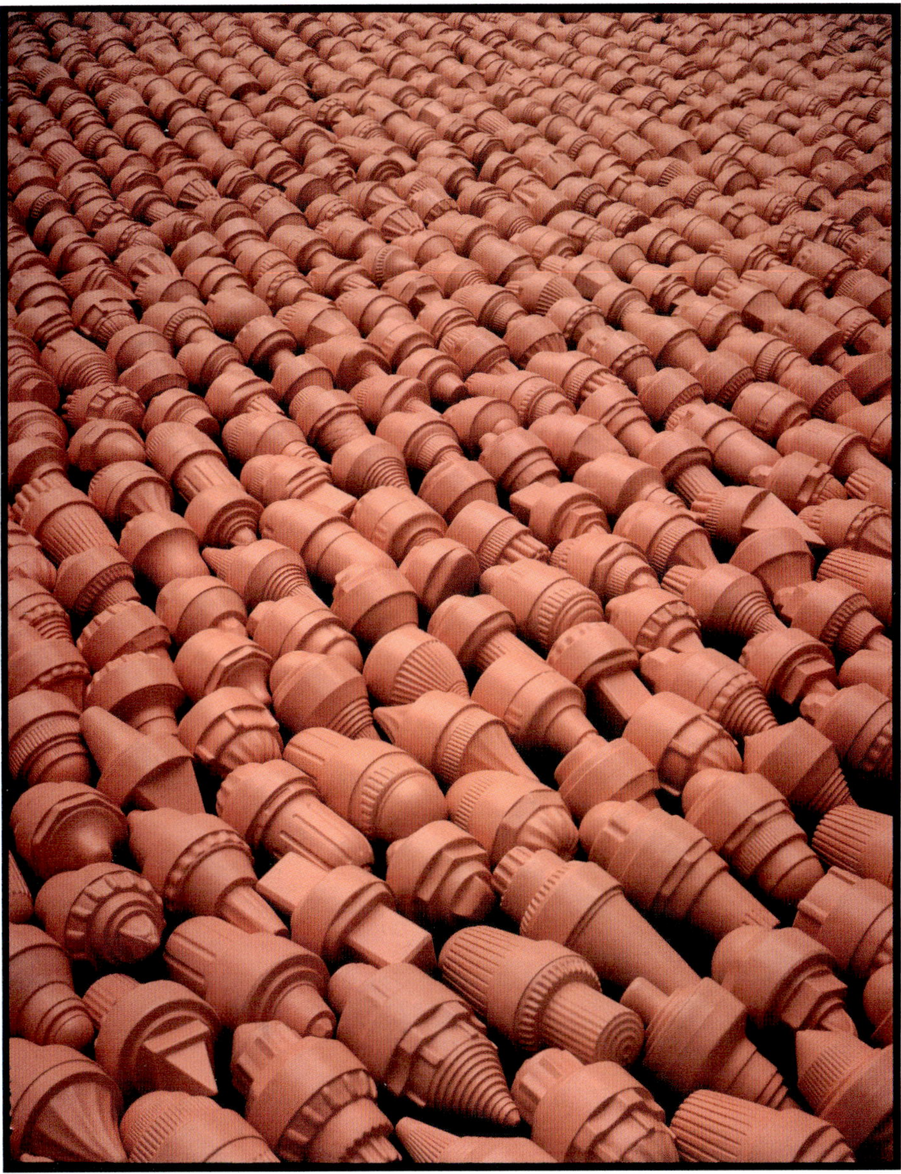

Plate 7 Allan McCollum, *Over Ten Thousand Individual Works* (detail), 1987/88. Acrylic enamel on cast hydrocal. Diameters 2 inches, lengths variable, each unique. Courtesy of the artist and Petzel Gallery, New York.

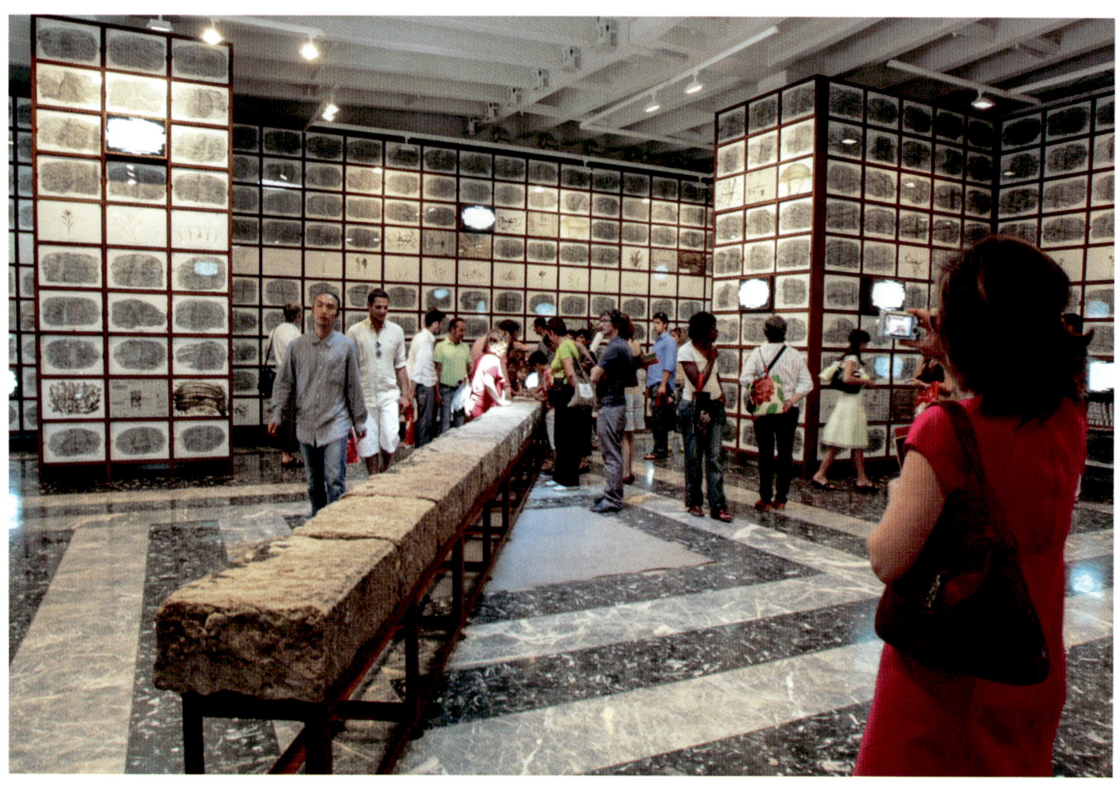

Plate 8 Masao Okabe, *Is There a Future for Our Past? The Dark Face of the Light*, 2007. Japanese Pavilion, 52nd Venice Biennale. Photo: Elisabetta Villa. Licensed by Getty Images.

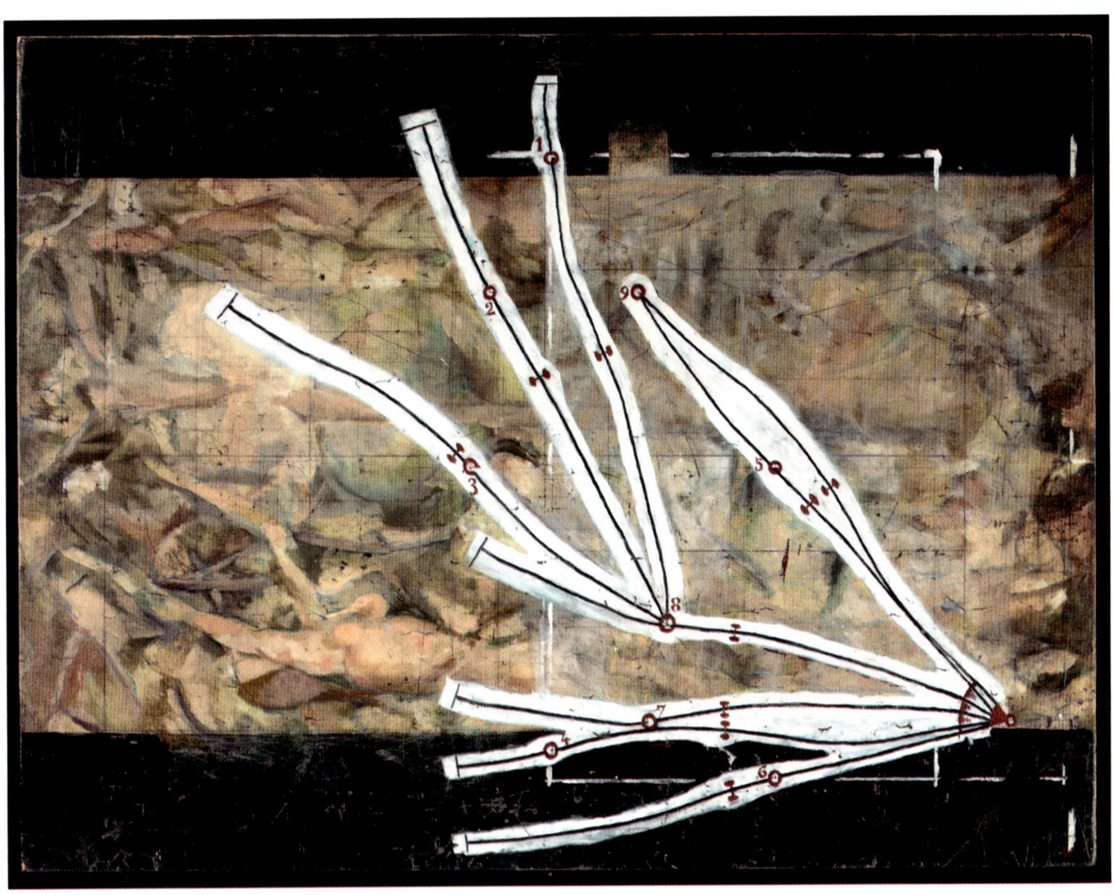

Plate 9 Marcel Duchamp, *Network of Stoppages*, 1914. Oil and pencil on canvas. 148.9 × 197.7 cm (58⅝ × 65⅝ inches). Museum of Modern Art (MoMA), New York. Abby Aldrich Rockefeller Fund and gift of Mrs. William Sisler. 390.1970© 2012. © Succession Marcel Duchamp/ADAGP, Paris/DACS, London 2015. Digital image, Museum of Modern Art, New York/Scala, Florence.

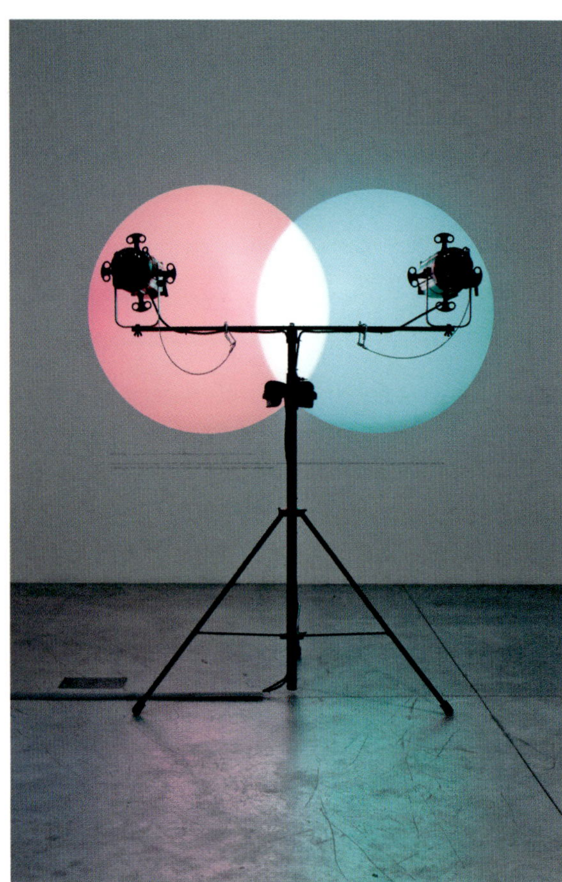

Plate 10 Amalia Pica, *Venn Diagram (Under the Spotlight)*, 2011. Spotlights, motion sensors, and text. Courtesy of the artist and Marc Foxx Gallery, Los Angeles. Photo © Kiki Triantafyllou.

Plate 11 Brian O'Doherty, *Duchamp Boxed*, 1968. Electrocardiographic tracing, cardboard box. 3 × 10 × 5.5 cm. Courtesy of Brian O'Doherty and Galerie Thomas Fischer, Berlin.

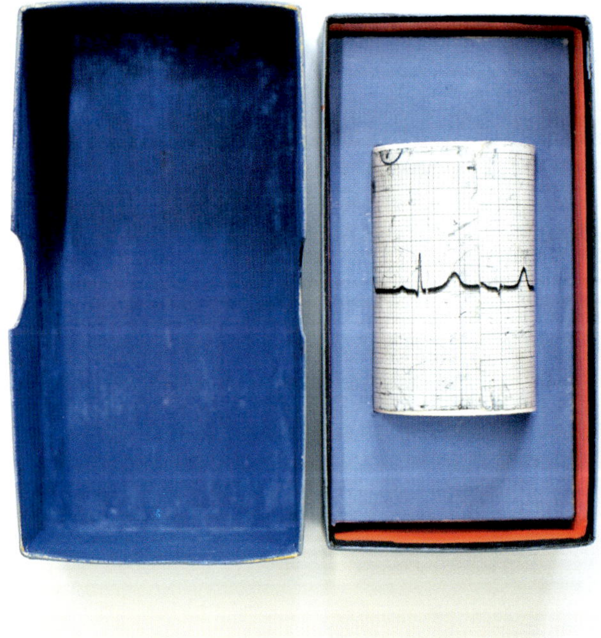

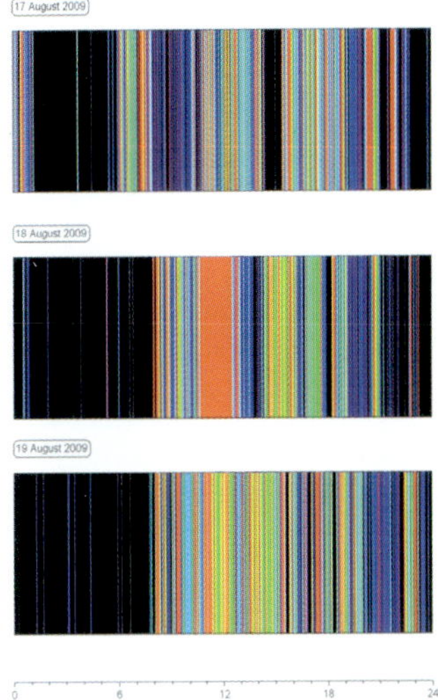

Plate 12 Susan Morris, *Three Days/ Newcastle*, 2009. Actigraph. Archival inkjet on paper. 46 × 34 cm. © Susan Morris.

Plate 13 Susan Morris, *SunDial: NightWatch_Sleep/Wake_2010*, 2011 (Flanders Tapestries version). Tapestry: silk and wool yarn. 170 × 282 cm. No. 1 in a series of 5 (spanning five years). © Susan Morris.

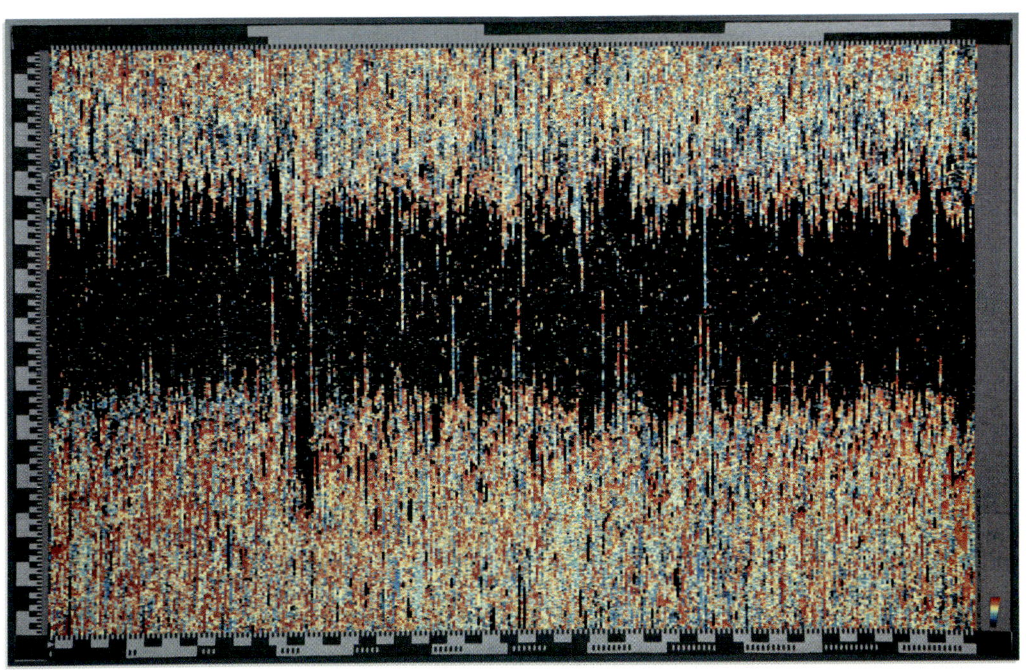

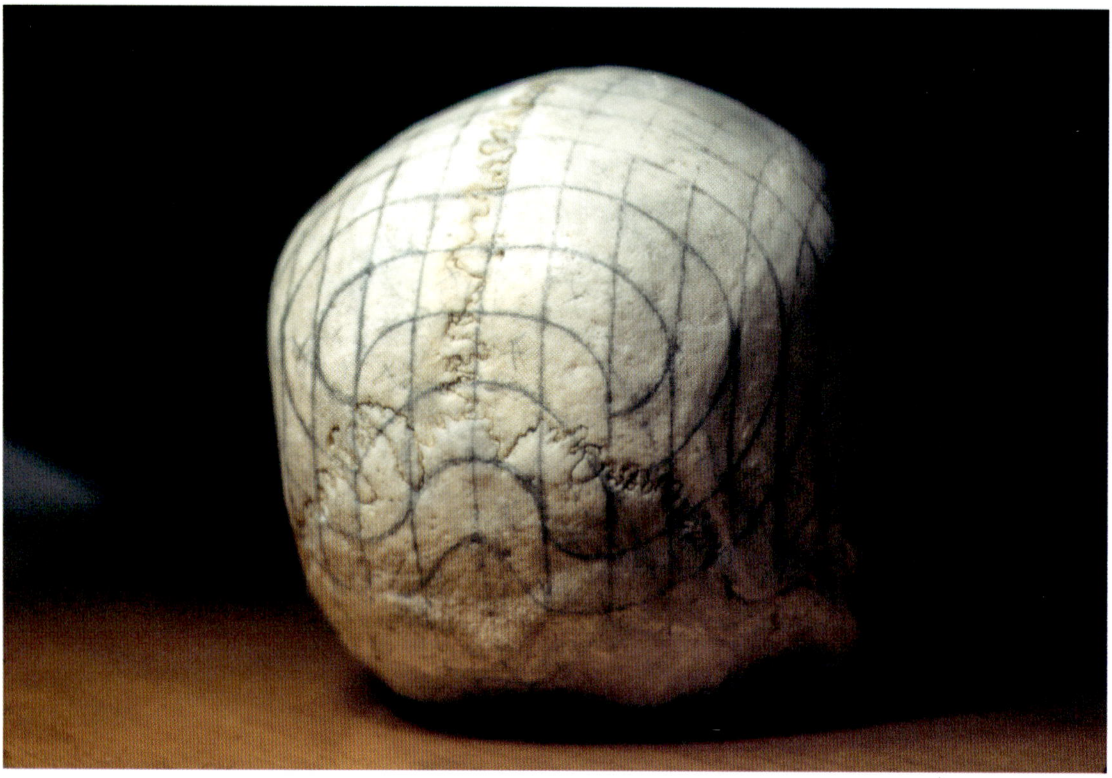

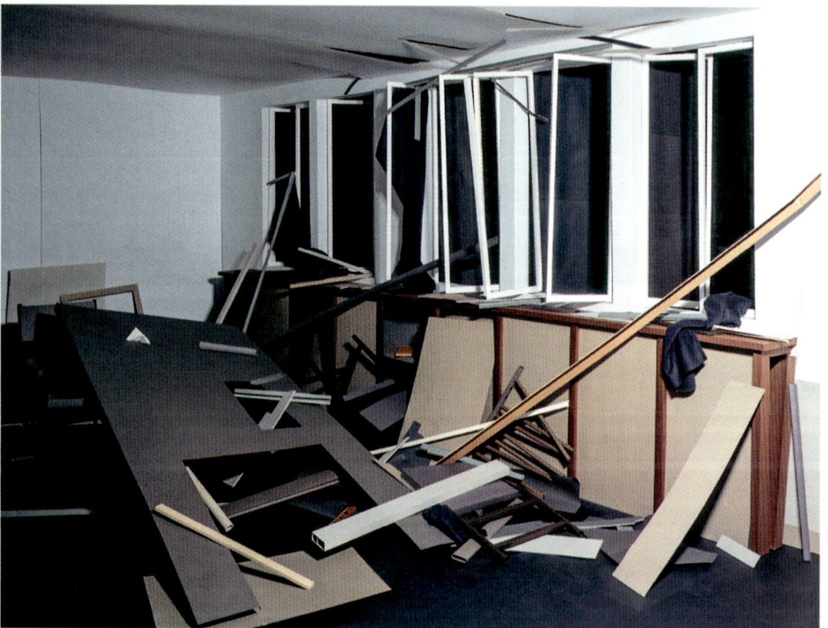

Plate 14 Gabriel Orozco, *Path of Thought*, 1997. Silver dye bleach print. 40.6 × 50.8 cm (16 × 20 inches). Courtesy of the artist and Marian Goodman Gallery, New York.

Plate 15 Thomas Demand, *Raum* (Room), 1994. C-print/Diasec. 183.5 × 270 cm. © Thomas Demand, VG Bild-Kunst, Bonn/DACS, London. Courtesy of Sprueth Magers.

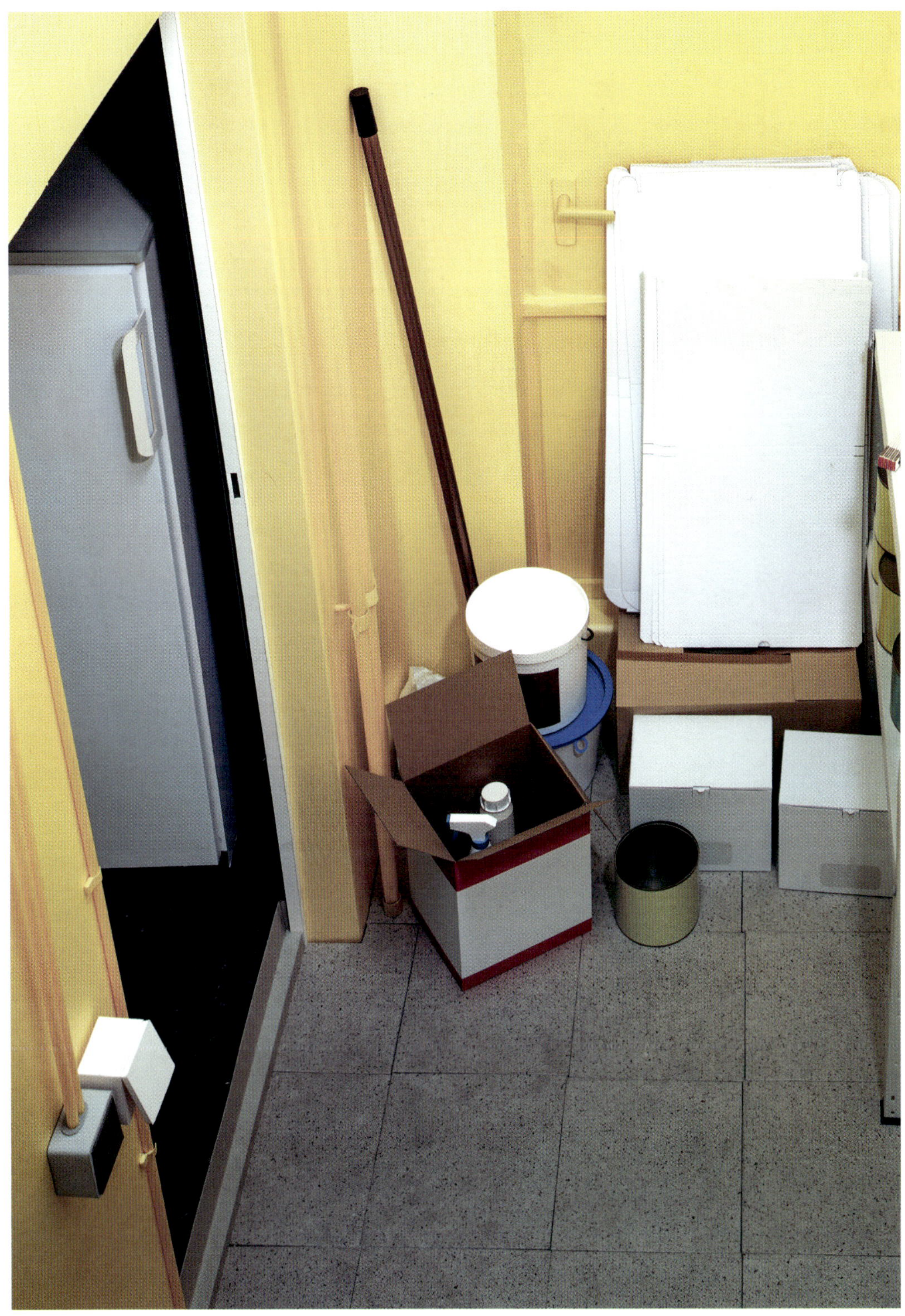

Plate 16 Thomas Demand, *Klause V* (Tavern), 2006. C-print/Diasec. 197 × 137 cm. © Thomas Demand, VG Bild-Kunst, Bonn/DACS, London, 2015. Courtesy of Sprueth Magers.

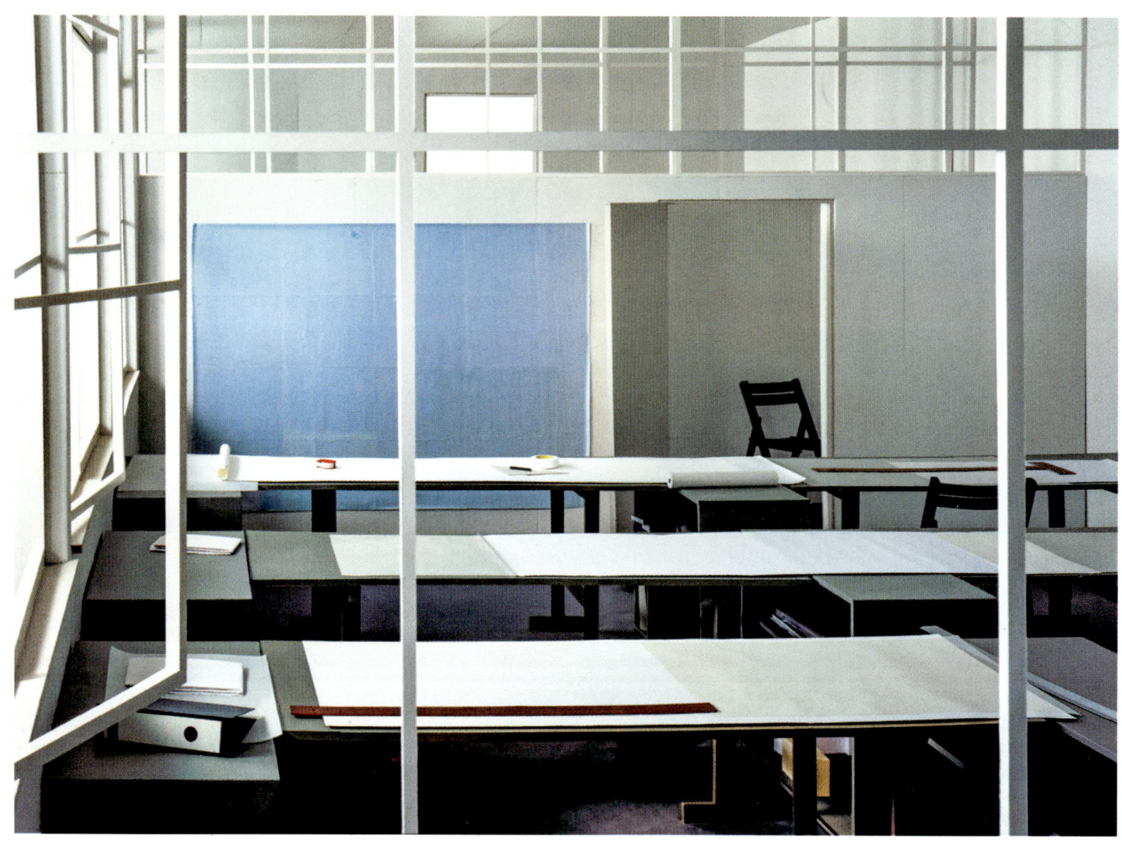

Plate 17 Thomas Demand, *Zeichensaal* (Drafting Room), 1996. C-print/Diasec, 183.5 × 285 cm. © Thomas Demand, VG Bild-Kunst, Bonn/DACS, London, 2015. Courtesy of Sprueth Magers.

"I am alone with this thing," he confides.[15]

Steinberg's comments help to illuminate a well-known, resonant passage from Johns's notebook: "An object that tells of the loss, destruction, disappearance of objects. Does not speak of itself. Tells of others. Will it include them? DELUGE."[16] Several writers on Johns have cited this passage, but strangely, they leave out the closing word in full caps, "Deluge." The word clearly invokes destruction on a mythic or biblical scale, like the eruption of Vesuvius. Leonardo made a series of drawings of the biblical Deluge, with great waves breaking over a city; Johns's work seems to concern itself with traces of an antediluvian world—the remainders of a ruined culture. They might plausibly be understood in relation to Benjamin's insight that in the modern age, technical progress has accelerated at such a rate that even everyday commodities soon become "hollowed out."[17] These emptied, obsolete objects reappear in Johns's casts as something like fossils dredged from the bottom of the sea. This intuition is supported by Johns's note that he wanted to find stands for his sculptures of the sort used for displaying shells.

Art historian Joshua Shannon devotes a chapter of his book *The Disappearance of Objects* to Johns, and attempts to position his work in relation to 1950s American consumerist culture. The aim of advertising in the period, Shannon argues, was to associate products with a variety of abstractions— linking soap, for example, with purity, femininity, or motherhood—and this precipitated a crisis of the object, a dematerialization of things. Johns's concern about this situation, Shannon continues, led him to make objects that could provide a counterweight to the abstraction of the mass-produced object. He aimed to rescue objects and redeem America from "the postmodern forces of etherialization."[18] This argument, I think, works rather well for *Painted Bronze (Ale Cans)* (1960), which really is weighty, especially in view of the fact that disposable beer cans had only recently replaced returnable glass bottles. Casting empty beer cans in solid bronze does suggest an ironic riposte to a throwaway culture.

On Shannon's account, Johns's early work responded to or compensated for the whirlwind of change. In a world in which, as Marx said, "all that is solid melts into air," Johns asserted the permanence and stability of things. Yet, as we have seen, Johns's casts have the deathly pale of fossils from a lost civilization, a condition that seems to me incompatible with any simple notion of material weight or referential stability. Furthermore, this interpretation does not take into account the cast's double valence. The process of casting actually *participates* in serial repetition, in mass production; Johns's work, then, evinces both melancholic acknowledgment of and resistance to this condition. Nor can the work plausibly be seen as just a response to consumerism, waste, and planned obsolescence, for it addresses a more general threat to our attachment to things, to other people, and to life itself. Johns made casts of the faces of friends, and, because you can't really tell the difference between a life mask and a death mask, they are highly ambivalent objects. His *Memory Piece (Frank O'Hara)* is a complicated construction that involves a cast of the poet's foot and three drawers that contain sand. The sole of the foot is able to make impressions in the sand and so to repeat and preserve, in an artificial way, the memory of O'Hara's visits to Edisto Beach, South Carolina, where Johns has a house. But, of course, footprints in the sand are a well-known figure of transience. Or, better, because a footprint in the shifting sand is an index of past presence, it serves as an emblem of transience.[19]

RACHEL WHITEREAD

Rachel Whiteread's work is often considered in relation to Bruce Nauman's concrete *A Cast of the Space under My Chair* (1965–68). Although Whiteread follows Nauman in making a positive cast of the space in or surrounding domestic furniture, I believe her work has far more in common with Johns's. Like Johns, she is engaged in a project that involves preserving traces of things that are succumbing to what Benjamin bitterly called Progress. In other ways, of course, her work is quite different. For example, she is clearly interested in the formal grid arrangement and simple shapes characteristic of the minimalist sculpture of Donald Judd, Carl Andre, and Sol LeWitt. Her work also sometimes has some of the irregularity and translucency of the work of Eva Hesse, who also made extensive use of casting. The comparison with Hesse is particularly apt in the case of Whiteread's resin casts in rainbow colors of the variegated spaces under different chairs, such as *Untitled (Twenty-five Spaces)* (1994; plate 6). Yet, unlike Hesse, Whiteread makes reference to items of domestic use, furniture, and architecture. This reference to everyday domestic life is a constant theme in the literature on her work, but, in my view, it would be more accurate to say that her interest is in the *ex-domestic*.[20]

Whiteread's practice involves trawling through secondhand furniture shops in London for items that have been *thrown out of the home*. She casts the interior or in-between spaces of things that have been *cast out*. The literature is curiously insensitive to the period in which the things she uses as molds originated. Her early work included casts of a *moderne* 1940s sideboard with glass top and a 1950s kitchen table complete with a strip of its original Formica top. It is said that *Ghost* is a cast of the interior space of a Victorian sitting room but, judging by the shape of the fireplace, it is more likely to be of interwar vintage. Freestanding wardrobes have been deeply unfashionable since the 1960s, when people started installing built-in wardrobes for storing clothes. Some of Whiteread's work is cast from things literally slung out of the house: Londoners who can't afford to have the local council pick up dead mattresses often dump them on the street, where they lie for weeks—an abject spectacle. Other items she selects to cast are things overtaken by the advance of technology, like the hot water bottle. The threat of obsolescence could also explain the casts of the irregular spaces above books on shelves, one example of which is called *Pulp*—which is what happens to unwanted books. Whiteread's resistance to the digitization of everything is clear in her comment, "I love books, I love the smell and feel of books, I don't believe books are going to disappear."[21]

Whiteread's attention to whatever is cast out of the house reaches a climax with *House* (1993–94; fig. 14), a concrete cast of the interior of a Victorian terrace house slated for demolition, produced *in situ* on Grove Road, Bow, East London, close to the infamous Enterprise Zone of Docklands. Its construction involved spraying the interior space with a reinforced concrete skin and then removing the building-mold.[22] The majority of Whiteread casts, then, are of the unwanted, outmoded, obsolescent, and derelict. A subtheme in her work is the casting of places that we tend to cast out of our consciousness—the neglected space under the floorboards, the spaces behind the bath enclosure and under the bed. These hidden spaces might be said to return uncannily in the inverted unfamiliar form of the cast space. But I'm inclined to think that the things Whiteread uses as molds are not so much repressed as thoughtlessly disposed of during successive waves of modernization. Deluge. Her sculptures are memorials to a world we are losing. And, ironically, Whiteread's process administers the *coup de grace*, for the mold has to be destroyed for the cast to be released. Of course, another thing that is cast out of consciousness or disavowed is death, which explains why Whiteread's work often makes reference to antique tombs and Egyptian funerary monuments.

We have seen that Johns's future fossils occupy an imaginary time when today's domestic items have become archaeological artifacts. This, as Steinberg remarked, "intimates our own absence." Similarly, Whiteread's process of casting interior spaces of the ex-domestic implies a lost object, which the viewer has to imagine. Her work projects a world of things that no longer exist, and, for the viewer, this has the effect of undermining any secure sense of self.

ALLAN MCCOLLUM

Apart from one series of photographs, Allan McCollum's work consists exclusively of casts; it is a sustained enquiry into the questions raised by the tension between our notions of the unique, authentic object and the mass-produced commodity. This has been a recurrent theme at least since the industrial revolution, and an insistent one since the advent of the ready-

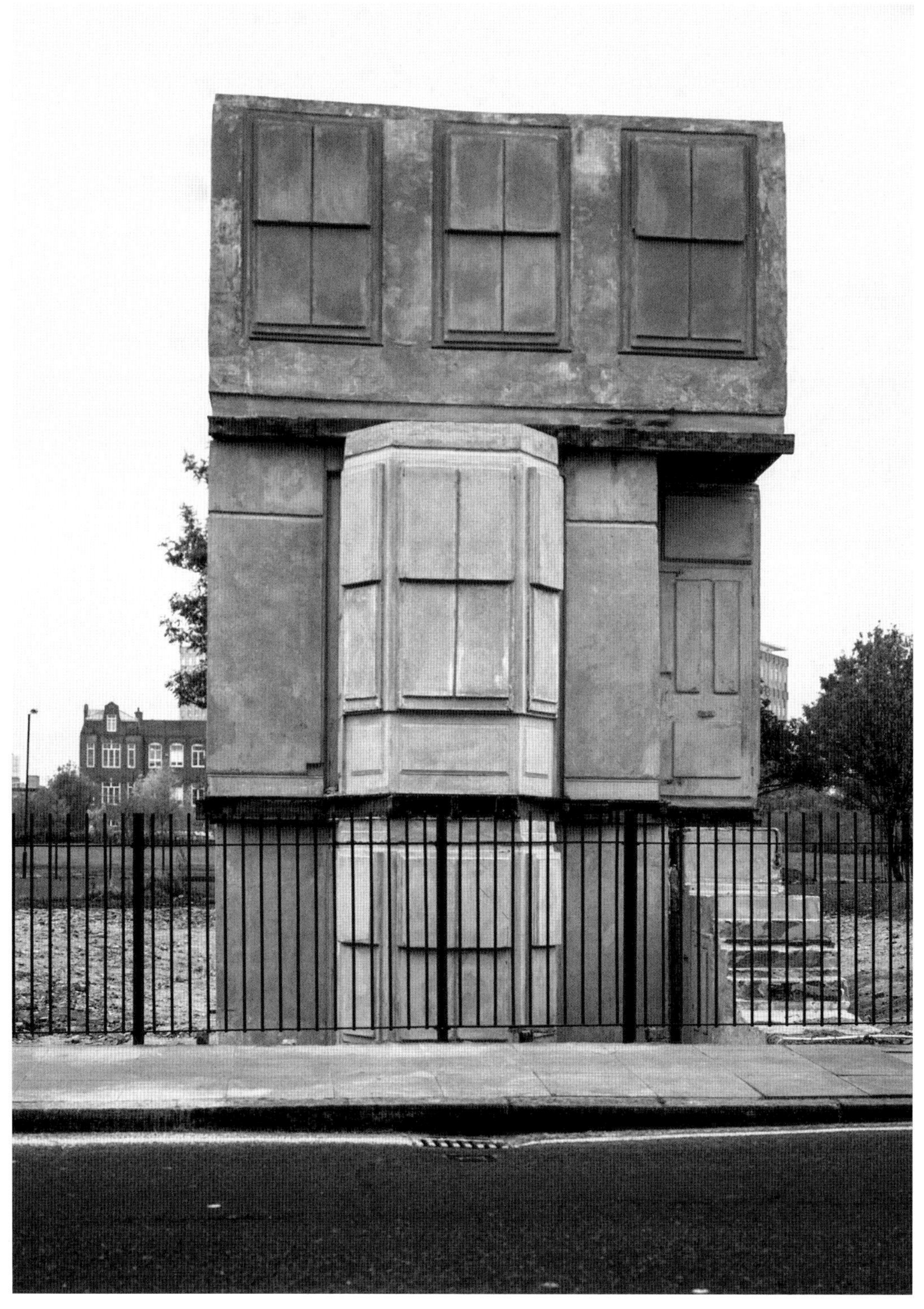

Figure 14 Rachel Whiteread, *House*, 1993. 193 Grove Road, London E3. October 25, 1993–January 11, 1994. © Rachel Whiteread. Courtesy of Gagosian Gallery. Photo: Sue Omerod.

made. What makes McCollum's work particularly relevant in this context, however, is that he is interested in what sorts of psychic investment are engendered by this couple. What feelings are evoked, for example, by seeing a sea of unique handcrafted objects, as presented in *Over 10,000 Individual Works* (plate 7)? The molds for this installation were made by systematically splitting and recombining the forms of everyday machine-made objects, such as a pocket flashlight or a vitamin bottle. Each piece is unique, but all are similar. By cross-contaminating the mass-produced object and the unique work of art, McCollum demonstrates how these concepts are mutually defining and unstable. He diagnoses the anxiety this causes: we tend to define what is most human in us by contrasting ourselves with the machine, and because art is called upon to render what is most human, it must eschew industrial techniques. But this raises more worries: it is evident, for example, that human behavior is not lacking in repetition—humor, sex, and psychosis readily come to mind. Moreover, we vainly attempt to fashion some modicum of individual identity by consuming mass-produced things. That McCollum sees his project in relation to Johns's is hinted at in a photo of his studio with a prominently positioned can of Ballantine Ale.

Given his interest in the desires and fears that circulate around the object, it is not surprising that McCollum was drawn to the famous cast of a dog from Pompeii. His installation *The Dog from Pompei* (1991; fig. 15), comprising multiple casts of a copy from the Vesuvius Museum, is closely related to another, *Lost Objects* (1991), made up of casts of fossilized dinosaur bones. With these two works, McCollum addresses his sense of the dissatisfaction and alienation that people often feel in a world of copies:

> We are constantly in a state of *banishment*, from the imaginary 'source' of things—from the more 'authentic' things that these copies seem to replace. . . . We live in a physical world that's filled with copies and representations made from molds, printing processes, templates, dies, and so forth. We live in a world filled with substitutions for things that are absent because every copy, in a certain sense, only exists because the original is gone. So copies are always about something that's absent, and in that sense they carry a sense of mourning, death, or loss. This is one way to look at our environment—maybe a particularly psychoanalytic way.[23]

He doesn't elaborate what he means by "psychoanalytic" in this context, but I take it he is referring to Freud's claim that the finding of an object is always a refinding, or, to put it another way, a finding of a substitute for the permanently lost object that is the mother. The mass-produced things that surround us evoke a sense of some original lost thing, which they simulate and which is nowhere. "So in a sense, absence is everywhere. So sometimes I ex-

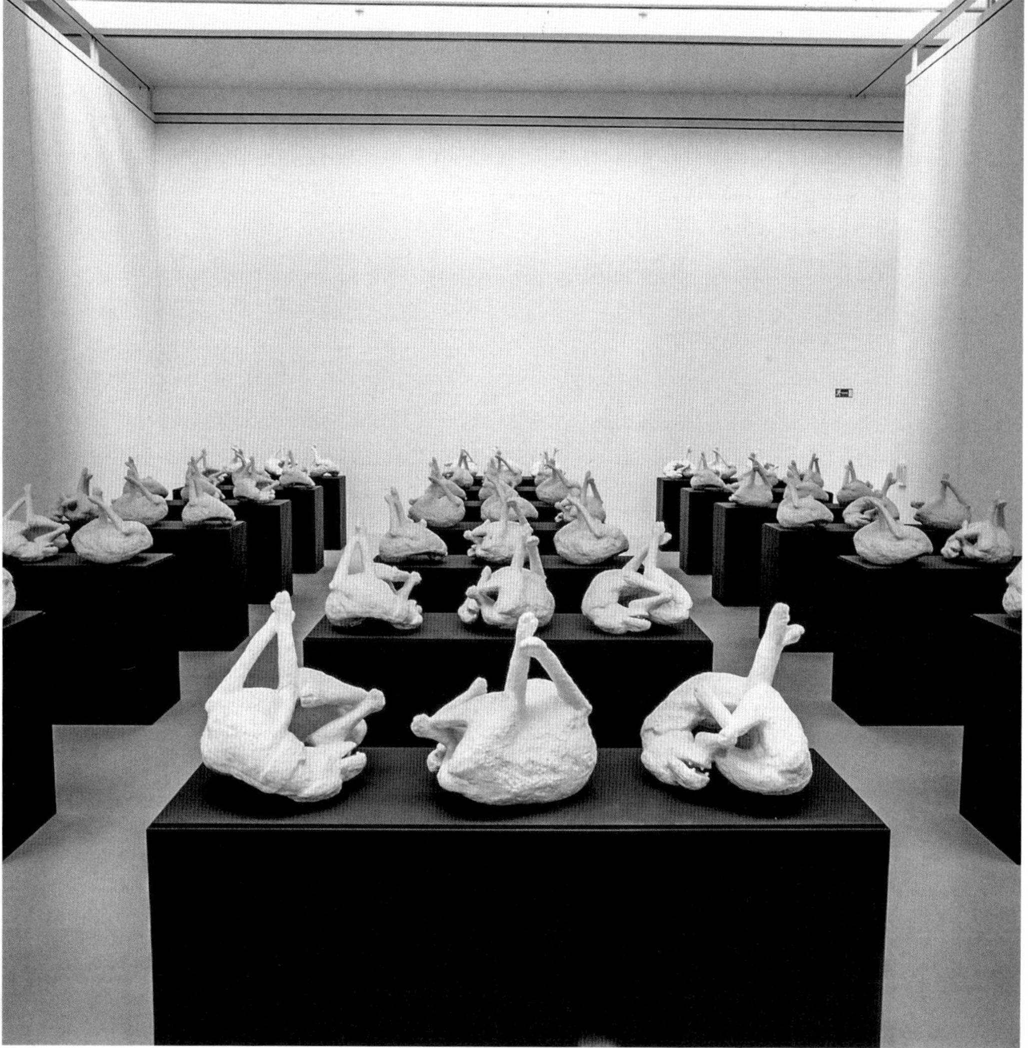

Figure 15 Allan McCollum, *The Dog from Pompei*, 1991. Cast glass-fiber-reinforced Hydrocal. Approx. 21 × 21 × 21 inches each. Installation view at Sprengel Museum, Hannover, Germany, 1995. The replicas, made from a mold taken from the original plaster cast of a dog smothered in ash from the explosion of Mount Vesuvius in 79 AD, were produced in collaboration with the Museo Vesuviano and the Pompei Tourist Board, Pompei, Italy, and Studio Trisorio, Naples, Italy.

perience living in the world as a kind of mourning, or as a kind of longing for the things that are always absent. The presence of so many copies seems to amplify this feeling for me." McCollum chose the dog from Pompeii and the dinosaur bones, both natural copies, because he thought our attraction to fossils to be symptomatic of a need to bridge the gap between original and copy. Fossils are collected and saved because they satisfy or appeal to certain emotional needs or desires. They are the physical evidence of a desire to be connected to the past, and they assuage a sense of estrangement from it. The dinosaur bones, for example, "represent this enormous, monumentally sad absence of a whole world we'll never retrieve again." The fossil relieves this sense of loss as it "comes to us as a copy but still has that direct, indexical relationship to the past." McCollum's work helps us to understand how casting generates melancholy because of its double valence: its close proximity to the authentic object is contaminated by being the process of multiple replication, mass production.

MARCEL DUCHAMP

Although he worked extensively with molds and casts during the lengthy period of his work on *Étant donnés* (1946–66), so far I have said nothing about Duchamp's practice of casting. The reason is that I don't think it forms part of the body of work considered here. In fact, this is what sets my project apart from *Part Object Part Sculpture*, a groundbreaking 2005–6 exhibition, curated by Helen Molesworth, that took Duchamp's late sculpture as a starting point—particularly the odd erotic casts he made, such as the negative cast of female genitalia, *Female Fig Leaf* (1950).[24] The exhibition explored the legacy of these objects among subsequent artists. As my starting point is trauma, not eroticism, I have a somewhat different perspective on some of the same works. Duchamp was interested in the erotic connotations of the cast, with its concavities and convexities, the snug fit of mold and cast. He was not particularly drawn to the archaeological aspect of the cast and its connection with trauma, loss, and memory—in short, its pathos. Yet these categories are not mutually exclusive. One of the most famous early finds at Pompeii was a finely delineated negative cast of a woman's breast. It was found in 1777, before the technique of filling the negative casts with plaster was invented, and is now lost. Nevertheless, Duchamp may have had it in mind when he made a plaster cast of the breast of his then-lover Maria Martins as a study for *Prière de toucher*, his design for the cover of the catalogue for the 1947 surrealism exhibition.

The most compelling example, however, of a Pompeian moment in Duchamp's oeuvre is not literally a cast. I'm referring to the entrance he designed in 1937 for Gradiva, Breton's temporary gallery in Paris. The story of Gradiva, written by Wilhelm Jensen and analyzed by Freud, concerns a young archaeologist, Norbert Hanold, who falls in love with an ancient relief of a young woman and travels to Pompeii, where he falls in love with a woman he fancies is the ancient Pompeian girl returned from the dead, Gradiva *rediviva*. The story has a happy ending as Zoe, actually a forgotten childhood sweetheart, manages to cure Norbert of his delusion while retaining his love for her.[25] Taking his cue from the name, Duchamp cut the shape of a couple out of a large pane of glass, an opening large enough for gallery-goers to walk through. This threshold is commonly interpreted as the happy couple arm in arm. But that fails to consider the negative form of the couple. Given that Gradiva's story is set in Pompeii, known for its negative casts of the victims of a volcanic eruption, it seems likely that Duchamp's design also refers to a couple who tried unsuccessfully to escape. There is a well-known marble statue by the Italian neoclassical sculptor Giovanni Maria Benzoni, *Flight from Pompeii* (1893), that extrapolates from archaeological evidence to imagine just this scene. If I am right, then visitors who passed through the entrance to Galerie Gradiva had an unknowing brush with death as their living bodies briefly filled the negative cutout. Duchamp may have been invoking the idea of the threshold as a liminal transition between two states, such as life and death.

Rubbing

Rubbing as a drawing technique is analogous to casting as a sculptural technique. In this discussion, I use the common English term "rubbing," rather than the French word "frottage," in part because one meaning of the latter is the act of rubbing up against another person in a sexual way, which is not a connotation I welcome in this context—although I do like one example of rubbing that draws on this connotation, a series of frottages by Gabriel Orozco of the tiled wall of a Paris Metro platform, *Havre-Caumartin* (1999). Moreover, frottage is a term invented by Max Ernst and so, for my purposes, is too closely associated with his particular take on the technique, that is, as a way of stimulating visions of strange creatures, plants, and landscapes. He took rubbings from diverse materials, combining them in a collagelike fashion to form highly articulated images.[26] Surprisingly, there is not a very strong tradition of frottage even within surrealism, although Henri Michaux made some interesting examples he called "apparitions."

The next important moment in the history of rubbing is the 1970s. As we saw in chapter 2, Rosalind Krauss made reference to it in part 2 of "Notes on the Index" (1977).[27] The exhibition *Rooms* (1976) included a work by Michelle Stuart, *East/West Wall Memory Relocated*, that involved rubbing sections of the wall on both sides of a corridor and then displaying them on the opposite sides. Stuart began her career as a cartographic draftsman, making maps based on aerial photographs. In 1969, she made a gridded drawing after the first photograph of the surface of the moon. Although, as a feminist, she deplored the world's violent history of conquest and colonialism, she was inspired by the idea of travel to unknown places. Many of her subsequent works incorporated rocks and dirt from far-flung sites.[28] Her best known pieces are large rubbings of the ground made on long scrolls of paper. One such ground rubbing, *#1 Woodstock, NY* (1973), is made with graphite on paper and shows the overall irregular pattern of the terrain. In another sort of rubbing, as seen in *#28 Moray Hill* (1974), she worked muslin-backed paper with rocks and earth from a particular site and burnished the surface with added graphite to a dark luster.[29] Stuart thus plays on the ambivalence of the index between plenitude and loss, presence and absence, location and dislocation. She moved between photographically mediated mappings and works that insisted upon tactile presence, sampling, and imprinting.

MASAO OKABE

One artist who has made a career out of the technique of rubbing is the Japanese artist Masao Okabe, who makes rubbings from the street and has declared, "The city is a giant printing plate."[30] Born in 1942, Okabe began making street rubbings in 1977. In 1986, he was commissioned by the newly opened Hiroshima City Museum of Contemporary Art to make a work called *Hiroshima*. The ensuing series of projects includes his installation for the Japanese pavilion at the 2007 Venice Biennale. *Is There a Future for Our Past? The Dark Face of the Light* showed some of the thousands of rubbings Okabe has made in and around Hiroshima (plate 8). These projects, and those outside Japan, have involved the participation of many people. At Venice, he included curbstones from the site of some of the rubbings, an old railroad station undergoing demolition, and provided materials for visitors to make their own rubbings. The work is thus more than a product; it is a collaborative project of rubbing the traces left by the past on the streets and walls of the urban environment. It concerns violence, trauma, amnesia, and collective memory. To signal this commemorative function, each rubbing and dried plant specimen taken from the site is labeled with the words "The Platform of the Old Ujina Station, Hiroshima, 1894/1945/2001"—the year the station and track, intended to carry military material and soldiers to Ujina Harbor, were completed; the year of the atomic bombing of Hiroshima; and the year of the rubbing.[31] The essay for the catalogue, by Chihiro Minato, raises the issue of the trace as the physical externalization of memory, in writing and other forms. Computerization, he claims, vastly increases the capacity of externalized memory but at the same time puts it in danger, for digital code cuts memory free from a material base as it flows through space: "We live in an age fraught with uncertainty about the future of memory—hence the title of the Venice installation: *Is There a Future for Our Past?*"[32] In Venice some of the rubbings were transferred to acetate and displayed on lightboxes. Since the rubbings were made across the gap between paving stones, they look like chest X-rays, an allusion perhaps to the lethal radiation released by the bomb – its "dark light." The installation preserves a shadow of a structure, dismantled to make way for a freeway, which once served as "a mute physical testimony of the past vanished."[33]

ANNA BARRIBALL

When I began writing this chapter, I had no conception of the range of styles and techniques of rubbing. For instance, Ernst's collagelike practice aimed at stimulating reverie is completely at odds with Okabe's methodical, rhythmic scanning of surfaces for information. The final case I want to consider is different again. Anna Barriball is an English artist who has made rubbing her signature, though not exclusive, technique. If, as I argued earlier, carving and rubbing have certain aims in common, then this is especially true of Barriball's approach. At one point in *Stones of Rimini*, Adrian Stokes more or less identifies the two, noting that carving is essentially a thinning of the stone with abrasives; the point, claw, chisel, and drill are tools used to prepare the stone for rubbing. This is why both the block in carved sculpture and the ground in relief always remain visible.[34] Obviously, Barriball does not literally abrade a surface, but her work is distinctly relieflike. She puts a thin sheet of paper on a surface and, using a 2B pencil that she keeps well-sharpened, assiduously, almost obsessively covers the entire sheet. The unusually hard pencil lead she uses registers the slightest detail.

Her first rubbing, like Ernst's, was of a wooden floor—*One Square Foot*, 2001. She later judged the piece too "pictorial," by which she meant that it has a contrived aesthetic effect and also not a large enough scale to become a thing in space rather than something to look at.[35] She subsequently avoided this arbitrariness by fitting her paper to cover a whole surface, like a bricked-up doorway or a paneled door (fig. 16). Yet the choice of these two subjects (and others) seems motivated: they are both closed apertures or thresholds. The things she chooses to rub are resistant, impenetrable, like stone. She also makes rubbings of textured glass, such as *Window* (2002), which turn what was an aperture into a shieldlike barrier; the metallic sheen of the graphite only heightens our sense of the thing's dense otherness. Although they are technically drawings, they are also shallow reliefs, formed by pressing the paper into patterns and groves. As Barriball noted in an interview, "It's the point of the pencil that pushes the paper almost like a carving process."[36] This is particularly true of a remarkable pair of rubbings entitled *Shutters* (2011; fig. 17). While at first they may look like readymade shutters or photographs, at close range one can see that the paper was put under extreme pressure as the sharp pencil poked and tore at the surface. One gets the feeling that the obduracy of the object and its awkward slats provoked a sort of intense struggle with the medium. Stokes says that actual objects in-

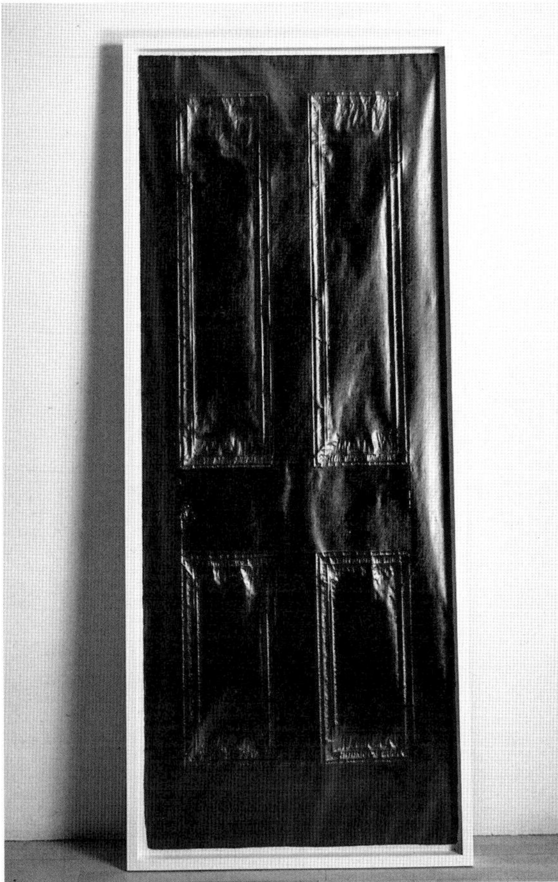

Figure 16 Anna Barriball, *Door*, 2004. Pencil on paper. 208.5 × 88 × 6 cm. Courtesy of the artist and Frith Street Gallery, London.

corporated into art undergo a change as they are given an "opaque identity that has eluded our possessiveness."[37] A comparison might be made here with Jasper Johns's transformation of the flag motif, which predetermines the picture's shape and dimensions and evokes an uncanny otherness.[38] The dark opacity of Barriball's rubbings of ordinary domestic fixtures and fittings resist our grasp. We are shut out by the large, looming shutters.

Stokes tended to understand carving as bound up with the symbolic formation of whole objects and so as a resolution of the paranoid-schizoid part-object relations that inform modeling. Yet he underplayed the painful side of separation. In his book *Earth and the Reverie of Will: An Essay on the Imagination of Matter* (1948), Gaston Bachelard describes what he calls "the dialectics of hard and soft." He observes that the resistance of hard material has the effect of awakening our energy: "the resistant material world summons our aggression"; it summons our "incisive will, our will concentrated at the cutting edge of a tool." Contrasted with this incisive gesture is the "gratuitous or unopposed gesture that claims to express our inner rhythm."[39] This formu-

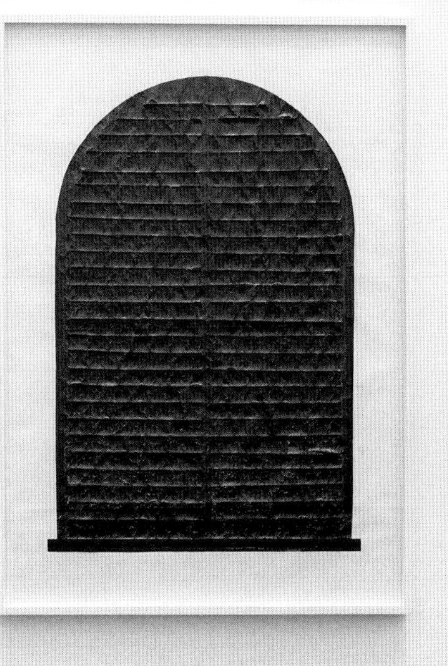

Figure 17 Anna Barriball, *Shutters*, 2011. Two framed works, pencil on paper. 143 × 90 cm (framed, 177 × 126 cm). Courtesy of the artist and Frith Street Gallery, London.

lation is close to Stokes's distinction between carving and modeling, except that Bachelard emphasizes the aggression, even sadism, provoked by resistant matter. Barriball's work seems to want to get as close as possible to the object by collapsing the space of drawing; yet, at the same time, she demonstrates its flinty resistance to our overweening "incisive" will.

We saw that, for Stokes, the situation of modern art is conditioned by the hallucinatory, fragmentary nature of contemporary experience—a condition, of course, vastly accelerated in recent decades by the digitization of everything. Things lose their materiality, their durability, their tactile, haptic resistance. In these circumstances, some artists have proposed through their work an alternative model of experience. The examples of casting and rubbing we've examined are ways of acknowledging this condition, mourning the losses incurred, yet also attempting to restore our sense of objects' resistant thingness.

Index, Diagram, Graphic Trace   5

The index and the diagram are, on the face of it, incompatible types of sign. While the index has a close, causal or tactile, connection with the object it signifies, the diagram is a form of representation that often involves statistical abstraction from phenomena, such as trends in the stock market or the weather. Yet the graphic trace is a hybrid form of representation: it is an *indexical diagram*. It takes from the index a registration of something unique—the impress of an individual—while incorporating the diagram's abstraction from what is immediately given in perception. In this chapter, works of art that incorporate the graphic trace are elucidated in relation to those that make use of the index or the diagram.[1]

Rilke's Primal Sound

A graph or diagram converts statistical data into lines, bars, or pie charts, or it translates temporal relations into spatial relations. Some forms of diagrammatic representation, however, are generated more or less directly by their object. For instance, the cardiograph and the seismograph respond to one's heartbeat and the earth's tremors, respectively. These beats and tremors are registered on a graph showing variations over time as a spiky line, and this is the sort of diagram I'm calling a graphic trace. An essay by the German poet Rainer Maria Rilke, "Primal Sound" (1919), concerns just this sort of conversion of tremors into what he calls "another field of sense."[2] He begins by recalling a physics lesson at school, shortly after the phonograph was invented. The children made a funnel of cardboard that was closed at the small end with paper, through which they stuck a bristle from a brush. The bristle was put in contact with a cylinder covered in wax that could be rotated with a handle.

They spoke into the funnel, causing the endpaper to vibrate and the bristle to incise a fine, irregular line in the receptive, rotating surface of the cylinder. This wavy mark in the wax was then fixed with varnish, at which point the students were able to reverse the process. Rotating the cylinder caused the bristle, and in turn the paper diaphragm, to vibrate; the children listened intently as the primitive recording device played back the sound of their own voices through the funnel. The effect, wrote Rilke, was staggering. "We were confronting, as it were, a new and infinitely delicate point in the texture of reality."[3]

It was not only the recorded sound but also the graphic marks on the cylinder that impressed themselves on Rilke's memory. Years later, as an anatomy student in Paris, he cast a glance at a human skull bathed in candle light. In that half-light, the coronal suture became strikingly visible and reminded him of the wavy line scratched on the cylinder by the primitive phonograph. He wondered, "What if one changed the needle and directed it on its return journey along a tracing which was not derived from the graphic translation of sound, but existed of itself naturally . . . along the coronal suture, for example."[4] Any line could be put under the needle and one would be able to hear the sound as it made itself felt, "transformed, in another field of sense." The phonograph, for Rilke, was capable of opening up an audible unconscious, giving access for the first time to the melody of things.

Marey's Graphic Method

The phonograph was but one of several inventions of the nineteenth century that received and recorded subtle vibrations and waves—another was the camera. Walter Benjamin famously credited photography, and especially the chronophotography of Eadweard Muybridge and Étienne-Jules Marey, with revealing an "optical unconscious," a field otherwise unavailable to visual perception.[5] The two pioneers, one English, the other French, are often yoked in discussions of chronophotography as if they were more or less interchangeable. However, their aims and methods were quite different. Before he became interested in photography, Marey spent years developing and improving instruments that in a clinical setting could receive and record the small involuntary motions of the body, such as heartbeat, blood flow, and respiration (fig. 18). The instruments he devised and promoted picked up these sometimes barely perceptible vibrations and transmitted them to a stylus that would make corresponding marks on a rotating cylinder. He invented, for example, the sphygmograph, a portable gadget that attached to the wrist to measure the pulse. Marey hailed these machines as more sensitive than human perception, and the graphic trace as a direct language for communicating the information recorded.[6] It was a fundamentally new kind

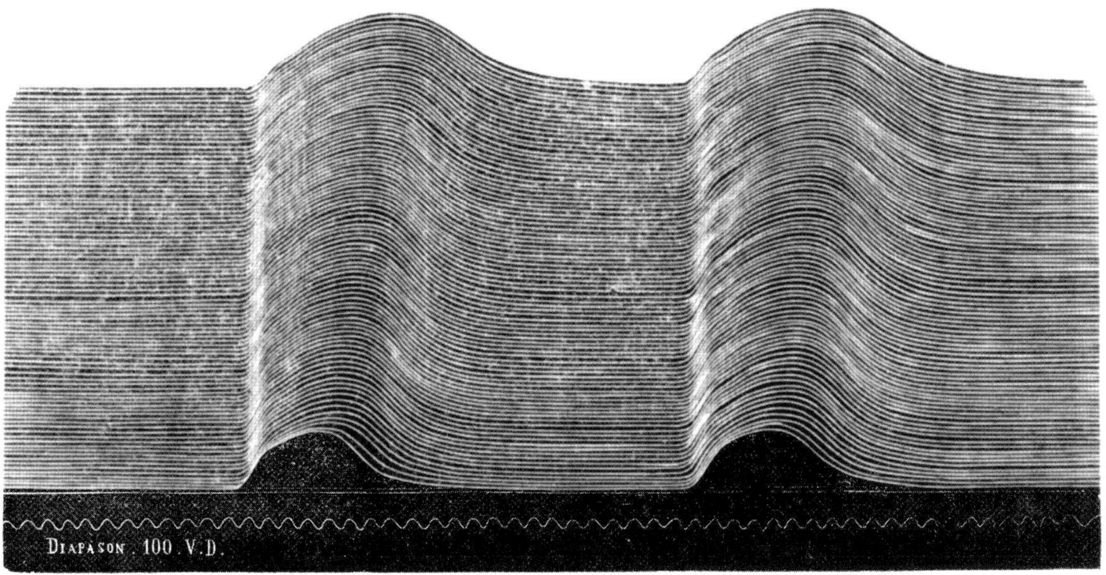

Figure 18 Étienne-Jules Marey, trace of repeated muscular contractions. From *La méthode graphique dans les sciences expérimentales et principalement en physiologie et en médecine* (Paris: G. Masson, 1885), 194.

of automatic writing that made sensible, as Friedrich Kittler writes, "the murmuring and whispering of the unconscious oracles."[7]

The image that Marey produced in this way was a single graphic field on which variations over time were displayed. When, in 1878, he saw Muybridge's photographic studies of human and animal locomotion, he recognized photography's potential for tracking large bodily movements, but also its disadvantages. Muybridge took still photographs in quick succession of a figure in motion. These could be displayed as a series of stills or projected as a short film. Muybridge's experiments led in the direction of realistic moving pictures, that is, an illusion of movement that mimics what is available to the senses. Marey's sensibility was more diagrammatic. He wanted to capture the *trajectory* of the moving body in a single field. When he tried to do so using a camera, however, the cumulative effect of overlapping photographic exposures tended to obscure the picture. To remedy this problem, Marey devised a way to blind the camera to all but the most essential movements: he dressed his model in black velvet cloth, attached silver buttons and metallic strips to the joints and limbs, and had his subject move in front of a wall painted black. He referred to this figure as *un homme squelette*, a skeleton man. As Mary Ann Doane notes in her book *The Emergence of Cinematic Time*, Marey moved "from graphic method to photographic method only to defamiliarize, de-realize, even de-iconize the photographic."[8] By filtering out excess information, Marey was able to produce a clean graphic trajectory of an action. The result was, like his graphic traces of inner bodily perturbations, something between an index and a diagram. It was also a startlingly beautiful new kind of picture.[9]

Although he was not aiming at artistic innovation, Marey's blinding of the camera and his spinning-disk shutter "sampled" phenomena at regular intervals, allowing variations over time to register on a single light-sensitive plate and *breaking up the temporal unity of the pictorial field*. As one commentator puts it, he "deconstructed the tableau-making, perspective-view of the camera," which was left untouched by Muybridge.[10] Some people think this set a precedent for cubism.[11] It certainly did for the Italian futurists and for Duchamp, whose *Nude Descending a Staircase* (1912) is an explicit adaptation of Marey's "geometric chronophotography."[12] What the painting captures are the cascading superimpositions of a skeletal figure, registered at temporal intervals but represented in the same field. She is a bride stripped bare of everything but a sort of armature and a graphic trace—*une femme squelette*. Equally significant is the way surrealists took up the graphic trace. André Breton may have actually used one of Marey's apparatuses in a medical capacity during World War I. What is certain is that artists and writers associated with the surrealist movement adopted the machines' impersonal automatism as a model to be imitated. This moment has been documented in detail by David Lomas in an important article whose title, "Modest Recording Instruments," is taken from the 1924 *Manifesto of Surrealism*, the essay that formally founded the group.[13] In a discussion of the successes and failures of attempts at automatic writing, Breton complained that most writers are too full of pride:

> But we, who have made no effort to filter, who in our works have made ourselves into simple receptacles of so many echoes, *modest recording instruments* who are not mesmerized by the drawings we are making, perhaps we serve an even nobler cause.[14]

Breton confuses here the automaticity of the process with a lack of (conscious) filtering, whereas we've seen that Marey's graphic trace depends on elaborate means of filtering unnecessary information.

Index and Diagram

As we saw in chapter 1, many works by Felix Gonzalez-Torres make use of the character of the index as witness to an anteriority. His *"Untitled"* (1991), for example, reproduced on billboards a photograph of an unmade double bed with two pillows bearing impressions of the heads of the bed's recent occupants. Here, as elsewhere, Gonzales-Torres used the power of the index as trace to evoke both past presence and present absence. Yet his approach dif-

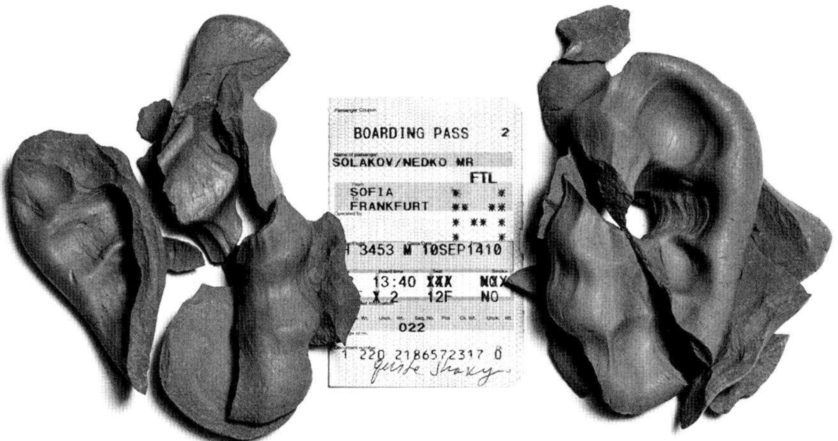

Figure 19 Nedko Solakov, *Fear* 2002–3. Terra-cotta; Alitalia, Austrian Airlines, and Lufthansa boarding pass stubs; ballpoint pen (ten pairs of sculptures, some of them in pieces). Dimensions variable. Courtesy of the artist. Photo © Angel Tzvetanov.

fers from the sort of artistic use of the index that picks up and records bodily or mental perturbations. A work by Bulgarian artist Nedko Solakov, *Fear*, exemplifies this capacity of the index (fig. 19). An extract from his statement about the work makes this clear:

> Between July 3rd and September 15th, 2002, I carried small balls of clay in my hands during all the flights I took to various destinations. To transform these balls into works of art was very easy. I just exploited my natural (and acquired) fear of flying and kept squeezing them all the time in my fists. Some of them were held for three hours, some for one. The sophisticated material captured the nervous convulsions of my terrified hands, triggered by all that bumping, babies crying and the moments of relatively quiet cruising (which are the worst because I expect something—For God's sake No!—to happen every minute).[15]

The morsels of clay imprinted by involuntary bodily convulsions, recalling the *Involuntary Sculptures* photographed by Brassaï in 1932, were fired and displayed alongside Solakov's boarding passes, examples of computerized automaticity. Some of the sculptures look like ears listening anxiously for the plane's engines to falter. Other pieces had exploded when Solakov fired them in his father's kiln; to allay his new fear that worry over the accident would aggravate his parents' heart conditions, he included the resulting fragments in the work as well. The ceramic pieces eloquently register the artist's fear of flying, but they cannot track or display his excitations as variations over time. This is the province of the diagram.

Peirce understood the diagram as a subspecies of the icon because there is a relation of similarity between the logical or temporal relations of the phenomenon and the spatial relations of the diagram. Following Peirce, Roman Jakobson explored the use of diagrams in everyday language. Some sentences take the form of mini-diagrams: for instance, Caesar's famous pronouncement "Veni, vidi, vici" (I came, I saw, I conquered) displays in a linear sequence the temporal order of his deeds.[16] Pictures may also display logical relations diagrammatically, as when the most important figure in a composition is depicted larger and centrally positioned. There is, of course, a measure of custom and convention in this arrangement, but it is not arbitrary; rather, it has an underlying diagrammatic logic. The art historian Meyer Schapiro wrote about these pictorial diagrams, observing the way the space around figures affects our sense of them. Referring to Edvard Munch, he noted that this is especially evident when several figures are presented, for "then the intervals between them produce a rhythm of body and void and determine effects of intimacy, encroachment, and isolation, like the intervals of space in an actual human group."[17]

During the twentieth century, Benjamin Buchloh argues, "one of the principal dialectical oppositions in the medium of drawing has been the authentic corporeal trace and the externally established matrix." On one side, drawing as desire—on the other, drawing "as self-critical subjection to pre-existing formulae."[18] His wide-ranging account of the diagrammatic paradigm singles out Duchamp's *Network of Stoppages* (1914) as pivotal because Duchamp overlaid a grid and a diagrammatic network of lines on top of a Cézannesque painting of nudes—one form of representation, as it were, displacing another (plate 9). Unlike prior models of drawing, the diagram would not trace desire, call forth corporality, or make a liberatory gesture; rather it would register "the disenchantment of the world and the total subjection of the body and its representation to legal and administrative control."[19] Changes in industrial technologies and the organization of labor in the late nineteenth century called for a synchronization of man and machine. Frederick W. Taylor's system of calculating a worker's most efficient movements using a stopwatch is only the most notorious example of the drive to rationalize labor by mechanizing man. Buchloh alludes to Muybridge and Marey in this context, stressing the adoption of their techniques for time and motion studies as means of disciplining labor. This is the dark side of chronophotographic visualizations of movement, obviously quite different from Benjamin's appreciation of its capacity to make visible phenomena below the threshold of ordinary perception.

In a short piece on the subject of technology, indexicality, and contingency, Mary Ann Doane writes:

> The emergence of photographic and phonographic technologies in the nineteenth century seemed to make possible what had previously been beyond the grasp of representation—the inscription of contingency. Any-

thing and everything in the order of materiality could be photographed, filmed, or recorded, particularly the unexpected, the rupture in the fabric of existence.[20]

The capacity of these technologies to capture the contingent, Doane argues, is owing to their indexical nature. The indexicality of photography as a medium is prized because it is partially outside of human control; it "registers without consciousness of registration," and so allows special access to contingency. She further suggests that photography and film are potentially means of "fulfilling a Utopian dream of resisting the naturalizing force of institutionalizing and regulating time."[21] This would include Marey's invention of a chronographic trace that records the contingencies of bodily movement.

Buchloh understands diagrammatic drawing, one-sidedly, as an artistic registration of modernity's evacuation of the body and subjectivity—or at least their disciplining and control. He concludes that Eva Hesse both adopted the diagrammatic and subverted its logic, contradicting the regulating pattern of graph paper by, for example, inscribing tiny ink circles in the squares of *No Title* (1967; fig. 20). As Briony Fer has observed, it was the varied pressure of her hand making little circular movements that produced the figure of a cross.[22] In other words, Hesse and other artists of this period adopt the diagrammatic mode in order to register their sense of the impossibility of any spontaneous, unmediated gesture, while at the same time subtly subverting the coercive regimes of the diagrammatic. This may well be an appropriate reading of a generation of artists in the 1960s and 1970s, struggling to find an alternative to the excesses of the abstract expressionism. The grid, in this context, figures an emphatically anti-expressionist impulse.[23]

A similar strategy can be found in Gonzalez-Torres's use of the diagram. In fact, his series *"Untitled" (Bloodworks)* (1989; fig. 21), with its ascending and descending diagonal lines on a hand-drawn grid, is formally much indebted to Hesse.[24] The lines are interpretable as registering daily counts of the immune systems T-cells and so tracking one of the well-known physiological manifestations of AIDS; in that light, the pair of images might be viewed as a diptych representing hope and despair. These spare but affecting works remind me of an illustration in *Roland Barthes by Roland Barthes*, in which a medical chart of the sort that is routinely kept at the end of one's hospital bed serves as a kind of nonmimetic portrait of the young tuberculosis sufferer. The Gonzalez-Torres piece fuses this medical context with the legacy of the grid in minimal and conceptual art.

An interesting take on the diagrammatic paradigm was exhibited at the 2011 Venice Biennale. As part of her thematic display devoted to subtle coercions of the classroom, the Argentine artist Amalia Pica showed a piece called *Venn Diagram (Under the Spotlight)* (2011; plate 10). The Venn diagram is a kind of mathematical graph that displays logical relations with two or

Figure 20 Eva Hesse, *No title*, 1967. Black ink on graph paper. 27.6 × 21.3 cm (10⅞ × 8⅜ inches). © The Estate of Eva Hesse. Courtesy of David Zwirner, New York/London. Photo: Adam Reich.

more overlapping circles. For example, if one circle denotes bipeds and a second creatures that can fly, then their overlap designates only those creatures that have two legs and can fly (e.g., birds and bats). In Pica's work, the overlapping circles projected by two spotlights with red and blue/green filters demonstrate both this simple logical schema and an elementary physics lesson on the phenomenon of colored lights mixing to form white light. In a caption, Pica outlines the diagram's logical relations of inclusion and exclusion and notes that during the period of the dictatorship in the 1970s in

her native Argentina, any group activity was closely monitored and Venn diagrams were banned from primary school curricula as they were suspected of
encouraging subversive thought. The lights are activated by separate motion
sensors such that if just one person is detected in the room, only one light
comes on. "It requires movement by one person or a combination of two or
more people in the room (a transitory collective) in order to see the inter-
section of the two lights." The sensors and the subtitle of the work, *Under
the Spotlight*, "refer to monitoring and surveillance of people."[25] The piece
is an illustration of the kind of paranoid irrationality characteristic of police
states, where the coincidence of two or more people in a room constitutes a
conspiracy and a Venn diagram takes on subversive political connotations.

We have seen how some artistic appropriations of the diagrammatic
paradigm aim to soften its unyielding abstraction with traces of the body.
Hesse's drawings on graph paper, Gonzales-Torres's *"Untitled" (Bloodwork)*
series, and Pica's *Venn Diagram* are examples of diagrams that respond to
the body. Art historian David Joselit argues that Duchamp's project too involved reinvesting the domain of the sign—language and the diagrammatic
mode—with the carnal and the tactile. If he is right, then Duchamp's *Network of Stoppages* represents not a replacement of one mode by another but

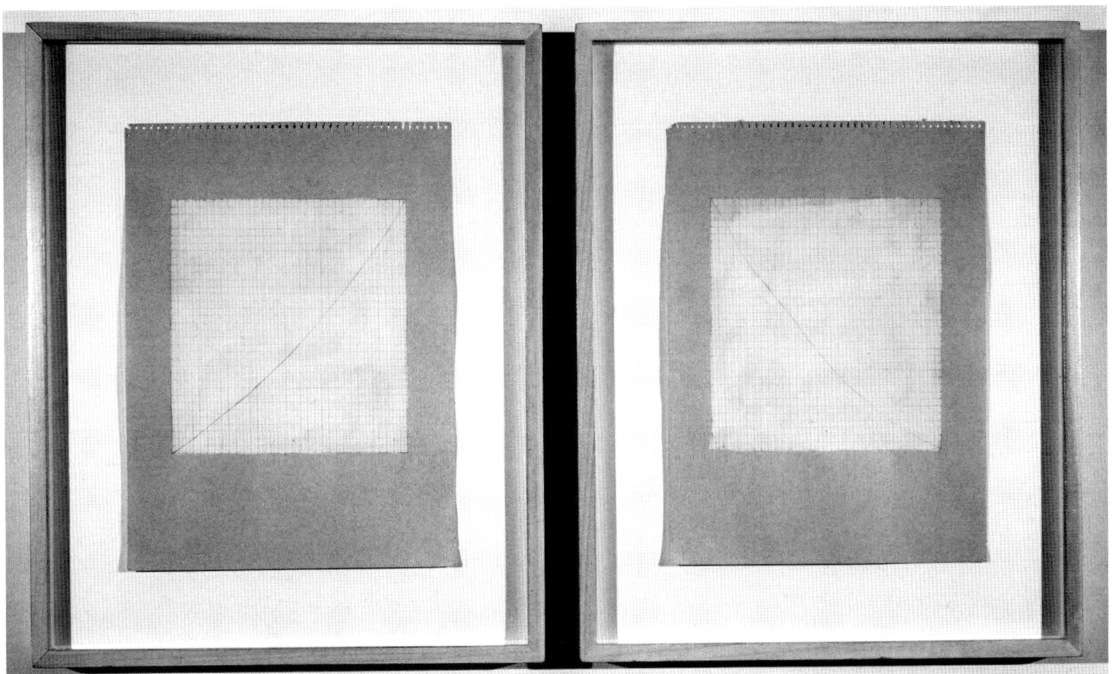

Figure 21 Felix Gonzalez-Torres, *Untitled (Bloodworks)*, 1989. Graphite, colored pencil, and
tempera on paper. Two parts: 121/4 × 9 inches each, 121/4 × 191/2 inches overall. © The Felix
Gonzalez-Torres Foundation. Courtesy of Andrea Rosen Gallery, New York.

a fusion of the diagrammatic and the corporeal, of line and flesh. As Joselit puts it, in *"Network of Stoppages*, the body is subjected to a standard of measurement, but one that collapses back into the carnal."[26] The network is based on the templates formed in Duchamp's earlier *Three Standard Stoppages* (1913–14), generated as directed by an elaborate and exacting instruction recorded in his box of notes for the year 1913: a thread one meter long was to be dropped from a height of one meter on to a horizontal plane, "distorting itself as it pleases," in order to create a new unit of measure—with "three examples obtained more or less similar conditions." The threads were affixed to a dark ground, and wooden templates or rulers formed in accordance with these new wavy units of length. The piece offers an ironic alternative to the standard meter, creating in its stead three unruly rulers. According to Joselit, this work should be understood as an experiment in giving a light, unruly, curvaceous body to a unit of measurement.[27] The white threads fixed on a dark ground allude, not just to the operation of chance, but to Marey's graphic trace; as such, they represent the *embodiment of line*, or rather, its reembodiment.

The Graphic Trace

The graphic trace is a diagram actually generated by the body; it combines the carnal and the symbolic, line and flesh, effortlessly, automatically. Two notable artistic appropriations of scientific graphic traces, created in the 1960s under the spell of Duchamp, involve the use of medical technology to make unconventional portraits. The first, Robert Morris's electroencephalographic self-portrait *Untitled (Hook, Track, Memory Dents)* (1963), consists of eight metal plaques naming the areas of the brain near where electrodes were attached along with EEG printouts recorded at each location. Morris discussed the piece in an interview with Robert Cummings, noting that during the EEG recording he was thinking about himself for the period of time it took for the graphic line to equal his height, thereby compounding its reflexivity:

> I went to N.Y.U. Medical Center and I had the electroencephalogram made. I wanted to make a self-portrait. So I calculated the numbers of—in one second the needle will travel so far. So I calculated the time I would have to think about myself for the needle to travel the length of my height. And that was considered a self-portrait. So I thought about myself for this time and used that kind of output as the drawing.[28]

Morris understood the piece as a nontraditional kind of drawing. As he says later in the interview, "Each one of those needles makes a little different kind of mark. The paper is very special. There are many lines. There are eight lines

I believe from eight parts of the brain. For me it's interesting to look at." The work was shown in the Green Gallery the year it was made along with a number of other pieces that, as Morris comments, "related to the body, my body, records of brain waves, photographs of myself, various objects involving recording actions like a hook dropped on plates of lead and drawn through plaster."[29] Morris implicitly makes a connection here between bodily indexical traces and process art involving material traces.

Morris's unusual self-portrait deserves further discussion, but I am also interested in a related work by Brian O'Doherty made in 1966—*Portrait of Marcel Duchamp: Mounted Cardiogram 4/4/66*.[30] O'Doherty greatly admired the older artist and made friends with him in the early 1960s. He was provoked, however, by Duchamp's pessimistic attitude toward the possibility of art surviving its moment of creation. Duchamp saw the museum as a graveyard: "When you put art on the wall of the museum, it begins to die."[31] O'Doherty thought about ways he could refute this skeptical claim. He had originally trained as a doctor and was at that time interested in the ethical issues and problems of identity that arose from the possibility of transplanting hearts (achieved in 1967) and other organs. It occurred to him that the perfect refutation of Duchamp's skepticism would be to capture the artist's beating heart and display it in a museum. Accordingly, he asked Duchamp to lie on a bed and have electrodes attached to his extremities in order to take readings with a hired electrocardiogram. In order to animate the cardiogram, O'Doherty devised a machine that simulated an oscilloscope in action displaying the characteristic trace of Duchamp's endlessly beating, immortal heart. According to O'Doherty, Duchamp suggested signing the piece "Brian O'Doherty, MD"—alluding to the young artist's medical training, but also slyly insinuating himself as coauthor. However, O'Doherty realized that the piece, far from being collaborative, had undertones of theft and fetishism. In 1968 Duchamp died, and O'Doherty paid tribute to him with *Duchamp Boxed*—a little blue cardboard casket into which he inserted a cylinder wrapped with a strip of the ECG printout (plate 11).

In retrospect, the technologies used by Morris and O'Doherty seem quite primitive. In contrast, British artist Susan Morris makes prints and tapestries using the very latest digital technologies of the graphic trace. Over the course of a five-year project, Morris constantly wore an "Actiwatch," a wristwatch-like diagnostic tool used, in a medical context, to collect data on the subject's sleep/wake patterns. The data is then fed into a computer to create color-coded graphs that display the subject's periods of activity and rest. In a series of prints, Morris repurposed these scientific info-graphic printouts, just as they came from the lab, to show her own periods of "being" and "fading" over time (plate 12). As she remarked, "The bright colours are the trace of my activity 'in the world' and the dark areas (the shadows) are when I'm 'out of it', sleeping and, quite probably, dreaming." What emerges from this series is an "intermittence" of the self—its memory blanks and involuntary recollections, its fluctuating presence and absence.[32]

When Morris was awarded a Wellcome Trust grant in 2010 to make a new work for the John Radcliffe Hospital in Oxford, she decided to make large tapestries based on data from the Actiwatch that had tracked her sleeping and waking patterns over long periods. Her choice of medium was prompted by a reading of "On the Image of Proust," in which Walter Benjamin claims that Proust's involuntary memory actually resembles forgetting. Generalizing from this, he remarks, "When we awake each morning we hold in our hands, usually weakly and loosely, but a few fringes of the tapestry of lived life, as loomed for us by forgetting." He inverts the story of patient Penelope, who unraveled by night the pattern woven during the day. Rather, Benjamin suggests, it is our purposive activity and remembering that unravels the patterns formed at night.[33] Although Morris's tapestries clearly show activity during both night and day, the device collects the data in the dark, so to speak, digitally registering an otherwise inaccessible behavioral unconscious.

Researchers into chronobiology have described our sleep patterns as being specific to an individual, a combination of genes, culture, and light exposure.[34] Sleep patterns are akin to fingerprints: unique and individual. It is possible, then, to think of this body of work in relation to automatic writing—or drawing—and to consider the graphs as involuntary, diagrammatic, displaced self-portraits. The tapestry illustrated here, *Sundial: NightWatch_Sleep/Wake_2010*, is one of three permanently installed in the Radcliffe Hospital (plate 13). The horizontal axis represents 365 days, while the vertical axis shows variation in activity over the course of the day: each day is 1,440 minutes long, and there is one thread per minute. What looks like a night sky or canyon down the middle of the tapestry indicates the low level of activity at night.[35] Although the tapestry is rigorously diagrammatic, it also has the intimacy of the index. One can clearly make out a time shift that, I discovered, registers a trip to New York, and a thin blue line crossing the dark canyon, which registers an all-night session writing a lecture. An important reference point for Morris's work is the ungovernable body of the hysteric in the nineteenth-century clinic, subjected to measure and confinement.

Morris was clearly attracted by the Actiwatch, which like Marey's camera, automatically filtered information, gathering specific data. She also liked the "readymade" colors of the printouts generated by the lab: red for maximum activity, black for stillness, and a graduated spectrum in between. In effect, the medical device created an aniconic self-portrait restricted to bodily motion in time. Equally important, for her, was the indexicality of the process, that is, the way it produces a shadow of even the most intimate moments of her daily life recorded over an extended period of time. Her highly coded, diagrammatic diary was literally generated by a "modest recording instrument."

On the one hand, Morris's tapestries register the effects of technological encroachment. As she has written, "The effects of electrical lighting, of orga-nising ourselves around a 'working day' and, more recently, of a 24-hour life-style, often operate at the expense of our natural sleep patterns; as current chronobiological research shows, the ensuing conflict risks damage to both mental and physical health." The Actiwatch might itself be seen as a rational-izing and regulating prosthetic device intended to enforce what the scientists call "sleep hygiene."

At the same time, however, they document the body's resistance to the rationalization of time in contemporary society. Morris says she wanted "to find a way of capturing things about my behaviour or mood, my feelings and my actions, that were unpredictable, erratic, accidental or irrational." And in-deed things that happened both inside and outside the regularity of calendar and watch time are inscribed across the grid of the tapestry-graph. This in-scription of contingency may be considered, as Doane says, a way of register-ing the body's resistance to "the naturalizing force of institutionalizing and regulating time." The diagram is disrupted; across the clear grid, a disorderly presence registers itself. As Morris writes:

> My hope is that when drawn upon to generate artworks these "tangled webs"—like illegible scribbles—can be seen as attempts to describe things that can't be put into words or easily represented; things to do with re-sisting bodies and non-compliant minds which, laid across a gridded field such as that within a calendar—the days, weeks, months of the year, plus the times of the day and of the night—record a body that goes its own way.[36]

*

Rilke speculated about the sound that would be emitted if one played, like a record, the coronal suture of the skull. But it is the skull as protective shield for the brain and the boundless activity of the mind that really interested him. The erratic suture is a metaphor for the inner workings of the psyche and particularly for the impact of trauma, described by Freud as the laying down of an indelible trace. In his "Eighth Duino Elegy" (1923), Rilke de-scribed the first panicky flight of a young bird: it "jerks though the air, as a crack goes through a cup. As the track of a bat tears through the porcelain of evening."[37] The fledgling's line of flight traces a jagged path through the sky, figured here as a cracked ceramic cup, registering distress in a form similar to the cardiograph or encephalograph. I think Gabriel Orozco alludes to this chain of associations in *Path of Thought* (1997; plate 14). For this photograph, he drew a graphlike, checkerboard grid on a skull and, using chiaroscuro effects, took a photo that highlighted the path of the coronal suture. He must have been aware that this image resembles a printout from some sensitive

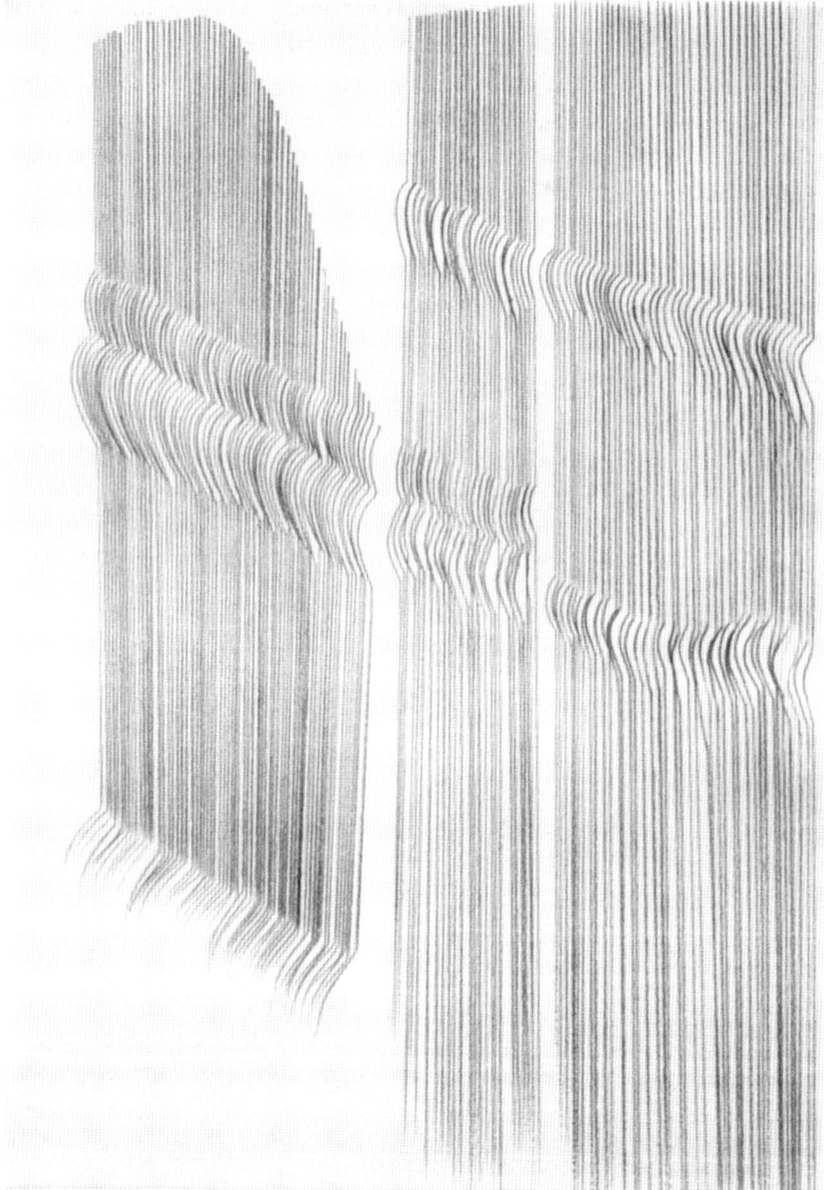

Figure 22 Gabriel Orozco, *Finger Ruler II*, 1995. Drawing on graph paper. Courtesy of the artist and Marian Goodman Gallery, New York.

recording instrument. Indeed, his *Finger Ruler II* (1995; fig. 22), which shows the regular intrusion of his fingertips into repeated ruled lines, closely resembles a plate from Marey's *La méthode graphique*. In Orozco's drawing, as in a graphic trace, bodily perturbations are registered on a grid that seeks to measure and fix them.

Orozco's simple drawing encapsulates the theme of this chapter. It implies that Marey's significance has nothing to do with the impression of movement, but rather with the invention of a kind of involuntary, bodily, and temporal language of drawing. Also, while Orozco's ruled lines allude, as Buchloh would say, to the way our lives are regulated, preprogrammed, by an external matrix, the bumps in them point to the body's insistent presence and the subject's desire to deviate from the straight line. Although the graphic trace was originally a scientific invention aimed at accurately measuring inner and outer bodily motions, and can still be used as a technique of power and control, there is nonetheless a *formal* tension between the jagged,

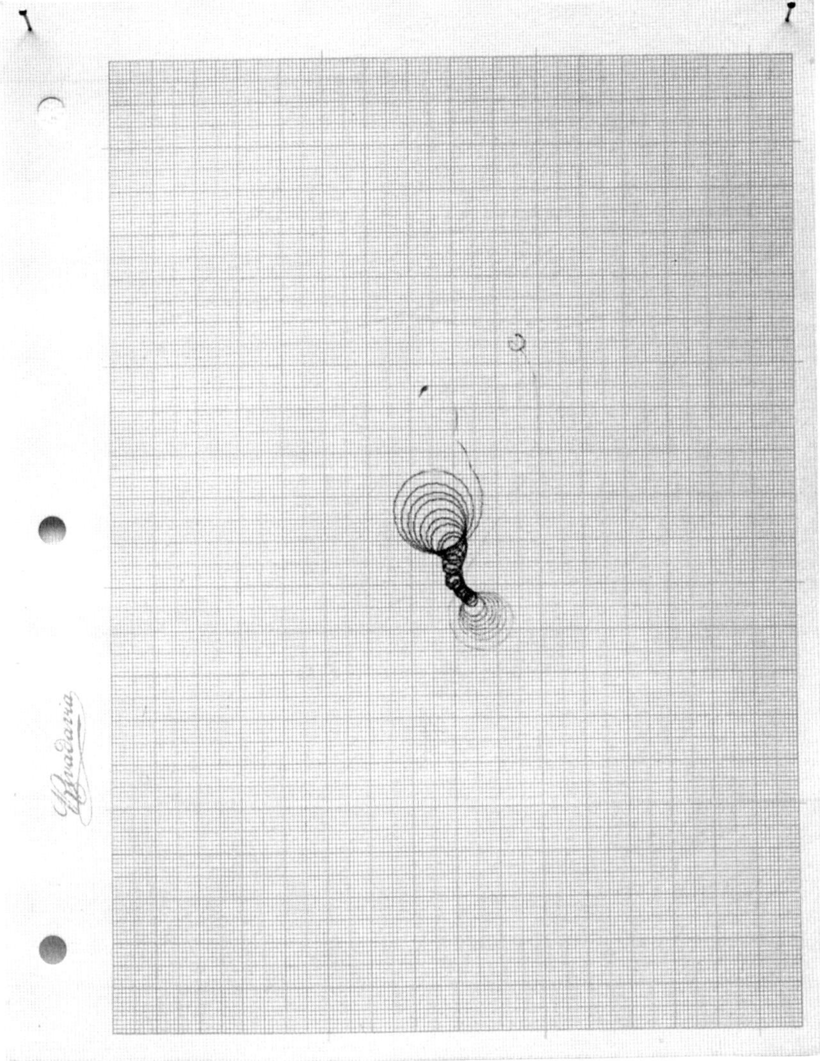

Figure 23 Amalia Pica, *Spinning Trajectory #2*, 2009. Felt-tip pen on graph paper. Courtesy of the artist and Marc Foxx Gallery, Los Angeles. Photo © Robert Wedemeyer.

irregular line of the graphic trace and the grid of the graph paper onto which it is often drawn. This tension is the theme of Amalia Pica's *Spinning Trajectories* (2009), a series of drawings made on graph paper with a felt-tipped spinning top (fig. 23). The top draws, not a jagged line registering trauma, but a skidding, twirling, irrepressible line across the page.

The "Unrepresentable" 6

According to Freud, trauma is produced by external stimuli powerful enough to break through the psyche's protective shield. This violent entry means that the stimulus is not properly experienced by the subject's conscious understanding. Since the impression is not assimilated, it remains confined to an unconscious limbo where, triggered by a later event, it causes the emotional pain of trauma. How could something so elusive be the subject of a work of art? One could argue that it is this very difficulty in relation to representability that puts trauma in touch with other aesthetic discourses, especially notions of the sublime, defined precisely as an aesthetic response precipitated by what is beyond our powers of imagination and understanding, like gigantic mountains or stormy seas. Artists, at least since the Romantic movement, have seemingly been attracted by whatever is at the margins of our intelligibilty and so incapable of being captured by conventional means of representation. The art of trauma, because it aims to represent in some fragmentary way something that eludes our grasp, often verges on the indecipherable. This is one reason why, as we have seen, so many artists have recourse to the subsymbolic index. Mary Ann Doane makes the point in a brief article on contingency, accident, and the index, where she writes, "It is the non-iconic, the non-figural, the opaque aspects of representation that, ironically, figure a grasp of contingency."[1] These considerations underscore the point I have stressed that the index has nothing to do with mimetic verisimilitude. Yet, as we shall see, despite the formal appropriateness of the trace in the context of the art of trauma, some recent interventions have been sharply critical of it. In the case of the devastating trauma of the Holocaust, the difficulty with respect to representation is compounded by moral compunction. Peter Weibel outlined the problem as follows:

> How can we represent what is, by its own definition, by its very nature un-representable, (without denying the traumatic experience and the cause of this experience, the evil, the terror,) without banalizing it, trivializing it, spectacularizing it, finally repressing it for a second time.[2]

In this chapter, I consider iconoclastic objections to representations of the Holocaust, and the French art historian Georges Didi-Huberman's response to them. In his book *Images in Spite of All: Four Photographs from Auschwitz* (2008), he introduces the concept of a torn or ripped image (*l'image déchirure*), which, he argues, can authentically represent, at least to some degree, the horror of the Holocaust. I then invoke his notion of the expressive potential of a partially effaced image in my comparative reading of the work of Gerhard Richter and Christian Boltanski. These two artists, in their very different ways, draw on the resources of the connotations that attach to the index and its aniconic opacity, but without abandoning representation.

Post-indexicality

An extended critique of the trace in the context of the contemporary art of trauma can be found in Lisa Saltzman's *Making Memory Matter: Strategies of Remembrance in Contemporary Art* (2006). The book is about artists whose work concerns memory and trauma, but who are skeptical about the use of indexical procedures. Indeed, Saltzman argues that artistic strategies since the 1990s have been predicated on absence rather than presence and marked by a "significant shift in the logic of the index."[3] Recent examples of the art of remembrance, she claims, invoke the index only to empty it: the work is "suspicious of the index, of the trace, of touch, as a privileged mode of encounter."[4] In particular, any physical connection to an object is scrupulously avoided. She instances the work of the African-American artist Kara Walker, who makes elaborate murals using silhouettes, an ancient technique of portraiture that involves tracing around a cast shadow of the subject's profile. The silhouette is thus "a pre-photographic contact image."[5] It would seem, then, that an indexical strategy is at work in Walker's work. Yet, Saltzman argues, Walker empties the index of any claim to authenticity by undercutting it with the utter phantasmagoria of her depictions of racist fantasy and stereotypes.

While this argument is ingenious, I would argue that Walker's work is far more closely related to the folk art tradition of intricate and fantastical paper-cutting or the phantasmagoria of shadow puppetry than to the polite tradition of silhouette portraiture. The silhouetted "shadows" of her imagery are, so to speak, phantasmagoria projected on the wall by a (white) viewer steeped in a culture of racism. If that is so, then it would be fairer to say that, in Walker's work, viewers find traces of their own psychic shades; the index is thus metaphorically invoked, rather than undercut. Saltzman also finds a "post-indexical" strategy in Rachel Whiteread's sculpture. Her work is claimed as post-indexical on the grounds that she makes casts of interior spaces rather than positive objects; thus her work "does not insist upon establishing presence. Rather, it insists on establishing absence."[6] However, as we saw in chapter 4, this argument neglects the fact that the normal process of making a positive cast of an object requires the preliminary stage of making a negative cast, just like a photographic negative. In both cases, it is this first step in the procedure, the negative, that entails more direct exposure to the object. As if to call attention to this proximity, Whiteread's plaster casts often bear traces of soot or color that has bled into the wet plaster. The negative cast, then, has a close, tactile relation to the object, even if it does not resemble it. One could go further and claim that one consequence of such close contact is the impossibility of resemblance, at least in the case of three-dimensional objects. Despite these objections, I think there are genuine cases of artists deploying Saltzman's "faked index," as we shall see in my discussion of the work of Boltanski.

Saltzman's notion of the faked index, which is a relative of Krauss's empty shifter, is indebted to the critique of presence and the originary trace mounted by Derrida in *Of Grammatology* and elsewhere.[7] A certain adoption of the deconstructive critique of logocentrism for the analysis of visual art informs a great deal of the critical commentary directed at the photograph as document. The photographic document, so it is claimed, encourages credulous belief in the truth of what is shown. Apparently operating without linguistic mediation or artistic convention, photography's promise of objectivity seems secured by its indexical genesis, that is, by its being a product of light reflected off objects onto light-sensitive paper. Photography, like speech, then, is likely to give us an illusory sense of unmediated presence.[8] This deconstructive critique of the illusion of presence was deepened by what Eric Santner refers to as the "ethical turn," when deconstructive strategies "became the site of resistance to any full symbolic metabolization of loss, which was itself posited as being in some fashion complicit with the fantasies of totalization."[9] The thought here is that to represent the Holocaust is to claim some privileged access while, at the same time, being immune to its devastating effects. As a result of this very influential critique, to make any claim to represent trauma authentically is to risk being accused of moral insensitivity. Consequently, for many writers, it has become necessary to redefine the index in such a way that it does not imply any immediate grasp or intuition or reference to an object or origin. Charles Merewether is another writer who is wary of the claims of the index to contact a world outside the sign: "The trace seeks to fascinate, to make us look back. . . . It seeks through offering an apparent plenitude of origins, to overcome detachment and distance, even plurality."[10] Merewether, following Derrida, resists this lure in favor of an interpretation of the trace that cannot be tied to an impression, an origin. Yet this line of thought, it seems to me, robs the index of the specificity and power that Peirce identified. Surely it is possible to hold open a gap between the index and its object by acknowledging that the index is a species of sign and so is inevitably caught up in a network of signs, while at the same time granting its specific referential weight.

Images in Spite of All

Deconstructive critiques of the trace and the photographic index, like the ones I've just sketched, are put under pressure when confronted by representations of traumatic atrocities. The status of unrepresentabilty may secure these events from trivialization, but problems arise when, in the face of denial, photographs are among the most convincing evidence that such events actually occurred. It is not surprising, then, that debates about photography, trace, and trauma form part of the very contentious atmosphere surrounding the representability of the personal and historical traumas of the Holocaust. These debates came to a head in 2001 when an essay by Georges Didi-Huberman appeared in the catalogue for an exhibition in Paris of photographs taken inside Nazi concentration and death camps. Organized by photography historian Clément Chéroux, the exhibition was called *Mémoire des camps: Photographies des camps de concentration et d'extermination nazis, 1933–1949*.[11] Didi-Huberman's contribution was critical of those who adopted an iconoclastic stance. The essay and the exhibition as a whole were vigorously attacked by reviewers in the prestigious journal *Les temps modernes*. Didi-Huberman's essay was subsequently republished in a book called *Images in Spite of All: Four Photographs from Auschwitz*, along with the author's defense of his position.[12] The original essay attended closely to just four photographs of Crematorium V at Auschwitz, taken in the summer of 1944 by Jewish members of the so-called *Sonderkommando*, a group of prisoners who were forced to carry out the gassing and incineration of their own people. Risking all, the photographer, known only as Alex, snatched a few blurred images of the scene of the crime — a group of naked women being hustled toward the gas chamber; a pile of corpses being readied for incineration (figs. 24 and 25). The roll of film was then smuggled out of the camp in a tube of toothpaste. It was hoped that the Polish resistance would be able to pass the photographs on to the Allies as evidence of what was happening in the camp, but they came to light too late.

The gist of Didi-Huberman's argument is that these poor, hastily taken images show us the truth, or at least a small portion of the truth, of the Holo-

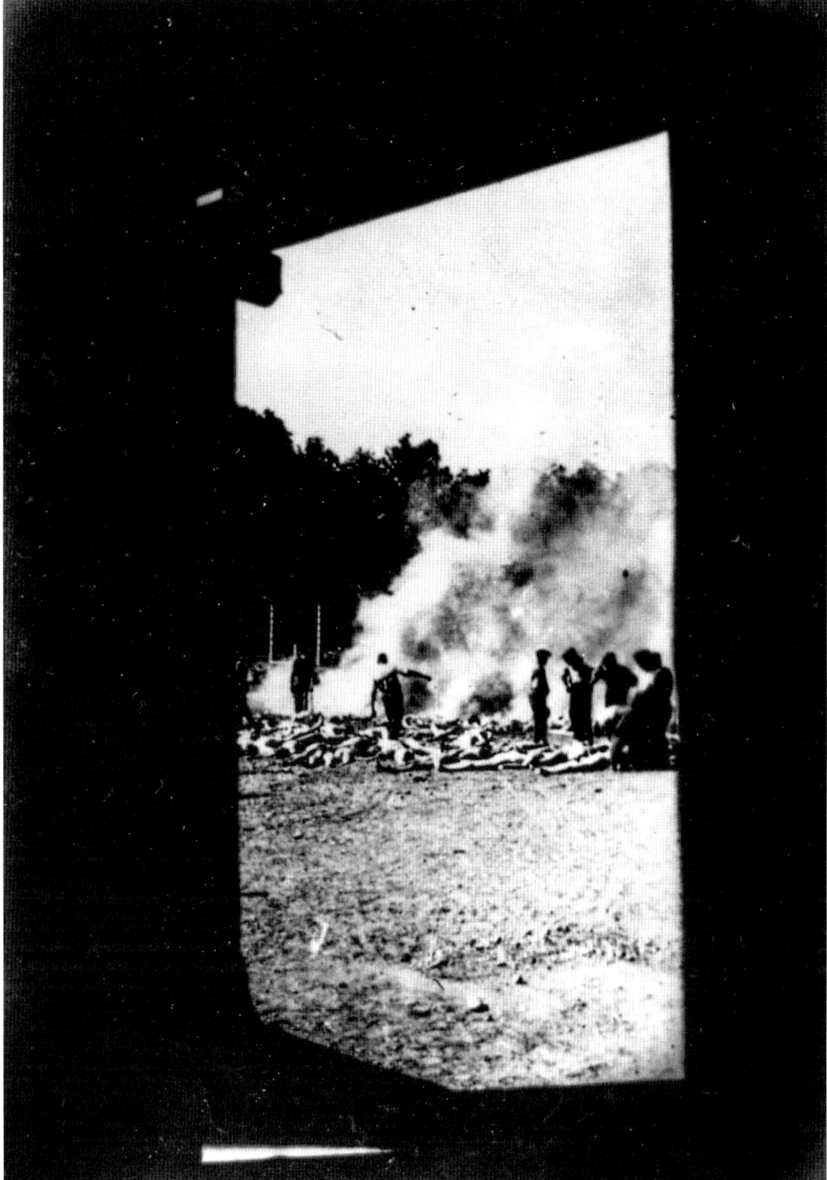

Figure 24 Anonymous (member of the *Sondercommando* of Auschwitz), cremation of gased bodies in open-air incineration pits in front of the gas chamber of crematorium V of Auschwitz, August 1944. Oswiecim, Auschwitz-Birkenau (negative no. 278).

caust. This may seem a modest claim, but it was aimed squarely at the widely held view that the horror of the death camps was so unspeakable that no mere image could possibly convey it. Any attempt to do so could only belittle and betray. The "in spite of all" (*malgré tout*) of the book's title refers, then, not only to the accomplishment of taking these particular four photographs

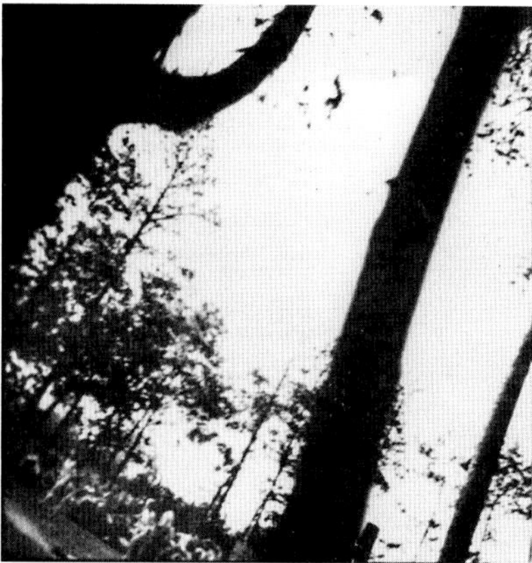

Figure 25 Anonymous (member of the *Sondercommando* of Auschwitz), women being pushed toward the gas chamber of crematorium V of Auschwitz, August 1944. Oswiecim, Auschwitz-Birkenau (negative no. 282).

despite strict prohibition, but also to the ability of the images to convey the truth despite all that is said about the falsification and illusory nature of the image. For Didi-Huberman, these pictures quite simply refute the negative aesthetics of the unrepresentablity of trauma.[13] He argues that we ask both too much and too little of images. We ask too much if we expect them to tell the whole truth—because all these photographs, or any photograph, can offer is a glimpse of the truth of the Holocaust. But we are also inclined to ask too little of images "by immediately relegating them to the sphere of the *simulacrum*."[14]

Didi-Huberman's essay was vigorously attacked by a Lacanian psychoanalyst Gérard Wajcman, whose article "De la croyance photographique" (Of Credulity towards Photographs) sought to guard against "referential illusion."[15] Wajcman aimed to protect the "unimaginablity" of the horror of the death camps, in keeping with the Lacanian dictum about the real being unrepresentable. Wajcman echoes the views of Claude Lanzmann, the editor of the journal *Les temps modernes*, where his review appeared. Lanzmann is the celebrated director of a nine-hour documentary about the Holocaust, *Shoah* (1985), which consists only of the testimony of survivors and perpetrators and shots of key sites as they were at the time of filming; there is no archival footage. Commenting on this exclusion, Lanzmann said, "I started precisely with the impossibility of recounting this history. . . . When I started the film, I had to deal with the disappearance of traces: there was nothing at all, sheer nothingness, and I had to make a film on the basis of this nothingness."[16]

It is precisely this sort of wholesale dismissal of surviving documentary evidence that Didi-Huberman so deplores. He suspects it is motivated by an overzealous and misguided adherence to certain poststructuralist and Lacanian orthodoxies, wherein the visual image is aligned with the Lacanian imaginary and condemned for propping up our narcissistic yearning for aesthetic coherence and referential stability. Yet this is Lacan's account of the role of the image, specifically the mirror image, in the formation of the ego; it is not his view of visual art or imagery in general. As Didi-Huberman admirably points out, Lacan claimed that it is precisely where words fail that a revelatory image may suddenly appear, for instance, in a dream. Furthermore, the four, almost illegible snapshots correspond well to Lacan's view that the real is manifested in the form of fragments, rags, part-objects—vestiges of a traumatic encounter. Countering the view that all images function as veils covering over a lack, and so are fundamentally fetishistic, Didi-Huberman argues that some images are more like a rip in a veil that allows a fragment of the real to escape.[17] The four photographs smuggled out Auschwitz are surely this latter kind of image.

Although Didi-Huberman hardly alludes to *Camera Lucida*, it seems to me clear that his conception of the image as a torn veil owes a great deal to Barthes's photographic punctum. He concludes, however, that while Barthes's idea of the photographic image as "that-has-been" has no doubt been exaggerated and abused, the skeptical rejection of the truth of the image by some poststructuralist theory "means losing sight of photographic power itself as well as the (problematic) point *where the image touches the real.*" Above all, the book pleads for the exercise of imagination in our thinking as an ethical responsibility. If we want to know the hell that was Auschwitz in the summer of 1944, we must "imagine it to the very end. We are *obliged* to that oppressive imaginable."[18] Although Didi-Huberman writes of "images," presumably to rhyme with "imagination," photography as a specific medium is considered, especially with respect to its indexicality and the importance of point of view. His book is a powerful defense of the capacity of the photographic document to capture something of the traumatic real. Yet he urges us to maintain a "lacunary" sense of the image's relation to truth.[19] To this end, he deplores the cropping and retouching of images to make them resemble more readable scenes, when the original photos "bear all the marks of extreme urgency and mortal danger."[20] Didi-Huberman makes the case for the representability of trauma with unusual force and sensitivity, albeit in relation to documentary images rather than art, if that distinction is tenable. *Images in Spite of All* nonetheless suggests a way of reconsidering two contemporary artists, Gerhard Richter and Christian Boltanski, whose work, based on photographic documents, bears on the subject of trauma and the Holocaust.

Gerhard Richter: *October 18, 1977*

A great deal has been written about Gerhard Richter's celebrated 1988 cycle of photo-paintings commemorating the deaths in prison of members of the Baader-Meinhof terrorist group. Yet no one, as far as I am aware, has discussed it in the light of Didi-Huberman's defense of the power of images to bear witness to traumatic historical events.[21] This approach is a promising one, partly because the German artist lives with a small, framed reproduction of one of the four photographs smuggled out of Auschwitz.[22] In a catalogue for a recent exhibition, we learn that Richter invited the art historian to his studio in December 2013. Didi-Huberman's contribution to the catalogue is an account of the visit in the form of an open letter to Richter. At the time of the visit, the studio walls were bare apart from four large blank canvases.

> On December 19 of last year, you had invited me to come to see that you had not yet painted four paintings: four paintings that would eventually measure up to these four photographs of Auschwitz-Berkenau.[23]

The paintings were never completed.

Richter has been thinking about making paintings after these photographs for some time. Since 1962, he has been compiling his *Atlas*, a collection of mainly found photographic images from magazines, newspapers, books, and family albums.[24] On a panel from 1967, a cropped version of one of the four photographs appears, along with other photographic documents of the camps (fig. 26). Most of the *Atlas* images are banal, and many allude to the "economic miracle" of postwar Germany. Benjamin Buchloh understands these images as agents of "psychic anaesthesia": "What becomes evident in Richter's archive of the imagery of consumption is the underside of this peculiar West German variation on the theme of banality: the collective lack of affect, the psychic armor with which Germans of the postwar period protected themselves against historical insight."[25] Yet, beside these pictures are horrific photographs of the Nazi death camps. Their presence casts a shadow over the banality of the other newspaper clippings, advertisements, and family snaps, giving them a disquieting character. As a young artist, Richter considered mounting an exhibition of Holocaust imagery alongside pornography, but fortunately decided against the idea. He has since insisted that he is unable to use photographs of concentration camps as the basis for photo-paintings. Yet this decision not to make explicit paintings based on photographs of the death camps has the effect of coloring his entire oeuvre; every image seems to have a shadowy underside. In some cases, this underside is explicit. For instance, family snaps taken in the 1930s and 1940s, collected in the *Atlas* and used as the basis for paintings in 1965, depict relatives of the artist who either were complicit with the Nazi regime (*Uncle Rudi*, posing in his Wehrmacht uniform; fig. 27) or fell victim to it (*Aunt Marianne*, killed in 1945 as part of a psychiatric euthanasia program). Views of mountain ranges are haunted by imagery of Hitler's Alpine retreat. Even the suspicion that the large abstractions, made by scraping wet paint with a squee-

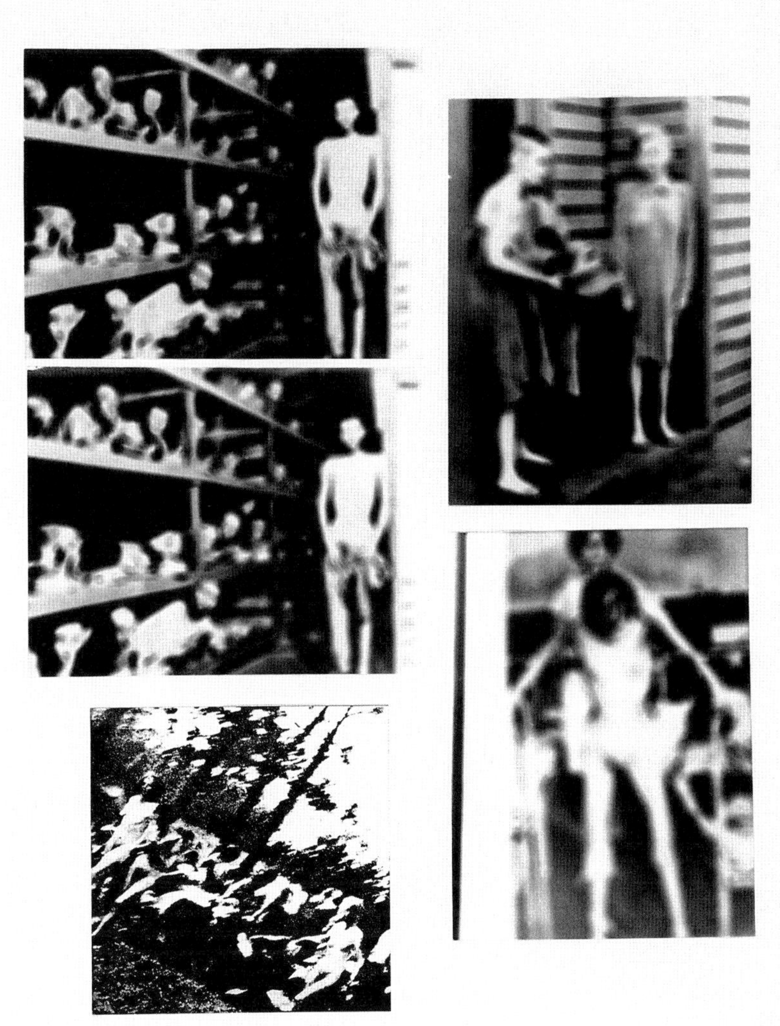

Figure 26 Gerhard Richter, *Atlas,* sheet 19, 1967. © Gerhard Richter 2015.

gee, efface figurative images is given credence by the artist's admission that a white and gray abstract painting called *Blanket* (1988) is an overpainted image from the Baader-Meinhof cycle, *Hanged*. The *Atlas* also reproduces studies for a mural commissioned for the Reichstag, the renovated capital building of the newly unified Germany in Berlin, which show death camp imagery. Given this, the abstract glass panel he eventually produced, *Black, Red, Gold* (1999), which shows only the colors of the German flag, is conceptually, although not literally, an overpainting.

Also collected in the *Atlas* are nine panels of blurred photographs documenting the activities and deaths in prison of members of the Baader-

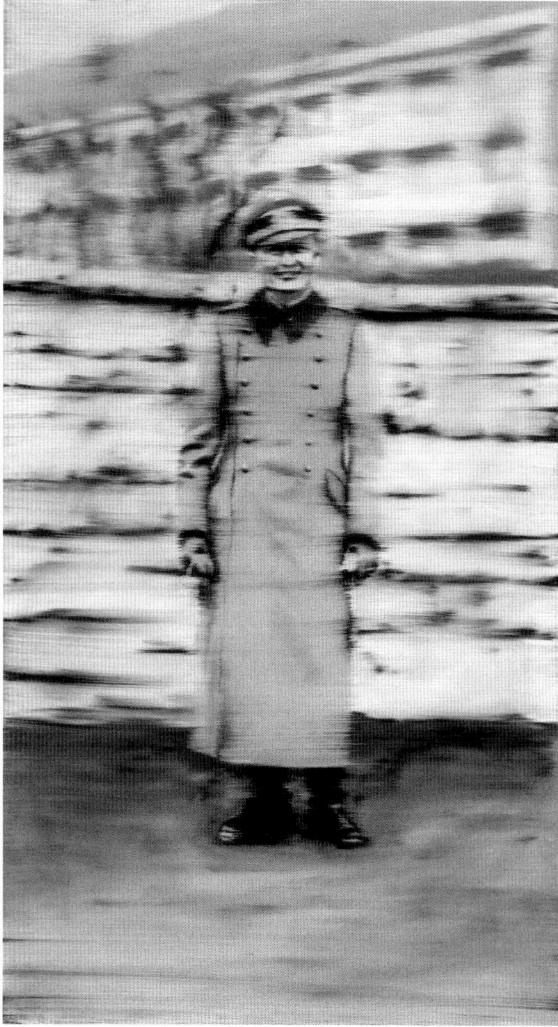

Figure 27 Gerhard Richter, *Uncle Rudi*, 1965. © Gerhard Richter 2015.

Meinhof, or Red Army Faction (RAF), group.[26] Selections from these photographs formed the basis for a suite of fifteen blurred gray paintings that must count as one of the twentieth century's greatest "history paintings," if we adapt the term to include paintings that do not idealize the past. The title of the cycle, *October 18, 1977*, refers to the date when three members of the ultraleftist terrorist group where found dead or dying in their cells in Stammheim prison in Stuttgart, although the events depicted cover a longer period. The cycle was painted ten years after the titular date, an interval in which the traumatic events of the mid-1970s, after a period of saturation coverage in the mass media and heated ideological dispute, had fallen from public view. Richter has said that the deaths of the terrorists, and related events both before and after, "stand for a horror that distressed me and has haunted me as unfinished business ever since, despite all my effort to suppress it."[27] In this light, the ten-year delay between the events and Richter's cycle mirrors the greater repression of and subsequent preoccupation with the Holocaust. Indeed, Richter has admitted that the cycle was a displaced means of making paintings about the Holocaust: "I realize that, perhaps, and surely not consciously, that was the only way for me to paint concentration camps."[28] The connection between the two moments, Holocaust and Baader-Meinhof saga, is not just circumstantial: it was postwar Germany's amnesia and incomplete denazification of its political and business elites that provoked the left-wing Baader-Meinhof group's terrorist activity against what they believed was a fascist state. As Weibel points out, "The RAF phenomenon was a social and political effect of the traumas of World War II and the Holocaust."[29]

Although the three deaths were officially declared suicides, the suspicion persists that the prisoners were in fact murdered by the state police. This uncertainty makes the RAF members both perpetrators of terror and possible victims of state power. Richter is careful to depict them neither as martyrs nor as monsters. In fact, this sort of polarization of ideological positions was something Richter aimed to defuse with this work. As a child under National Socialism and a young man in communist East Germany, Richter learned to distrust radical ideologies and utopian aspirations of both the left and the right. Why, then, did he chose to commemorate the RAF? Richter used press and police archive photographs as the basis for his paintings because, as he said, photographs are "more direct, more emotive, more intimate." But he also noted that while the photograph of a dead young woman induced horror, the blurred painting of it softened one's emotive response to sorrow.[30] His hope may have been that the rage provoked by the RAF on both the left and the right could be tempered though something like pity—incidentally, an emotion that Barthes closely associated with the photographic punctum.[31]

Much of the discussion of the painting concerns the furore over the group's activities and its members' deaths. When discussion focuses on the paintings themselves, it mainly concerns the extent to which they alter the photographic documents by cropping and blurring. What is particularly striking about the cycle is the great variety of blurring treatments, rendering the word "blur" hopelessly imprecise. For example, the painting of Ulrike Meinhof, based on a photo taken before she cofounded the RAF, is blurred by a soft feathering of wet paint and resembles the effect of air-brushing in a studio portrait. At the opposite extreme is the almost violent effect of vertical scoring down the painting of Andreas Baader's cell. Richter's photopaintings make the images less legible than the original photographs, but not in a painterly or expressionist way. It is as if he were attempting to use the resources of paint to convey something of the fragmentary, elusive, urgent character of the photographs smuggled out of Auschwitz.

What is less often considered in the critical literature is the formal variation and rhythm of the cycle as a whole. This extends to the images' size, proportions, point of view, blurring techniques, and other characteristics. I understand from the curators of the Tate Modern's retrospective of Richter's work in 2011 that the artist gave few instructions, within certain constraints, for the installation of the cycle. Robert Storr's monograph on the cycle, published by the Museum of Modern Art, assumes a broadly chronological sequence, and the text refers to this arrangement as if it were definitive.[32] Yet this fixity would seem to be counter to the artist's own sense of the cycle. While the fifteen paintings must be regarded as one work and must be hung in a single room, its installation comes with built-in indeterminacy. The variation of the paintings themselves precludes a systematic grid—a form of display common in the *Atlas*, the color charts, and many other Richter works. My suggestion is that Richter attempted to convey the affect of pity or mourning at the level of form, through not only through the gray tones but also a kind of "musical" rhythm of variation, modulation, repetition, and visual crescendos and diminuendos. This explanation of the formal character of the work seems to me more persuasive than Storr's suggestion that the cycle incorporates elements of cinematic form—stop motion, zoom, fade out.[33] This notion works best with the three images of Gudrun Esselin, called *Confrontation 1, 2,* and *3,* which are based on photographs shot at three consecutive moments and plausibly form a cinematic series. However, the three paintings, all titled *Dead* and based on a single image of Meinhof's head after her hanged body had been cut down, are usually shown in a series of diminishing size that has no cinematic counterpart (fig. 28).[34] It is this group that evokes most strongly in me a feeling of pity, but the cycle as a whole aims to convey a sense of wordless mourning. In his notes for the press conference for the first exhibition of *October 18*, Richter wrote:

> It is impossible for me to interpret the pictures. That is: in the first place they are too emotional; they are, if possible, an expression of speechless emotion. They are the almost forlorn attempt to give shape to feelings of compassion, grief and horror (as if the pictorial repetition of the events were a way of understanding those events, being able to live with them).[35]

Unfortunately, he does not comment on the unusual repetition and variation of size and proportion, which, in my view, help to convey this "speechless emotion." However, the cycle's visual musicality may be hinted at by the inclusion of a painting of Baader's record player.

Richter chose to depict an event around which views were polarized; he wanted the paintings to elicit an emotional response but also understanding, a space for thought or what Aby Warburg called *Denkraum*. One way artists have of creating that space, according to Warburg, is through the use of gri-

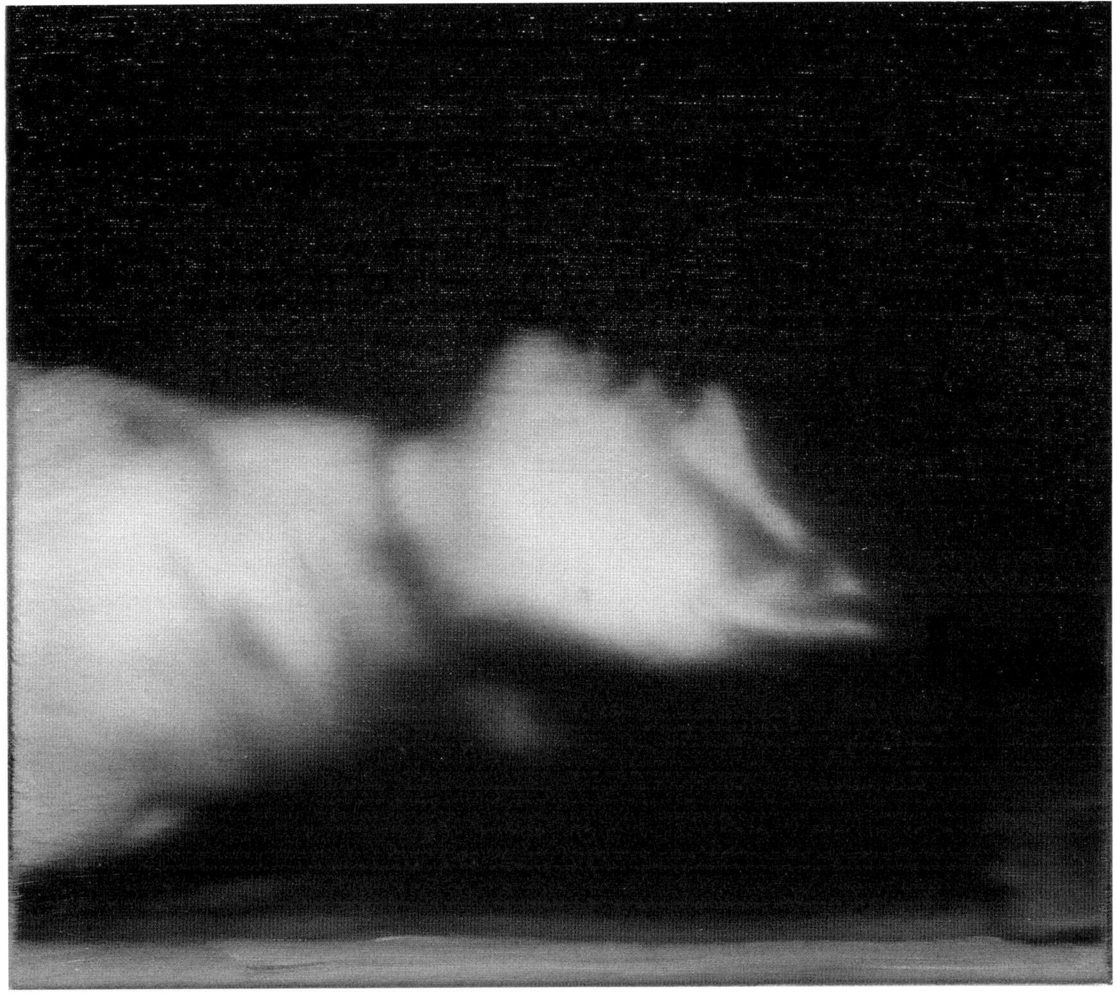

Figure 28 Gerhard Richter, *October 18, 1977*, 1988 (detail: *Dead*). © Gerhard Richter 2015.

saille; a horrific scene can be represented in gray tones so as to make it bearable. As Warburg observed in his *Grisaille Notebook* (1928–29): "The strength of the artist in keeping these forces at bay without forfeiting their vitalizing influence is symbolized in the artistic means of grisaille."[36] This potential of art to create psychic distance undoubtedly relates to Warburg's close reading of Friedrich Nietzsche's *The Birth of Tragedy*, especially the following passage: "Even the image of the angry Achilles is only an image to him whose angry expression he enjoys with the dreamer's pleasure in illusion. Thus, by this mirror of illusion, he is protected against becoming one and fused with his figures."[37] Richter draws on traumatic-mediatic material, the equivalent in the technological age of Warburg's dangerous and energizing classical imagery, and transforms it into something that can form the basis of meaningful experience and vivid memory.

Traumatic imprinting, disappearance, displacement, reemergence, acknowledgment, pity, and wordless mourning are all compressed in this complex cycle of paintings. Although Richter's paintings are figurative, they follow in the tradition of resisting transparent or literal artistic imaginations of traumatic material, a principle that has often led artists to invoke trauma negatively in the form of abstract art as, for example, in the works by Sol LeWitt, Ellsworth Kelly, and Richard Serra commissioned by the Holocaust Museum in Washington, DC, made to commemorate those who suffered and died.[38] Richter's cycle of paintings, like Didi-Huberman's book, is a powerful defense of the capacity of pictorial imagery to capture something of the traumatic real.

Christian Boltanski: *Lycée Chases*

A comparison between roughly contemporary works by Richter and by the French artist Christian Boltanski should prove instructive, as the work of both artists bears on the rise of National Socialism and the impact of the war in Europe. Boltanski was born in 1945, so did not, like Richter, live through the period, but his father, a secular Jew, is said to have spent a year of the Nazi occupation of France (1943–44) hiding under the floorboards in the family home in Paris. Also, Boltanski's photographic work is marked by the blurring of archival photographs, so an analysis of the differences between Richter's and Boltanski's use of documentary photographs and techniques of blurring may prove illuminating. In addition, both artists form part of a tradition that includes Duchamp, Joseph Beuys, and Andy Warhol.[39]

All commentators characterize Boltanski's work as crossed by contradiction, ambivalence, or paradox. Didier Semin analyzes his work in terms of tension between the Duchampian readymade and the relic, and describes his self-presentation as an oscillation between messiah and con man.[40] These observations help to capture something of the troubling ambivalence at the heart of Boltanski's work, an ambivalence associated with the index that was discussed at length in chapter 4. A typical Boltanski piece is a curious hybrid, taking the form of a pseudo-relic, a fraudulent fragment or trace of a simulated past. In fact, his work perfectly exemplifies Saltzman's category of the "faked index." For example, in 1969, he produced an artist's book called *Research and Presentation of Everything That Remains of My Childhood, 1944–1950*. Photographic documents of a lock of hair, a swatch of material, or a pile of building blocks are presented as if precious souvenirs of youth, but everything is fabricated. In an accompanying statement, Boltanski writes that he is saving these traces of his life in an effort to counteract his inevitable death. He apparently ridicules our impulse to shore up our frail existence by accumulating things: "So many years will be spent searching, studying, classifying, before my life is secured, carefully arranged and labelled in a safe place—secure against theft, fire and nuclear war—from whence it will be possible to take it out and assemble it at any point. Then, being thus assured of never dying, I may finally rest."[41] Elsewhere he has stated, "My idea was to hold on to traces, to struggle against death."[42] As if to underscore the extent of fiction and fabrication in his collection, a year later he produced *Attempts to Reconstruct Objects That Belonged to Christian Boltanski between 1948 and 1954* (1971), which consists of forty clay models based on his memories of blankets, ink bottles, and toys including paper airplanes, a water pistol, and building blocks, all displayed in metal trays. Boltanski invests these objects with a phony aura—and, as a consequence, he effectively mutually contaminates both the auratic relic and the mass-produced readymade.

The combination of the patina of age and the theme of death are put to powerful use in a series of installations that combine connotations of a chapel with some infernal bureaucratic archive. Found photographs such as one taken in 1931 of the graduating class of the Jewish Gymnasium in Vienna (*Lycée Chases*, 1986–87) are rephotographed, enlarged, and cropped. There are different configurations of the installation, but all include an altarlike arrangement of corroded tin biscuit boxes and clip-on desk lamps that shine directly into the photographed faces, plus straggling electric wires. The dim ambient light creates an atmosphere that is both sacred and threatening. The blurring caused by enlarging and rephotographing the original photographs gives them a weaker mimetic hold but does not affect the image's indexicality; indeed, the blurring of the photographic index can even testify to its authenticity, as we've seen with the Auschwitz photographs.

Boltanski's strategy of calling into question the authenticity of the document or other trace becomes problematic when it comes to his installations that allude to the Holocaust. His earlier work explored the ways in which pictorial rhetoric and gallery context can endow the banal with the aura of memory, loss, and death. For example, he created the series of installations called *Inventories* (1973–79) by instructing gallery curators to procure and display the possessions of a recently deceased, anonymous person. In fact, only one of the displays, in Baden-Baden (1973), was based on the possessions of a dead person. *Inventory of Objects That Belonged to a Resident of Oxford* (1973) was based on the possessions of a young man studying abroad for a year. Nevertheless, these objects wrenched from their context of everyday use are still capable of carrying an emotional charge. They are not just a collection of random items of consumption, but rather "personal effects" that seem to betray something about the individuality of their erstwhile owner. Of course, this may be an illusion; nevertheless, our relation to them is quite different from our attitude to pop or neo-Dada objects. This is partly owing to the fact that the used or secondhand object bears a patina that takes it out of the realm of mass production and consumption. The found object, as opposed to the readymade, is rarely new, and when such objects are presented as the orphaned possessions of a dead person, they become empty husks that signify absence or death.[43] Boltanski gave them a fragile reliclike aura, but our doubts about their authenticity mean that they are in constant danger of sliding back into utter insignificance—and this is precisely the point. Boltanski's work from the 1970s seemed designed both to arouse and to undercut the viewer's "credulity toward images," very much in the spirit of Saltzman's faked index. Yet when a found photograph of a Viennese Jewish high school class in 1931, many of whose members we must assume perished in the Holocaust, forms the basis of the work, is it an appropriate response to oscillate between credulity and skepticism?

As we have seen, the auratic effect of Boltanski's installations is carried partly by the blurring of found photographic documents. The blur in Boltanski's work signifies aging, transience, a slipping into the past and falling from memory, prompting us to cling all the more urgently to this seemingly last, fragile trace. Some of the faces are reduced by enlargement to skulls with dark eye sockets. Abigail Solomon-Godeau has persuasively argued that Boltanski's blurring generalizes the portrait face and thereby traduces the singular identity and particular historical circumstances of the person.[44] Yet this generalization of the face is, I think, symptomatic of a larger problem, which is that Boltanski's work generalizes the theme of death: the Jewish Austrian students in 1931 are given no privilege in relation to any other photograph of children. The artist made this clear in an interview:

> If people know the material is from the Holocaust, they can't think about anything else. The first time I showed *The Lycée Chases* was in Germany and everybody spoke to me about Nazis and all that. I said, "Yes, it's true, it's about that, but it's also about all of us." . . . In the same body of work which is called *Lessons of Darkness*, is the large piece of *The Children of Dijon*. Now, the children of Dijon look very happy and yet, that period of time has passed, and they are now adults. The photo we can see was made 12 years ago. That means the photo of this little boy, the face we see now, has disappeared; they no longer exist. . . . The Holocaust is only an example of dying.[45]

In other words, the blurring of the photo-document that generalizes the individual features is intended to allow us to project a generalized sense of human finitude and to contemplate our own mortality.

As we have seen, Richter's painterly blurring in *October 18, 1977* has a rather different aim. The cycle grapples with the problem of representing a traumatic past in a way that formally recognizes the difficulty of coming to terms with it. It is a form of painting "against itself" that acknowledges the limits of representation. It also alludes to the way both trauma and technologies of the image affect memory. His blurring of the images distances them, creating room for thought; it softens horror into pity and directs attention onto the formal rhythm of the cycle as a whole. In sum, Richter understands that a purely transparent representation of traumatic events would betray them just as much as one so generalized that the subject becomes human mortality as such, rather than a specific, tragic historical event.

Invisible Traces 7

POSTSCRIPT ON THOMAS DEMAND

Thomas Demand may seem like an unlikely artist to feature in a book about the trace. As is well known, he does not photograph things in the world, or at least not directly. Rather, he photographs life-size models of scenes, often based on press photographs, which he and his assistants laboriously construct out of sheets of colored paper and card attached to wood or metal supports. The most common explanation given for this strange procedure is that Demand aims at undermining assumptions about photography's power to present an objective view of the world. The large size and superb quality of his analogue prints, displayed unframed behind Perspex, lures one into the mistaken belief that we are looking at a photograph of, say, a real interior, while the illusion of three-dimensionality invites us imaginatively to enter the space. Gradually, however, we begin to notice that the image lacks certain traces of human presence or signs or wear and tear. All signage and other textual materials are expunged. As evidence of the scene's paper construction emerges, realization of its wholesale artifice leads to a sense of disillusionment, perhaps tempered by admiration for the skill of the artist, with the result that our habitual credulity toward images is dashed. On this account, Demand's photographs insistently repeat the already well-rehearsed poststructuralist lesson that the photographic image is a construction, with no indexical ground in an original.[1]

Another well-known explanation for the procedure, advanced by Michael Fried, agrees that Demand's practice is aimed at undercutting photographic indexicality. However, for Fried, this elaborate exercise in distancing the image from any referent is done in the service of a particular view of photography as an art. On this account, the paper construction serves as a guarantee that every aspect of the photograph is through and through intentional. Demand's images, he writes, are "divested of every hint of indexicality" and are "saturated with his intentions," so that there is no room for anything but a recognition of "madeness."[2] Demand's practice thus declares the autonomous nature of his art, against a view of photography as dependent on an anterior reality and crossed by contingency. Fried proposes that Demand uses photographic sources precisely because analogue photography is a medium characterized by being "weak in intentionality," as John Berger put it.[3] Demand's counterimages are thus able to "allegorize intendedness as such."

While it is perfectly true that Demand does not really "do" aleatory process, Mark Godfrey has pointed to the role that chance plays in his finding of a subject—a point to which I will return.[4] Moreover, Fried's argument fails to explain why Demand bases his models, not just on photographs, but on found images that circulate in the mass media and document events very much crossed by contingency and death. Despite their very different points of view, then, neither the poststructuralist nor the modernist reading explains why Demand's procedure is so often carried out on scenes that are related to atrocities of one kind or another. The vast majority of his photographs concern traumatic historical events, often from Germany's troubled past. Why would the artist want to call into question the veracity of documents relating to these events? Why would he choose documentary and press photographs as the basis for an autonomous art? Clearly, the practice of making and photographing models needs to be understood in a way that can also account for Demand's particular choice of spaces haunted by the past. Of course, it is arguable that Demand's art performs the equivalent of "critical historiography," a practice that reminds us that our relation to the past is always mediated and constructed, our understanding limited and partial. This reading of the work explains the elaborate artifice and the subject matter, yet does not seem to me to get at its specific visual character.

The one thing Demand's models conspicuously lack is any trace of the events that took place in the spaces represented, even when those events famously left traces that can, in fact, be seen in the source photographs. A murder scene is stripped of all evidence; Jackson Pollock's studio is totally dripless. The philosopher Nigel Warburton has argued that what is characteristic of the experience of Demand's photographs is just this disquieting sense of absence. The spotless space in *Corridor*, for example, lacks all trace of the horrors that occurred in the space on which it is modeled. And, in any case, the photograph does not represent the interior of the Milwaukee apartment where serial killer Jeffrey Dahmer murdered and cannibalized his seventeen victims, but the corridor outside. Of course, this displacement can be explained by the fact that forensic pictures of the interior of the apartment were so appalling that they were never published. Perhaps Demand's purging of detail and trace relates to the way mass media both sensationalize and sanitize current events?

Another possibility is that the tracelessness of the images indicates some kind of deficit with respect to memory. Writing of Marcel Proust's theory of involuntary memory, Walter Benjamin noted of its opposite, voluntary memory, that "the information it gives us about the past retains no trace of that past."[5] The sort of memory that relies on deliberate recall, is hollow, simulacral; as Samuel Beckett remarked in his book on Proust, "It presents the past in monochrome."[6] While Demand's photographs are certainly not monochrome, they do call attention to the limitations of memory in modern times, where information is fully accessible but the texture, the scent, the tactile quality of memory is voided. There is no taste of a madeleine dipped in lime-blossom tea. As Godfrey puts it, the work's lack of specificity may relate to "an intensification of a process of loss of historical consciousness already underway in the culture at large."[7] This loss has particular resonance in a German context, where the combination of National Socialism and the Holocaust, wartime destruction, and rapid postwar reconstruction encouraged wholesale forgetting. It is hard to see, however, how images so drained of the texture of the past could long sustain our attention.

Yet the idea that Demand's work is concerned with the contemporary situation of memory is confirmed by some of the artist's statements. In a conversation with the novelist Daniel Kehlmann, Demand spoke of his fears of an impending crisis of memory. In the age of Facebook, he notes, the distinction one formerly drew between collective and personal memory is collapsing. In theory, one could publicly document and post one's entire life online. Demand observed that one could construct "a lifelong photo album in the Cloud":

> But that also means you are storing your own deepest memories offsite. These days this most private aspect of human life is being commercialized. . . . We know we've got all these photos readily accessible, so we forget them. And what happens in the long term with the human mind if it now structures knowledge according to how it can be accessed and retrieved? After all, you for one, are still more interested in the contents of Proust's work than in knowing where the book is on the shelf.[8]

In response, Kehlmann offers a useful analogy between the current situation of knowledge and the use of satellite navigation in cars. Satnav or GPS navigation allows you to find your way around a city without knowing its geography. So also in the case of knowledge: you can find information so fast that "very quickly you lose any deeper understanding of connections and contexts."[9] Yet the concern over a crisis of memory long predates digitization. Demand's statement quoted above recalls part of Benjamin's essay "On Some Motifs in Baudelaire" (1939), where Benjamin observed that technologies such as photography, which make it easy to retain and retrieve an event, have a deleterious effect on our capacity for long experience and substantive memory. Because our prosthetic devices can remember for us, our power of recall is weakened. "The techniques inspired by the camera and subsequent analogous types of apparatus extend the range of the *mémoire volontaire*" and thus inevitably reduce the play of involuntary recollection.[10] It is surely no accident that, in precisely this context, Demand mentions Proust—the person who coined the term *mémoire involontaire* and whose writing is a testimony to its power to make recollection vivid. In "On the Image of Proust," Benjamin claimed that Proust's involuntary memory actually more closely resembles forgetting, for it is in dreams that we weave meaningful patterns from disparate threads. Our conscious, purposive daytime activity unravels the patterns formed at night.[11] Beckett made the same point when he remarked that "the most trivial experience . . . is encrusted with elements that logically are not related to it and have consequently been rejected by our intelligence."[12] The formation of meaningful patterns is what Benjamin refers to as experience proper (*Erfahrung*)—that is, experience tied to meaning, the unconscious, memory. According to Benjamin, "Proust's work *A la recherche du temps perdu* may be regarded as an attempt to produce experience . . . in a synthetic way under today's social conditions."[13]

It seems clear from these exchanges that Demand sees his own work as a response to a crisis of memory tied to technologies of representation. Do its hollowness, indeterminacies, and artifice serve to make us conscious of the generalized and superficial character of our experience and memory? This is a plausible supposition. Yet, again, it does nothing to explain the visual fascination of Demand's photographs. Although the actual scenes in his photographs are often banal, they nonetheless have a compelling quality. This quality, I suggest, is partly owing to the fact that Demand chooses imagery that is imprinted on our memory by the mass media in the form of highly mediated traumatic witnessing. We are dominated by imagery mediated via multiple technologies of reproduction, so authentic experience, as Benjamin defined it, is becoming increasingly rare. In a conversation with theorist, filmmaker, and storyteller Alexander Kluge, Demand observed, "I gain a large part of my experience exclusively through this media based narrative on the world and not, as one would have done one or two generations ago on 'primary experience.'" Or, again: "I'm at the end of an entire chain of worlds of images that present themselves to me. All experience, all I essentially am, is largely the upshot of things passed on to me."[14] Given that our experience is inevitably mediated, the question then becomes: is it possible in such a technological environment to retrieve something analogous to authentic experience? Can the technical, mediatic image be made memorable?

In the same conversation with Kluge, Demand revealed that many of the

Figure 29 Thomas Demand, *Tunnel*, 1999. 35 mm film loop, Dolby SR, 2 min. © Thomas Demand, VG Bild-Kunst, Bonn/DACS, London, 2015. Courtesy of Sprueth Magers.

images he uses have a particular personal charge. *Room* (1994; plate 15), for example, shows a destroyed office, which, we learn, is based on a photograph documenting the unsuccessful attempt on Hitler's life by Wehrmacht officers in 1944. It makes reference to a photograph that hung in Demand's schoolroom, and presumably many other German schoolrooms. For those who grew up in postwar Germany, this scene has more than merely historical interest: Demand says it "had been seared in my mind."[15] The same is true of a more recent and global incident that he made the basis of a short film. *Tunnel* (1999; fig. 29) is unusual in that it is an extrapolation of still photographs everyone saw of both ends of the Pont de l'Alma tunnel in Paris, where Princess Diana's car crashed two years earlier. Using a mock-up of the scene, Demand created a two-minute, 35-millimeter film loop that takes us around the bend and into the mouth of the tunnel fifty-two times. Shot from the point of view of someone in the car, it is a scene everyone imagined; as Demand noted, "The imagination pans through the tunnel." He has said that his interest in this sort of event is prompted by the way people construe it as part of their own biography; he is interested in the way "people turn this event into their own story."[16] Like other signal events, such as the assassination of John F. Kennedy and the attacks of 9/11, it is both collectively experienced and a privately remembered:

What it's about is the place that has been seared in our memories via a sense of reality that has nothing to do with real experience but which consists of stories we've heard.[17]

The idea of experience and memory being bound up with stories links Demand's practice to that of the storyteller. The storyteller, according to Benjamin, is a figure in steep decline. Storytelling is about sharing experience, and, since experience is waning, so also is the practice of storytelling.[18] Experience in the deepest sense is adversely affected by the rise of technologies of reproduction and the shocks of modern life. Just as shocks on the battlefield left World War I soldiers unable to communicate their experience, so the torrents of media imagery to which we are exposed leave us poorer in experience—that is, in the ability to assimilate, communicate, and share. We have instant access to information, but, unlike a story, it does not stick. Benjamin observes that the story, unlike information, does not expend itself, but rather remains open, ambiguous, and enigmatic:

> Every morning brings us news from across the globe, yet we are poor in noteworthy stories. This is because nowadays no event comes to us without already being shot through with explanation.[19]

The story is free from explanation. Consequently, "it preserves and concentrates its energy and is capable of releasing it after a long time." This is partly because the story is passed down from mouth to mouth and also because the storyteller always impresses the story with his own personal history. "Thus, traces of the storyteller cling to the story the way the handprints of the potter cling to the clay vessel."[20]

Does Demand aim to transform our exposure to mass-media imagery into something like authentic experience, retroactively? Is he a storyteller in this sense? Certainly he leaves behind nothing like the potter's handprints—on the contrary. But Benjamin's simile has to do with the way the storyteller or artist impresses something personal on the otherwise external thing— tying it, indexically, to a given context. In Demand's case, this might mean invoking his personal memories in relation to a public event. In his conversation with Kluge, he commented directly on this aim of relating personal experience to the public sphere:

> I believe my work is a matter of oscillating between the two: applying my private, intimate experience to the public, and seeing whether there's a place for me there, whether I can kindle something within the public sphere.[21]

What particularly interest him are signal events, circulated in the media, indirectly witnessed by us, which leave invisible traces on our minds. These images are "seared in our memories," as he says more than once.[22] Referring to his *Tavern* cycle of photographs, which relates to the abuse and murder of a boy in a small German village, he says, "For me, what is decisive are the blurred traces left in the media by these incidents" (plate 16).[23] Demand chooses "blurred" mass-media images that have affected us, and so form part of our personal biographies, and which also circulate in the public sphere. Through the process of making models, he detaches the images from mass-media information and makes them enigmatic, prolonging our attention. This is also what the storyteller does. In a story, things are reported with accuracy, but, Benjamin notes, "the psychological connections of the events are not forced on the reader." It is left up to him to interpret things as he understands them, and thus the narrative "achieves an amplitude that information lacks." The story is bare; it "has a chaste compactness which precludes psychological analysis."[24] This could well describe Demand's process: he takes a mediatic image, drains it of information, and so enables our associations. Ulrich Baer touched on this point when he observed that the effect of Demand's elimination of anecdote is to open up "these places' sense of historical significance as a process of discovery and revision. . . . Historical meaning is given in these images not as something known and understood."[25]

Benjamin characterized aura as "the associations which, at home in the *mémoire involuntaire*, tend to cluster around the object of perception."[26] Demand's *Drafting Room* (1996; plate 17) exemplifies this principle. It is based on a found photograph of a postwar architectural studio directed by a man who, it turned out, was known to Demand's grandfather. "Now there was suddenly a web of connections around this image," he notes, "thanks to which my personal environment became linked up to public history."[27] This is reminiscent of Benjamin's sense of how experience in the deepest sense is fostered; it involves a negotiation of public and private spheres, of personal and collective memory: "Where there is experience in the strict sense of the word, certain contents of the individual past combine in the memory with material of the collective past."[28] There is, however, a paradoxical twist in Demand's choice of this particular example, for the architecture of this Bauhaus-style drafting room is a perfect example of a space devoid of traces. In his 1933 essay "Experience and Poverty," Benjamin proposes a new sort of poverty caused by war and technology that results in a loss of legacy and tradition. This lack, he suggests, might also be an opportunity for creativity; it is a chance to start from scratch. All these constructors of the new need, Benjamin says, is a drafting table.[29] However, this radical call to erase the traces is at odds with the main thrust of his writing on memory, experience, and storytelling. For Benjamin, the storyteller is a craftsman whose task is to "fashion the raw material of experience."[30] Demand's whole practice involves making paradoxical objects—hand-crafted documentary images. "Things must be slowed down," he says, "and for me that involves making something with my hands."[31]

In his essay "The Surrealist Situation of the Object" (1935), André Breton declared that even those surrealist paintings that "seem to be most free can naturally come into being only through their return to 'visual residues' stemming from perception of the outside world."[32] These "residues" are visual impressions that have attracted constellations of formerly dissociated thoughts, giving them an unusual density and opacity. The phrase "visual residues" is derived from Freud's notion of the "day's residues," which coalesce in the formation of dreams.[33] Demand must have had something similar in mind when he refers to the sedimentation or chain of images deriving from a remote event. This is why his photographs can be so affecting. They take as raw materials the psychic traces of mass-media imagery, our half-unconscious "visual residues," and turn them into "stories"—to be remembered, communicated, passed on. In an interview, Demand made this clear: he said that his art involved "pulling true facts into fiction."[34] On this account, then, Demand's photographs have the clarity, intense color, and lack of specificity that is characteristic of hallucination or dream.[35] Another way to understand the transformation he achieves is in terms of Barthes's distinction between the generally interesting information provided by the *studium* of a photograph and the affective force and personal meaning provided by the *punctum*. Demand may be alluding to this idea when he remarks that he attempts to "privatize the public world of memory," that is, to give it subjective significance.[36] This is a very far cry from Fried's insistence on "sheer artistic intention," or on "the conscious process" of choosing a subject, or the idea that the viewer "is called upon by the image to do nothing more than register the 'madeness' of the objects on view."[37] On my account, insofar as the recognition of madeness is an important feature, it is to signal Demand's intention to craft a story rather than convey information.

My account of Demand's work has wider ramifications. We recall that Gerhard Richter is also interested in retrieving moments in the recent past that combine personal and political history. His painting *Uncle Rudi*, for example, is based on an image from the family photo album, no more than a snapshot, now made public through another paradoxical object—the hand-painted photograph. One could cite, too, his transformation of photojournalistic images related to the arrest and deaths of members of the Baader-Meinhof group into a cycle of paintings, a quasi-narrative, that can absorb our interest for extended periods. And these are not the only artist-storytellers working against the grain of media imagery. Perhaps we might consider Andy Warhol's *Death and Disaster* series in this light, although the automatic repetitions of his photo-silkscreen technique and the shock content of the images give them a rather different character from the work with which I'm concerned.[38]

Richard Hamilton's *Kent State*, a series of prints from 1971, seems a better case of an artist engaging with mass-media imagery in a transformative way. Although the image represents one of the students shot by Ohio National Guardsmen at a demonstration against the Vietnam war, Hamilton's statement relating to it concentrates on the many stages of mediation involved in its eventual transmission to the screen of his new color television, where he photographed it and then subjected it to further technical transformation—a description of the technological complexity of what Demand refers to as "the chain of images" that is passed on to us and now constitutes our experience of the world. As Mark Godfrey points out, Hamilton's print shows the rounded edges of the TV screen, a framing that seems to engage with the discourse surrounding the medium's annihilation of memory. Television must refresh its flickering screen immediately to receive a new image—like consciousness bereft of memory. "How," Godfrey asks, "could Hamilton oppose the aspect of the discourse, creating mnemonic art works from an experience of a technology whose function had been to destroy the mnemonic?"[39] How could he isolate a single image from the flow of signals and give it weight? He did this by selecting one undramatic image of a student lying on the ground and, using photo silk-screen print technologies, analyzing it into its component colors. These formed the basis for the series of variations building up to the complete, though still blurry, image comprising fifteen layers of pigment.

Other artists relevant in this context include Vija Celmins, who in 1967–68 made painstaking *trompe l'oeil* drawings of photographs ripped from newspapers. *Bikini* (1968), for example, is a clipping of a captioned photo of a mushroom cloud formed by the testing of a nuclear weapon at Bikini Atoll in the South Pacific in 1946. One might also cite Vik Muniz's *Drawings from Memory after the Best of Life Magazine* (1989–91). All of these artists draw on and transform traumatic-mediatic material that forms the basis of experience in a technological age.

The gist of my argument is that Demand's work appropriates hypermediated but personally affecting images and transforms them into the object of experience proper.[40] If that is so, then photography has the potential to restore the link, severed by the shock effects of modern life, between voluntary and involuntary memory, between the individual and the collective. In a sensitive reading of Benjamin's essay "The Storyteller," Peter Brooks glosses what it might mean to transform information into a memorable story. Interestingly, he stresses what is left out:

What may need to be scrutinized in narrative is less its "message," less its ostensible affirmations, and much more its interstices, its gaps, its moments of passage, the moment when something falls silent to indicate a transference, the moment when one begins to hear other possible voices in response.[41]

As this passage intimates, genuine experience involves openness to otherness. The root word in the German *Erfahrung* is *fahren*, meaning "to travel," which, as Miriam Hansen points out, includes a degree of risk for the subject, or what I earlier referred to as exposure.[42]

Throughout this book, I have been guided by an alternative account of Benjamin's theory of photography—one that attempts to recuperate something of his response to early photography and his sense that the viewer's experience of it is a kind of aesthetic experience laced with trauma. This rereading is made possible by the fact that early photography is, for him, marked precisely by the spark of contingency, the accident, the inconspicuous spot, the locus of pain. As such, it offers us a model of technical-auratic experience, quite different from the shock effects that, as Hansen puts it, "seal human consciousness in a permanent state of psychical defence."[43] Hansen is referring here to Freud's conception of consciousness as a protective shield against excessive stimuli, figured as the clear plastic cover of the mystic writing pad, which does not retain traces. Benjamin glossed Freud's point as follows: "The greater the shock factor in particular impressions, the more vigilant consciousness has to be in screening stimuli. The more effectively it does so, the less these impressions enter experience."[44] Conversely, only those (traumatic) impressions that evade consciousness can enter experience. On this account, modernity may destroy the contemplative distance usually associated with aura, but it may also open up the possibility of another kind of auratic-traumatic experience, which Benjamin closely associated with surrealism's "profane illumination." One cultural response to modernity's traumatic effects upon the human sensorium is to present found material, indexical traces and mass-media imagery in ways capable of mobilizing unconscious processes and so producing experience in a synthetic way under today's social conditions.

Notes

Chapter 1

1 Sigmund Freud, "A Note upon the 'Mystic Writing Pad'" (1925), in *The Standard Edition of the Complete Psychological Works of Sigmund Freud*, ed. James Strachey (London: Hogarth Press, 1956–74), 19:226–32.

2 Sigmund Freud, *Beyond the Pleasure Principle* (1920), in *Standard Edition*, 18:25 (italics in original).

3 Sigmund Freud, *Moses and Monotheism: Three Essays* (1939), in *Standard Edition*, 23:3–132.

4 Walter Benjamin, "The Work of Art in the Age of Its Technological Reproducibility: Second Version," in *The Work of Art in the Age of Its Technological Reproducibility and Other Writings on Media*, ed. Michael Jennings, Brigid Doherty, and Thomas Levin (Cambridge, MA: Belknap Press/Harvard University Press, 2008), 37.

5 Benjamin Buchloh, "Refuse and Refuge," in *Gabriel Orozco*, ed. Yve-Alain Bois, October Files 9 (Cambridge, MA: MIT Press, 2009), 15n4.

6 Gabriel Orozco, *Photogravity* (Philadelphia: Philadelphia Museum of Art, 1999), 103.

7 Freud, *Beyond the Pleasure Principle*, 25.

8 My emphasis is on instances of trauma in the public domain rather than those of infantile sexuality and childhood development.

9 Cathy Caruth, *Unclaimed Experience: Trauma, Narrative, and History* (Baltimore: Johns Hopkins University Press, 1996), 132n5 (chap. 3).

10 Freud, *Moses and Monotheism*.

11 I have been guided in my thinking about the art of trauma by a number of excellent books, anthologies of essays, and exhibition catalogues. I list some here: Mieke Bal, Jonathan Crewe, and Leo Spitzer, eds., *Acts of Memory: Cultural Recall in the Present* (Hanover, NH: University Press of New England, 1999); Jill Bennett, *Empathic Vision: Affect, Trauma, and Contemporary Art* (Stanford, CA: Stanford University Press, 2005); Shelly Hornstein and Florence Jacobwitz, *Image and Remembrance: Representation and the Holocaust* (Bloomington: Indiana University Press, 2003); Lisa Saltzman, *Making Memory Matter: Strategies of Remembrance* (Chicago: University of Chicago Press, 2006); Lisa Saltzman and Eric Rosenberg, eds., *Trauma and Visuality in Modernity* (Hanover, NH: University Press of New England, 2006).

12 Sigmund Freud, "From the History of an Infantile Neurosis" (1918 [1914]), in *Standard Edition*, 17:37–38.

13 Sigmund Freud, "Construction in Analysis" (1937), in *Standard Edition*, 23:260.

14 André Breton, *Mad Love*, trans. Mary Ann Caws (Lincoln: University of Nebraska Press, 1987), 23.

15 André Breton, "Max Ernst," in *What Is Surrealism? Selected Writings*, ed. Franklin Rosemont (London: Pluto Press, 1978), 7.

16 Walter Benjamin, "Little History of Photography," in *Walter Benjamin: Selected Writings*, vol. 2, *1927–1934* (Cambridge, MA: Harvard University Press, 1999), 510. The German text reads: "mit dem dei Wirklichkeit die Bildcharakter gleichsame durchgesengt hat." The verb combines *sengen*, to burn or scorch, with the word *durch*, meaning through. Walter Benjamin, *Gesammelte Schriften*, ed. Rolf Tiedemann and Hermann Schweppenhauser (Frankfurt am Main: Suhrkamp Verlag, 1977), 2:371. See my book on the artistic and theoretical legacies of Freud's *Beyond the Pleasure Principle*: Margaret Iversen, *Beyond Pleasure: Freud, Lacan, Barthes* (University Park: Pennsylvania State University Press, 2007), esp. chap. 7, "What Is a Photograph?," on Lacan, Barthes, and photography, which includes an account of Barthes's debt to Benjamin.

17 For an overview of the contradictions inherent in Benjamin's thinking about photography, see Kathrin Yacavone, *Benjamin, Barthes and the Singularity of Philosophy* (New York: Continuum, 2012).

18 Ann Banfield, "L'imparfait de l'objectif: The Imperfect of the Object Glass," *Camera Obscura* 24 (September 1990): 85.

19 Ibid., 78. I am grateful to Susan Morris for alerting me to this point.

20 Mary Ann Doane, "Notes from the Field: Contingency," *Art Bulletin* 94, no. 3 (September 2012): 348.

21 Peter Geimer, "Notes from the Field: Contingency," *Art Bulletin* 94, no. 3 (September 2012): 351.

22 Moyra Davey, "Photography and Accident," in *Long Life Cool White: Photographs and Essays* (Cambridge, MA: Harvard University Art Museums; New Haven, CT: Yale University Press, 2008), 86.

23 Geimer, "Notes from the Field," 352.

24 Roland Barthes, *Camera Lucida: Reflections on Photography*, trans. Richard Howard (New York: Hill and Wang, 1981), 5; *La chambre claire: Note sur la photographie* (Paris: Cahiers du Cinéma, Gallimard, Seuil), 1980.

25 Laura Mulvey, "The Index and the Uncanny: Life and Death in the Photography," chap. 3 of *Death 24x a Second: Stillness and Moving Image* (London: Reaktion Books, 2006), 65.

26 Iversen, "What Is a Photograph?," in *Beyond Pleasure*. Reprinted in Geoffrey Batchen, ed., *Photography Degree Zero: Reflections on Roland Barthes's Camera Lucida* (Cambridge, MA: MIT Press, 2009), 57–74.

27 Barthes, *Camera Lucida*, 4.

28 Jacques Rancière, *The Future of the Image* (London: Verso, 2007), 10.

29 Eric L. Santner, *On Creaturely Life: Rilke, Benjamin, Sebald* (Chicago: University of Chicago Press, 2006).

30 Never, not for a single day, do we have
before us that pure space into which flowers

endlessly open. Always there is World
and never Nowhere without the No: that pure
unseparated element which one breathes
without desire and endlessly knows. A child
may wander there for hours, through the timeless
stillness, may get lost in it and be
shaken back. Or someone dies and is it.
For, nearing death, one doesn't see death; but stares
beyond, perhaps with an animal's vast gaze.
Lovers, if the beloved were not there
blocking the view, are close to it, and marvel . . .
As if by some mistake, it opens for them
behind each other . . . But neither can move past
the other, and it changes back to World.

Rilke, "The Eighth Elegy," in *Duino Elegies*, trans. Stephen Mitchell, in *Ahead of All Parting: The Selected Poetry and Prose of Rainer Maria Rilke* (New York: Modern Library, 1995), 377. See also Rilke, *Duino Elegies*, trans. C. F. MacIntyre (New York: Dover, 2007). The *Elegies* were written between 1912 and 1922.

31 For a recent commentary, see Giorgio Agamben, *The Open: Man and Animal*, trans. Kevin Attell (Stanford, CA: Stanford University Press, 2004).

32 Benjamin, "The Storyteller: Observations on the works of Nikolai Leskov" (1936), in *Selected Writings*, vol. 3, *1935–1938*.

33 W. G. Sebald, *Austerlitz* (London, Penguin Books, 2001), 2–3.

34 W. G. Sebald, "As Day and Night, Chalk and Cheese: On the Pictures of Jan Peter Tripp," in W. G. Sebald and Jan Peter Tripp, *Unrecounted*, trans. Michael Hamburger (London: Penguin Books, 2004), 78–79. The original German of this essay can be found in Sebald, *Logis in einem Landhaus* (Frankfurt am Main: Fischer Verlag, 1989).

35 Marcel Proust, *The Way by Swann's*, in *In Search of Lost Time*, trans. Lydia Davis (London: Penguin Books, 2002), 47.

36 W. G. Sebald, "St. Jerome Lecture 2001: W. G. Sebald in Conversation with Maya Jaggi and Anthea Bell," *In Other Words: The Journal of Literary Translators* 21 (Summer 2003): 13.

37 Sebald, *Austerlitz*, 2–3.

38 Chantal Akerman, *Autoportrait en cinéaste*, exh. cat. (Paris: Cahier du cinema et Centre Pompidou, 2004), 37.

39 See Akerman's two-part installation *To Walk Next to One's Shoelaces in an Empty Fridge* (2004) in which she and her mother discuss the contents of the filmmaker's maternal grandmother's adolescent diary. Both her maternal grandparents and other relatives, Polish Jews, perished at Auschwitz.

40 For a brilliant fictional evocation of intergenerational trauma in the context of American slavery, see Joan Brady, *Theory of War* (London: Andre Deutsch, 1992; New York: Alfred Knopf, 1993).

41 Interview with Chantal Akerman, in Ivone Margulies, *Nothing Happens: Chantal Akerman's Hyperrealist Everyday* (Durham, NC: Duke University Press, 1996), 199.

42 Griselda Pollock, *After-affects/After-images: Trauma and Aesthetic Transformation in the Virtual Feminist Museum* (Manchester: Manchester University Press, 2013), 327.

43 Nancy Spector, *Felix Gonzalez-Torres*, exh. cat. (Guggenheim Museum, New York, March 3–May 10, 1995).

44 Ibid., 122.

45 Rainer Maria Rilke, *The Notebooks of Malte Laurids Brigge*, trans. M. D. Herter Norton (New York: W. W. Norton, 1964), 27. See also Rilke, "Blood-Remembering," in *Rilke on Love and Other Difficulties*, trans. John J. L. Mood (New York: W. W. Norton, 1975), 93–94. The passage is printed in full in Dietmar Elger, Andrea Rosen, Roland Waspe, et al., *Felix Gonzalez-Torres: Catalogue Raisonné*, 2 vols. (Berlin: Hatje Cantz Verlag, 1997).

46 Rilke, *Notebooks of Malte Laurids Brigge*, 26.

47 Rosalind Krauss, "Notes on the Index: Seventies Art in America," 2 parts, *October* 3 (Spring 1977): 68–81; *October* 4 (Fall 1977): 58–67. Reprinted in Krauss, *The Originality of the Avant-Garde and Other Modernist Myths* (Cambridge, MA: MIT Press, 1985).

48 Hal Foster, "Death in America," *October* 75 (Winter 1996). Revised version in Foster, *The Return of the Real: The Avant-garde at the End of the Century* (Cambridge, MA: MIT Press, 1996.)

49 Georges Didi-Huberman, *L'empreinte*, exh. cat. (Paris: Éditions du Centre Georges Pompidou, 1997). See also Didi-Huberman, *La ressemblance par contact: Archéologie, anachronisme et modernité de l'empreinte* (Paris: Éditions de Minuit, 2008).

50 Mary Anne Doane, *The Emergence of Cinematic Time: Modernity, Contingency, the Archive* (Cambridge, MA: Harvard University Press, 2002).

51 Griselda Pollock, "New Encounters: Arts, Cultures, Concepts," in *Digital and Other Virtualities: Renegotiating the Image*, ed. Antony Bryant and Griselda Pollock (London: I. B. Tauris, 2010), xvii.

52 Hal Foster, "Trauma Culture," http://www.artnet.com/magazine. See also Foster, *Return of the Real*.

53 See, for example, *Trauma*, exh. cat. (National Touring Exhibition, Hayward Gallery, London, 2001); Jennifer Blessing and Nat Trotman, *Haunted: Contemporary Photography, Video, Performance*, exh. cat. (New York: Guggenheim Museum, 2010); Peter Eleey, curator *September 11*, exh. cat. (P.S. 1, Long Island City; MOMA, New York, September 11, 2011–January 9, 2012)).

54 The double meaning of exposure in English does not work in other languages, including German, which has two words: *Aussetzung* and *Belichtung*.

55 Catherine Malabou, *Ontology of the Accident: An Essay on Destructive Plasticity*, trans. Carolyn Shread (Cambridge: Polity Press, 2012), 43.

Chapter 2

1 Charles Sanders Peirce, "Icon, Index, Symbol," in *Collected Papers*, vol. 2, *Elements of Logic* (Cambridge, MA: Harvard University Press, 1960), paragraphs 283–91, pp. 161–65.

2 Peirce, *Collected Papers*, vol. 2, paragraph 361, p. 211.

3 Peirce, *Collected Papers*, vol. 4, paragraph 56, p. 39.

4 See Peirce, "Three Kinds of Sign," in *Collected Papers*, vol. 3, paragraphs 359–64. See also Charles Sanders Peirce, "Icon, Index, Symbol" and "Logic as Semiotic: The Theory of Signs," in *The Philosophy of Peirce: Selected Writings*, ed. Justus Buchler, 156–73, 98–119 (New York: Harcourt Brace, 1940).

5 Mary Ann Doane, "The Indexical and the Concept of Medium Specificity," *Differences* 18, no. 1 (special issue, "Indexicality: Trace and Sign," edited by Doane; 2007): 128–52.

6 Ibid., 136.

7 Doane, "Indexicality: Trace and Sign" (introduction to issue), *Differences* 18, no. 1 (2007): 2.

8 Roman Jakobson, "Quest for the Essence of Language," in *On Language: Roman Jakobson*, ed. Linda R. Waugh and Monique Monville-Burston (Cambridge, MA: Harvard University Press, 1990), 412.

9 Roland Barthes, *Camera Lucida: Reflections on Photography*, trans. Richard Howard (New York: Hill and Wang, 1981), 5. See also Meyer Schapiro, *Words and Pictures: On the Literal and the Symbolic in the Illustration of a Text* (The Hague: Mouton, 1973).

10 Jean-François Lyotard, *Discours, figure* (Paris: Editions Klincksieck, 1971), 3.

11 Ibid., 86, 27.

12 D. N. Rodowick, *Reading the Figural; or, Philosophy after New Media* (Durham, NC: Duke University Press, 2001), 6.

13 Peirce, "Icon, Index, Symbol," 159ff, and "Logic as Semiotic."

14 André Bazin, "The Ontology of the Photographic Image," in *What Is Cinema?* (Berkeley: University of California Press, 1967), 1:14.

15 See Diarmuid Costello, Margaret Iversen, and Joel Snyder, eds., "Agency and Automatism: Photography as Art since the Sixties," special issue of *Critical Inquiry* 38, no. 4 (Summer 2012).

16 Roman Jakobson, "Shifters, Verbal Categories, and the Russian Verb" (1957), in *Selected Writings*, vol. 2, *Word and Language* (The Hague: Mouton, 1971), 132.

17 Rosalind Krauss, "Notes on the Index," part 1, *October* 3 (Spring 1977): 70. Reprinted in Krauss, *The Originality of the Avant-Garde and Other Modernist Myths* (Cambridge, MA: MIT Press, 1986), 198. (Subsequent references are to the reprint.)

18 Ibid., 199.

19 Ibid., 203.

20 Man Ray, "The Age of Light," in *Classic Essays on Photography*, ed. Alan Trachtenberg (New Haven, CT: Leete's Island Books, 1980), 167.

21 Krauss, "Notes on the Index," 203.

22 Ibid., 205.

23 Ibid., 206.

24 Ibid., 209.

25 Alanna Heiss, the director of the organization behind the exhibition, notes in her forward to the catalogue that the work in the show "includes the space it's in; embraces it, uses it. Viewing space becomes not frame but material." Heiss, *Rooms*, exh. cat. (P.S. 1, June 9–26, 1976; Institute for Art and Urban Resources, 1977), 3.

26 Krauss, "Notes on the Index: Seventies Art in America," part 2, *October* 4 (Fall 1977). Reprinted in Krauss, *The Originality of the Avant-Garde and Other Modernist Myths*, 216.

27 Krauss does make brief reference to Barthes's sense of the temporality of the photograph as a "presence seen as past." Yet her reference to this phrase in "The Rhetoric of the Image" sits uneasily with her stress on the shifter's dependence on "sheer objectivity" and here-and-nowness.

28 Anna Lovatt, "Palimpsests: Inscription and Memory in the Work of Michelle Stuart," in

Michelle Stuart: Drawn from Nature, ed. Lovatt, exh. cat. (Djanogly Art Gallery, University of Nottingham; Berlin: Hatje Cantz Verlag, 2013), 9.

29 Mary Ann Doane, *The Emergence of Cinematic Time: Modernity Contingency the Archive* (Cambridge, MA: Harvard University Press, 2002), 70.

30 Leo Steinberg, "Other Criteria," in *Other Criteria: Confrontations with Twentieth-Century Art* (Oxford: Oxford University Press, 1972), 55–91. "Flatbed" refers to the horizontal bed of a printing press.

31 Ibid., 85, 90, 84.

32 Ibid., 88.

33 Ibid., 89, 88.

34 *Reizüberflutung*, the term used by Freud to signify the overload of stimuli leading to trauma, lies behind Benjamin's notion of shock (*Schockerlebnis*), although he does not use the term.

35 If that is the case, then the admittedly simulated gash in the canvas of *Tu m'* held together with real safety pins must carry some connotation of trauma, an iconography reinvented by punk rockers in the 1980s.

36 Steinberg, "Other Criteria," 90.

37 Leo Steinberg, "Reflections on the State of Criticism," *Artforum* 10, no. 7 (March 1972). This is an excerpt from "Other Criteria," published later that year in *Other Criteria*.

38 Rosalind Krauss, "Rauschenberg and the Materialized Image" (1974), in *Robert Rauschenberg*, ed. Branden W. Joseph, October Files 4 (Cambridge, MA: MIT Press, 2002), 52.

39 See David Campany, "Man Ray and Marcel Duchamp: Dust Breeding, 1920," in *Singular Images: Essays on Remarkable Photographs*, ed. Sophie Howath, 47–53 (London: Tate Publishing, 2005). He writes, "where photography was once the medium of movement, it now appears as a deliberate, forensic medium of traces" (53). See also Campany, *A Handful of Dust: From the Cosmic to the Domestic*, exh. cat. (Le Bal, Paris; London: Mack, 2015).

40 See Carolyn Steedman, *Dust: The Archive and Cultural History* (New Brunswick, NJ: Rutgers University Press, 2001), and the special issue on dust of *Cabinet* 35 (2009).

41 *Littérature* 5 (October 1, 1922).

42 Suzanne Pagé et al., *Gerhard Richter: Catalogue Raisonné 1962–1993* (Berlin: Hatje Cantz Verlag, 1993), 881–84. For a sensitive account of the context of this work see Mark Godfrey, "Damaged Landscapes," in *Gerhard Richter: Panorama: A Retrospective*, exh. cat. (Tate Modern, London; Nationalgalerie, Berlin; Centre Pompidou, Paris; London: Tate Publishing, 2011), 73–89.

43 Richter himself compared his close-up photographs in black and white of an abstract painting done in Halifax to *Dust Breeding*. See *128 Details of a Picture (Halifax 1978)*.

44 See Sophie Ristelhueber, *Aftermath: Kuwait 1991* (London: Thames and Hudson, 1992). Rauschenberg's *White Paintings* should be added to this series, especially as described by John Cage: "The white paintings were airports for the lights, shadows, and particles"; they "caught whatever fell on them." Cage, "On Robert Rauschenberg, Artist, and His Work" (1961), in *Silence: Lectures and Writings* (London: Marion Boyars, 1968), 102, 108.

45 W. G. Sebald, *The Immigrants* (1993), trans. Michael Hulse (London: Harvil Press, 1996), 161.

46 Eric L. Santner, *On Creaturely Life: Rilke, Benjamin, Sebald* (Chicago: University of Chicago Press, 2006), 102.

47 See Griselda Pollock, "Mary Kelly's *Ballad of Kastriot Rexhepi*: Virtual Trauma and Indexical Witness in the Age of Mediatic Spectacle," in *Digital and Other Virtualities: Renegotiating the Image*, ed. Antony Bryant and Griselda Pollock, 200–216 (London: I. B. Tauris, 2012).

48 Mary Kelly, *The Ballad of Kastriot Rexhepi*, exh. cat. (Santa Monica Art Museum, December 11, 2001–January 20, 2002).

49 Mary Kelly in conversation with the author, December 30, 2013.

50 See Juli Carson and Mary Kelly, "Mea Culpa: A Conversation with Mary Kelly," *Art Journal* 58, no. 4 (1999): 75.

51 Branden W. Joseph, "Preface to 'Reflections . . . ,'" in *Robert Rauschenberg*, ed. Branden W. Joseph, October Files 4 (Cambridge, MA: MIT Press, 2002), 3.

52 Steinberg, "Other Criteria," 91.

Chapter 3

1 Zoe Leonard, "Out of Time," *October* 100 (Spring 2002): 89.

2 There are actually three versions of *Analogue*: 412 photographs displayed as an installation, a book of 90 photographs, and series of dye-transfer prints that can be displayed in series or individually.

3 See, for example, William Mitchell, "Digital Images and the Postmodern Era," in *The Reconfigured Eye: Visual Truth in the Post-Photographic Era* (Cambridge, MA: MIT Press, 1992), 8–11.

4 Commenting on Gursky's *Rhine II* (1999), Matthew Biro notes, "Its indexical qualities have been weakened; and we perceive it as a metaphor for the dialectic between nature and technology, rather than a depiction of a particular geographic location." Biro, "From Analogue to Digital Photography: Bernd and Hilla Becher and Andreas Gursky," *History of Photography* 36, no. 3 (2012): 353–66.

5 For a balanced discussion of these issues see Phillip Rosen, *Change Mummified: Cinema, Historicity, Theory* (Minneapolis: University of Minnesota Press, 2001), esp. chap. 8, "Old and New."

6 On the disparity between prephotographic reality and the image, see, for instance, Joel Snyder, "Picturing Vision," *Critical Inquiry* 6, no. 3 (1980), and John Tagg, *The Burden of Representation: Essays on Photographic Histories* (Amherst: University of Massachusetts Press, 1988), 1–3.

7 Joel Snyder addressed these issues in a paper called "Photography, Chemical and Numerical," delivered to the American Society of Aesthetics, November 6, 2008.

8 See, for example, Sherrie Levine, whose recent works include *After Cézanne* (2007), eighteen pixelated photographic prints of reproductions of paintings by Cézanne.

9 Eric L. Santner, *On Creaturely Life: Rilke, Benjamin, Sebald* (Chicago: University of Chicago Press, 2006). See Tacita Dean's commentary on W. G. Sebald in *October* 106 (Fall 2003).

10 Thierry de Duve, "Time Exposure and Snapshot: The Photograph as Paradox," in *Photography Theory*, ed. James Elkins (New York: Routledge, 2007), 116.

11 Benjamin uses two German words where we have only the one word, "experience." *Erlebnis* and *Erfahrung* are usually translated as "isolated or immediate experience" and "long experience," respectively.

12 Benjamin, "On Some Motifs in Baudelaire," in *Walter Benjamin: Selected Writing 1938–1940*, vol. 4, ed. Howard Eiland and Michael Jennings (Cambridge, MA: Belknap Press/Harvard University Press, 2003), 202.

13 Ibid., 177, for Benjamin's discussion of *Schockerlebnis*.

14 As noted in chapter 1, conscious experience quickly expires, whereas memory traces are "often most powerful and most enduring when the incident that left them behind was one that never entered consciousness." Freud, *Beyond the Pleasure Principle*, in *Standard Edition*, 18:25.

15 Ibid., 298.

16 Leonard, "Out of Time," 89.

17 Walker Evans, "The Direct Pitch," *Fortune* (October 1958), 139–45.

18 Kaja Silverman, "The Author as Receiver," *October* 96 (2001): 17–34. George Baker pursues a similar line of argument in a piece about Leonard, Dean, and Sharon Lockhart. Baker, "Lateness and Longing," in Daniel Birnbaum, ed., *50 Moons of Saturn: T2 Torino Trienniale* (Milan: Skira, 2008), 64.

19 Gabriel Orozco, "Gabriel Orozco in Conversation with Guillermo Santamarina," in *Gabriel Orozco*, exh. cat. (Museo Nacional Centro de Arte Reina Sofia, Madrid, 2005), 143. For more on chance and contemporary art, see Margaret Iversen, ed., *Chance*, Documents of Contemporary Art (Cambridge, MA: MIT; London: Whitechapel Gallery, 2010).

20 Email correspondence with Zoe Leonard, May 26, 2010.

21 Zoe Leonard, "Salvage," unpublished manuscript.

22 Zoe Leonard, "Recollection," unpublished manuscript.

23 Beth Dungan, "An Interview with Zoe Leonard," *Discourse* 24, no. 2 (Spring 2002): 80.

24 Zoe Leonard, "A Thousand Words: Zoe Leonard Talks about Her Recent Work," *Artforum* 37, no. 5 (January 1999): 100–101.

25 Email correspondence with Zoe Leonard, May 26, 2010.

26 Leonard, "Thousand Words."

27 Email correspondence with Zoe Leonard, March 10, 2011.

28 Leonard comments on why she works in both mediums: "In both cases, I work with found objects and found images, things I notice." Dungan, "Interview with Zoe Leonard," 79.

29 Benjamin, "Little History of Photography," in *Walter Benjamin: Selected Writings*, vol. 2, part 2, *1927–1934* (Cambridge, MA: Harvard University Press, 1999), 514.

30 Tacita Dean, "Analogue," in *Analogue: Drawings 1991–2006*, ed. Theodora Vischer and Isabelle Friedli (Gottingen: Schaulager/Steidl, 2006), 8.

31 Email correspondence with Tacita Dean, September 22, 2010.

32 One exception is Ed Krčma, "Cinematic Drawing in the Digital Age," *Tate Papers*, no. 14 (Autumn 2010).

33 Tacita Dean, *An Aside*, National Touring Exhibitions (Hayward Gallery, London, 2005), 4.

34 Mark Godfrey, "Photography Found and Lost: On Tacita Dean's *Floh*," *October* 114 (Fall 2005): 90–119.

35 Tacita Dean, "Floh," in *Tacita Dean: Selected Writings, Seven Books* (Paris: Musée de la Ville de Paris; Göttingen: Steidl, 2003).

36 *Tacita Dean* (Barcelona, 2001), 97.

37 Tacita Dean, "And He Fell into the Sea," in *Selected Writings, Seven Books*.

38 Michael Newman, "Salvage," in Dean, *Selected Writings, Seven Books*.

39 Tacita Dean, "Disappearance at Sea II—Voyage de guérison," in *Tacita Dean*, exh. cat. (Museu d'Art Contemporani de Barcelona, 2001), 44.

40 See Roland Groenenboom, "A Conversation with Tacita Dean," in *Tacita Dean*, exh. cat. (Museu d'Art Contemporani de Barcelona), 104. I have not mentioned the sound tracks of Dean's films. They are analogue, optical sound recordings of ambient, found sound edited in the studio. "Digital silence," she complains, "has a deadness," unlike the "the prickled sound of mute magnetic tape." Tacita Dean, "Artist Questionnaire: 21 Responses," *October* 100 (special issue, "Obsolescence"; Spring 2002): 26.

41 For an interesting discussion of this piece, see Marina Warner, "Light Drawing In: The Art of Tacita Dean," in *Gehen* (Walking), ed. Theodora Vischer and Katrin Grogel, exh. cat. (Basel: Shaulager; Göttingen: Steidl, 2008).

42 Dean, *An Aside*, 4.

43 Groenenboom, "Conversation," 91.

44 Marina Warner, "In Conversation with Tacita Dean," in Marina Warner, Jean-Christophe Royoux, and Germaine Greer, *Tacita Dean* (London: Phaidon, 2006), 44.

45 Dean, "Analogue," 8.

Chapter 4

1 Georges Didi-Huberman, *La ressemblance par contact: Archéologie, anachronisme et modernité de l'empreinte* (Paris: Éditions de Minuit, 2008), 20.

2 Adrian Stokes, *Stones of Rimini*, in *The Critical Writing of Adrian Stokes*, ed. Lawrence Gowing, vol. 1, *1930–1937* (London: Thames and Hudson, 1978), 235, 238.

3 Ibid., 247–48.

4 Ibid., 248.

5 Stokes, *Reflections on the Nude* (1967), in *Critical Writing*, vol. 3, *1955–1967*, 303.

6 Ibid., 321.

7 Stokes, *Stones*, 186.

8 Ibid., 186.

9 Georges Didi-Huberman, "The Order of Material: Plasticities, Malaises, Survivals," in *Sculpture and Psychoanalysis*, ed. Brandon Taylor (Surrey: Ashgate Press, 2006), 203.

10 Stokes, *Stones*, 236.

11 Stokes, *Reflections*, 321.

12 Jasper Johns, *Jasper Johns: Writings, Sketchbook Notes, Interviews*, ed. Kirk Varnedoe (New York: Museum of Modern Art, 1996), 163.

13 Fairfield Porter, "The Education of Jasper Johns," *Artnews* 62, no. 10 (February 1964): 44–45, 61–62.

14 Leo Steinberg, "Jasper Johns: The First Seven Years of His Art," in *Other Criteria: Confrontations with Twentieth-Century Art* (New York: Oxford University Press, 1972), 29–30.

15 Leo Steinberg, "Contemporary Art and the Plight of Its Public," in *Other Criteria*, 14, 15.

16 Johns, *Jasper Johns: Writings*, 27.

17 Walter Benjamin, *The Arcades Project*, trans. Howard Eiland and Kevin McLaughlin (Cambridge, MA: Belknap Press/Harvard University Press, 1999), 466.

18 Joshua Shannon, *The Disappearance of Objects: Art and the Rise of the Postmodern City* (New Haven, CT: Yale University Press, 2009), 82–87.

19 In his commentary on Dürer's *Melencolia I*, Benjamin wrote of the withdrawal of the mournful person for whom "the most simple object appears to be a symbol of some enigmatic wisdom because it lacks any natural, creative relationship to us." He pointed out how, in the Dürer engraving, "the utensils of active life are lying around unused on the floor, as objects of contemplation"—in this case tools of carpentry and metallurgy. Walter Benjamin, *The Origins of German Tragic Drama*, trans. John Osborne (London: New Left Books, 1977), 140. Johns did create a petrified version of the tools of his trade with his bronze cast of a Savarin coffee can stuffed with brushes.

20 See Anthony Vidler, *The Architectural Uncanny: Essays in the Modern Unhomely* (Cambridge, MA: MIT Press, 1992), especially the chapter on Pompeii.

21 Rachel Whiteread, "Rachel Whiteread Interviewed by Andrea Rose," exh. cat. (47th Venice Biennale, 1997), 34.

22 James Lingwood, ed., *Rachel Whiteread: House* (London: Phaidon, 1995).

23 "Allan McCollum Interviewed by Thomas Lawson," originally published in *Allan McCollum* (Los Angeles: A.R.T., 1996), http://allanmccollum.net/allanmcnyc/Lawson_AMc _Interview.html. Quotations in the following paragraph are also from this interview.

24 Helen Molesworth, *Part Object Part Sculpture*, exh. cat., Wexner Center for the Arts, Ohio State University (Philadelphia: Pennsylvania University Press, 2005). See particularly Molesworth's introductory essay and her entries on Rachel Whiteread and Allan McCollum.

25 Sigmund Freud, "Delusions and Dreams in Jensen's 'Gradiva'" (1907), in *Standard Edition*, 9:1–96.

26 See Max Ernst, "Beyond Painting," in *Max Ernst, Beyond Painting and Other Writings by the Artist and His Friends*, ed. Robert Motherwell (New York: Wittenborn, Schulz, 1948), and Werner Spies, ed., *Max Ernst Frottages*, trans. Joseph M. Bernstein (London: Thames and Hudson, 1969). Writing in 1945, Duchamp refers to Ernst's use of an "old Chinese" frottage or rubbing technique as a form of automatic drawing that contributed to "the literary surrealist exploration of the subconscious." Marcel Duchamp, *The Essential Writings of Marcel Duchamp*, ed. Michel Sanouillet and Elmer Peterson (London: Thames and Hudson, 1975), 149. For centuries, the Chinese used a very specific rubbing technique to transfer carving, and particularly calligraphy, from stone onto paper: a sheet of paper is soaked to loosen the fibers, then pressed into the incised pattern on a stele, molding it to the shape of the patterns or characters. When ink is applied to the surface, the rubbing serves as a simple printing plate.

27 The two-part article is reprinted in Rosalind Krauss, *The Originality of the Avant-Garde and Other Modernist Myths* (Cambridge, MA: MIT Press, 1985), 196–220.

28 See Christine Filippone, "Cosmology and the Transformation of the Work of Michelle Stuart," in *Woman's Art Journal* 32, no. 1 (Spring/Summer 2011): 3–12.

29 Anna Lovatt, "Palimpsests: Inscription and Memory in the Work of Michelle Stuart," in *Michelle Stuart: Drawn from Nature*, ed. Lovatt, exh. cat. (Djanogly Art Gallery, University of Nottingham; Hatje Cantz, 2013). See also Sarah Kent, *Michelle Stuart: Paperwork* (London: ICA, 1979).

30 Chihiro Minato, "Is There a Future for Our Past?" in *Masao Okabe, Is There a Future for Our Past? The Dark Face of the Light*, ed. Chihiro Minato (Tokyo: University of Tokyo Press, 2007), 186.

31 Ibid., 188–89.

32 Ibid., 183.

33 Masao Okabe, "Question's Form Vanishes: The Loss of Physical Testimony," in *Masao Okabe*, 4.

34 Stokes, *Stones*, 232.

35 Anna Barriball and Anthony Spira, "In Conversation," in *Anna Barriball*, exh. cat. (Milton Keynes: MK Gallery; Edinburgh: Fruitmarket Gallery, 2011), 88–89.

36 Ibid., 89.

37 Stokes, "Reflections," 322.

38 In conversation, Barriball told me that Jasper Johns is an artist she admires. April 21, 2016.

39 Gaston Bachelard, *Earth and the Reverie of Will: An Essay on the Imagination of Power* (1948), trans. Kenneth Haltman (Dallas: Dallas Institute of Humanities and Culture, 2002), 14, 28–29.

Chapter 5

1 This chapter is an expanded version of a paper written for a symposium organized by Margaret Iversen and David Lomas, "Involuntary Drawing: Time, Motion Capture, the Body," held at the University of Westminster, February 18, 2012, and supported by the AHRC Centre for the Study of Surrealism and Its Legacies. It was published in *Tate Papers*, no. 18 (Autumn 2012), along with other papers delivered at the event.

2 Rainer Maria Rilke, "Primal Sound," in *Rodin and other Prose Pieces*, trans. G. Craig Houston (London: Quartet Books, 1986), 130.

3 Ibid., 128.

4 Ibid., 129.

5 Benjamin, "Work of Art," 37.

6 Étienne-Jules Marey, *La méthode graphique dans les sciences experimentales, et principalement en physiologie et en médicine* (Paris, 1885). See also Francois Dagognet, *Étienne-Jules Marey: A Passion for the Trace*, trans. Robert Galeta with Jeanine Herman (New York: Zone Books, 1992), and Marta Braun, *Picturing Time: The Work of Étienne-Jules Marey* (Chicago: University of Chicago Press, 1994).

7 Friedrich A. Kittler, *Discourse Networks, 1800–1900*, trans. Michael Metteer with Chris Cullens (Stanford, CA: Stanford University Press, 1990), 229. He alludes to Rilke's "Primal Sounds" on page 281. See also Kittler, *Gramophone, Film, Typewriter*, trans. Geoffrey Winthrop-Young and Michael Wutz (Stanford, CA: Stanford University Press, 1999).

8 Mary Ann Doane, *The Emergence of Cinematic Time: Modernity, Contingency, the Archive* (Cambridge, MA: Harvard University Press, 2002), 54.

9 A 2011 exhibition at the Royal Academy, *Degas and the Ballet: Picturing Movement*, revealed the way in which Degas, under the influence of Marey, became interested in abstracting the figure in order to bring out the trajectory of a line. In his experiments with photography, Degas used lighting to transform a three-dimensional likeness into a graphic line. He compared the effect to moonlight, again showing how the restriction of the visible field can be revelatory.

10 Michael Marrinan and John Bender, *The Culture of the Diagram* (Stanford, CA: Stanford University Press, 2010), 202.

11 See, for example, Braun, *Picturing Time*, 281–82.

12 See Duchamp's remarks on Marey in Pierre Cabanne, *Dialogues with Marcel Duchamp* (New York: Viking Press, 1971), 34.

13 David Lomas, "'Modest Recording Instruments': Science, Surrealism and Visuality," *Art History* 27, no. 4 (September 2004): 627–51. Lomas discusses some examples of the surrealists' appropriation of the graphic trace, including a collage by Max Ernst and a Salvador Dalí etching. See also Lomas, "Becoming Machine: Surrealist Automatism and Some Contemporary Instances," *Tate Papers*, no. 18 (Autumn 2012), http://www.tate.org.uk/research/publications/tate-papers/18/becoming-machine-surrealist-automatism-and-some-contemporary-instances (accessed November 20, 2012).

14 André Breton, "Manifesto of Surrealism" (1924), in *Manifestoes of Surrealism*, ed. and trans. Richard Seaver and Helen R. Lane, 27–28 (Ann Arbor: University of Michigan Press, 1972).

15 Nedko Solakov, "Fear" (2003), http://nedkosolakov.net/content/fear/story/index_eng.html, paragraph 5 (accessed October 6, 2012).

16 Roman Jakobson, "Quest for the Essence of Language," in *On Language: Roman Jakobson*, ed. Linda R. Waugh and Monique Monville-Burston (Cambridge, MA: Harvard University Press, 1990), 412.

17 Meyer Schapiro, "On Some Problems in the Semiotics of Visual Art: Field and Vehicle in Image-Signs" (1969), in *Theory and Philosophy of Art: Style, Artist, and Society* (New York: George Braziller, 1994), 12. For more discussion of this topic, see Margaret Iversen and Stephen Melville, "Seeing and Reading: Lyotard, Barthes, Schapiro," in *Writing Art History: Disciplinary Departures*, 129–50 (Chicago: University of Chicago Press, 2010).

18 Benjamin Buchloh, "Hesse's Endgame: Facing the Diagram," in *Eva Hesse Drawing*, ed. Catherine de Zegher (New York: Drawing Center; New Haven, CT: Yale University Press, 2006), 117.

19 Ibid., 119.

20 Mary Ann Doane, "Notes from the Field: Contingency," *Art Bulletin* 94, no. 3 (September 2012): 348.

21 Ibid., 348.

22 Briony Fer, *The Infinite Line: Remaking Art after Modernism* (New Haven, CT: Yale University Press, 2004), 124.

23 For more on this topic see Margaret Iversen, "Desire and the Diagrammatic," *Oxford Art Journal* 39, no. 1 (2016): 1–17.

24 See Nancy Spector, *Felix Gonzalez-Torres*, exh. cat. (Guggenheim Museum, New York, March 3–May 10, 1995), 120.

25 Email correspondence with Amalia Pica, November 16, 2011.

26 David Joselit, *Infinite Regress: Marcel Duchamp, 1910–1941* (Cambridge, MA: MIT Press, 1998), 61. See also Joselit, "Dada's Diagrams," in *The Dada Seminars*, ed. Leah Dickerman (Washington: National Gallery of Art), 2005.

27 Joselit, *Infinite Regress*, 29.

28 Paul Cummings, "Oral History Interview with Robert Morris, 1968 Mar. 10," *Archives of American Art*, Smithsonian Institution, http://www.aaa.si.edu/collections/interviews/oral-history-interview-robert-morris-13065.

29 Ibid.

30 For more information on the sixteen components making up O'Doherty's 1966–67 *Por-*

trait of Marcel Duchamp, see *Patrick Ireland: The Duchamp Portrait, 1966/67*, exh. cat. (Washington, DC: Corcoran Art Gallery, 1974).

31 Brian O'Doherty, "Taking Duchamp's Portrait," unpublished transcript of lecture delivered at the Edgar P. Richardson Symposium on Portraiture, Donald W. Reynolds Center for American Art and Portraiture, Washington, DC, March 27, 2009. The symposium was held in conjunction with the opening of the exhibition, *Inventing Marcel Duchamp: The Dynamics of Portraiture*, at the Smithsonian's National Portrait Gallery. I am grateful to O'Doherty and the National Portrait Gallery for sending me the transcript.

32 The quotations are based on recorded conversations with the artist.

33 Walter Benjamin, "On the Image of Proust," in *Walter Benjamin: Selected Writing 1927–1934*, 2, ed. and trans. Michael William Jennings, Marcus Paul Bullock, Howard Eiland, Gary Smith, Rodney Livingstone, and E. F. N. Jephcott (Cambridge, MA: Belknap Press/ Harvard University Press, 1999), 238.

34 Russell Foster, "Take a Survey Comparing the Sleeping Habits of Germans and Britons," *Guardian* online (April 27, 2012).

35 This information comes from Morris's artist's book *Sun Dial: Night Watch* (2015), about the production of the tapestries and related projects. It includes the essay "Susan Morris: Marking Time" by Margaret Iversen, which is available online: https://drawingroom .org.uk/resources/susan-morris-marking-time. There is also a book about this project and others by Morris with essays by Briony Fer, Margaret Iversen, and Ed Krčma; see Deirdre O'Dwyer, ed., *Susan Morris, Sontag Montag* (London: Five Years, 2009).

36 Ibid.

37 Rainer Maria Rilke, *Duino Elegies*, trans. C. F. MacIntyre (New York: Dover, 2007), 65.

Chapter 6

1 Mary Ann Doane, "Notes from the Field: Contingency," *Art Bulletin* 93, no. 3 (September 2012): 348.

2 Peter Weibel, "Repression and Representation: The RAF in German Postwar Art," in *Art of Two Germanys/Cold War Cultures*, ed. Stephanie Barron and Sabine Eckmann (New York: Abrams, 2009), 256.

3 Lisa Saltzman, *Making Memory Matter: Strategies of Remembrance* (Chicago: University of Chicago Press, 2006), 104n31. See also Saltzman, "Faraway, So Close: Mythic Origins, Contemporary Art: The Case of Kara Walker," in *Contemporary Art and Classical Myth*, ed. Isabelle Wallace and Jennie Hirsh, 19–39 (Surrey: Ashgate, 2011), and Saltzman, *Anselm Kiefer and Art after Auschwitz* (Cambridge: Cambridge University Press, 1999).

4 Saltzman, *Making Memory Matter*, 13.

5 Ibid., 58.

6 Ibid., 92.

7 Jacques Derrida, *Of Grammatology*, trans. Gayatri Chakravorty Spivak (Baltimore: Johns Hopkins University Press, 1976).

8 For example: "Photography's constitutive discourses situate photography as a metaphysical project founded upon a desire for presence secured through an unmediated transcription of the real." David Phillips, "Photo-Logos: Photography and Deconstruction," in *The Subjects of Art History: Historical Objects in Contemporary Perspectives*, ed.

Mark Cheetham, Michael Ann Holly, and Keith Moxey (Cambridge: Cambridge University Press, 1999), 155.

9   Eric L. Santner, *On Creaturely Life: Rilke, Benjamin, Sebald* (Chicago: University of Chicago Press, 2006), 52n9.

10 Charles Merewether, "A Lasting Impression," in *Trace* (1st Liverpool Biennial of International Contemporary Art and Tate Gallery Liverpool, curated by Anthony Bond, 1999), 164.

11 Clément Chéroux, ed., *Mémoire des camps: Photographies des camps de concentration et d'extermination nazis, 1933–1999*, exh. cat. (Hôtel de Sully, Paris, 2001).

12 Georges Didi-Huberman, *Images in Spite of All: Four Photographs from Auschwitz*, trans. Shane B. Lillis (Chicago: University of Chicago Press, 2008).

13 Ibid., 27.

14 Ibid., 32.

15 Gérard Wajcman, "De la croyance photographique," *Les temps modernes* 56, no. 613 (2001): 47–83. Didi-Huberman cited passages from Wajcman's book *L'objet du siècle* (Paris: Verdier, 1998) in the catalogue essay.

16 Claude Lanzmann, "Site and Speech: An Interview with Claude Lanzmann about *Shoah*," in *Claude Lanzmann's Shoah: Key Essays*, ed. Stuart Liebman (Oxford: Oxford University Press, 2007), 39. Lanzmann has gone so far as to say that if he were to discover footage of Jews being asphyxiated in gas chambers, he would destroy it. See Dominick la Capra's critique of Lanzmann's iconoclasm in "Lanzmann's *Shoah*: 'Here there is no Why,'" *Critical Inquiry* 23, no. 2 (Winter 1997): 231–69.

17 Didi-Huberman, *Images in Spite of All*, 80; see also p. 38, on the real as manifested in fragments.

18 Ibid., 70, 3 (italics in original).

19 Ibid., 73.

20 Georges Didi-Huberman, "Out of the Plan, Out of the Plane," in *Gerhard Richter: Pictures/Series*, ed. Hans Ulrich Obrist (Fondation Beyeler; Riehen, Basel: Hatje Cantz, 2014), 171.

21 One exception is an article by my former PhD student Aline Guillermet, who acknowledges an early unpublished version of this chapter. Guillermet, "Memory, Forgetting and the Representation of History in Gerhard Richter's *18 October 1977*," published in French in *OwnReality* (Centre Allemand d'Histoire de l'Art; www.ownreality.org), Autumn 2014.

22 See the transcript of the conversation between Richter and Nicholas Serota, "I Have Nothing to Say and I'm Saying It," in which he mentions the image and Didi-Huberman's book. In *Gerhard Richter: Panorama, A Retrospective*, 25, exh. cat. (Tate Modern, London; Nationalgalerie, Berlin; Centre Pompidou, Paris; London: Tate, 2011).

23 Didi-Huberman, "Out of the Plan, Out of the Plane," 171.

24 Richter has an excellent website which reproduces his work including *Atlas*: http://www.gerhard-richter.com/art/atlas/. *Atlas* has also been published in book form: Gerhard Richter, *Atlas*, ed. Helmut Friedel (London: Thames and Hudson, 2006).

25 See Benjamin Buchloh, "Gerhard Richter's Atlas: The Anomic Archive," *October* 88 (Spring 1999): 141. A comprehensive account of the cycle is Gerhard Richter and Robert Storr, *Gerhard Richter, October 18, 1977* (New York: Museum of Modern Art, 2002). See

also the exhibition catalogue *October 18, 1977* (London: ICA and Anthony D'Offay Gallery, 1989). A thought-provoking essay is by Peter Wollen, "October 18, 1977," in *Paris/ Manhattan: Writings on Art* (London: Verso, 2004), 75–86. For a collection of texts relating to art and the archive see Charles Merewether, ed., *The Archive*, Documents of Contemporary Art (Cambridge, MA: MIT Press; London: Whitechapel Art Gallery, 2006).

26 The very blurred images arranged in a grid give some idea of the wealth of documentary photographs Richter collected for the cycle. See *Atlas*, plates 470–79.

27 Gerhard Richter, *Text: Writings, Interviews and Letters, 1961–2007*, ed. Dietmar Elger and Hans Ulrich Obrist (London: Thames and Hudson, 2009), 202.

28 Richter, "Interview with Gregorio Magnani" (1989), in Gerhard Richter, *Text*, 224.

29 See Weibel, "Repression and Representation," 258.

30 "Interview with Jan Thorn-Prikker," in Richter, *October 18, 1977*, 18. See also Stefan Germer's essay in this catalogue, "Unbidden Memories," 4–6.

31 Roland Barthes, *Camera Lucida: Reflections on Photography*, trans. Richard Howard (New York: Hill and Wang, 1981), 116–17.

32 Richter and Storr, *Gerhard Richter, October 18, 1977*.

33 Ibid., 106.

34 This is imprecise; the dimensions of the three are 62 × 67 cm, 62 × 62 cm, and 35 × 40 cm.

35 Richter, *Text*, 202.

36 For citations from unpublished notes in the Warburg archive, see E. H. Gombrich, *Aby Warburg: An Intellectual Biography* (Chicago: University of Chicago Press, 1988), 96.

37 Friedrich Nietzsche, *The Birth of Tragedy and The Case of Wagner*, trans. Walter Kaufmann (New York: Random House, 1967), 46. Warburg's annotated copy of *Die Geburt der Tragödie* (Leipzig, 1886) is in the Warburg Institute.

38 On this topic see Mark Godfrey, *Abstraction and the Holocaust* (New Haven, CT: Yale University Press, 2007).

39 See Abigail Solomon-Godeau, "Mourning or Melancholia: Christian Boltanski's *Missing House*," *Oxford Art Journal* 12, no. 2 (1998): 1–20. See also Boltanski's statement "You know I am an artist of the second part of the 20th century and that means two of my grandfathers were Beuys and Warhol," in "Interview with Christian Boltanski by Irene Borger," *BOMB* 26 (Winter 1989), http://bombmagazine.org/article/1148/christian-boltanski.

40 Didier Semin, "From the *Impossible Life* to the *Exemplary Life*," in Didier Semin, Tamar Garb, and Donald Kuspit, *Christian Boltanski* (London: Phaidon, 1997), 19.

41 Christian Boltanski, *Recherche et présentation de tout ce qui reste de mon enfance, 1944–1950* (Research and Presentation of All That Remains of My Childhood, 1944–1950) (Paris: Éditions Givaudan, 1969).

42 Christian Boltanski and Catherine Grenier, *The Possible Life of Christian Boltanski*, trans. Marc Lowenthal (Boston: Museum of Fine Art Publications, 2007), 45.

43 For a discussion of this point, see Margaret Iversen, "Readymade, Found Object, Photograph," *Art Journal* 63, no. 2 (special issue, "Aesthetics/Anti-aesthetics," edited by James Meyer; Summer 2004): 44–57.

44 Solomon-Godeau, "Mourning or Melancholia," 11.

45 Boltanski, "Interview."

Chapter 7

1   See, for example, Andreas Ruby, "Thomas Demand, Memoryscapes," *Parkett* 62 (2001).

2   Michael Fried, *Why Photography Matters as Art as Never Before* (New Haven, CT: Yale University Press, 2008), 268, 271.

3   John Berger and Jean Mohr, *Another Way of Seeing* (New York: Pantheon, 1982), 90.

4   Mark Godfrey, "Nationalgalerie," in *Thomas Demand, Nationalgalerie* (Göttingen: Steidl/Mack, 2009), 3.

5   Walter Benjamin, "On the Image of Proust" (1929), in *Walter Benjamin: Selected Writing 1927–1934*, vol. 2, part 1, ed. Michael William Jennings, Howard Eiland, and Gary Smith (Cambridge, MA: Belknap Press/Harvard University Press, 1999), 238.

6   Samuel Beckett, *Proust* (London: Chatto and Windus, 1931), 19.

7   Godfrey, "Nationalgalerie," 6.

8   Thomas Demand, "Model Making: Demand in Conversation with Daniel Kehlmann," *Art Review* 88 (April 2012): 77.

9   Ibid., 80.

10 Benjamin, "On Some Motifs in Baudelaire," in *Walter Benjamin: Selected Writing 1938–1940*, vol. 4, ed. Howard Eiland and Michael Jennings (Cambridge, MA: Belknap Press/Harvard University Press, 2003), 337.

11 Benjamin, "On the Image of Proust," 238.

12 Beckett, *Proust*, 55.

13 Benjamin, "On Some Motifs," 315.

14 Thomas Demand, "A Conversation between Alexander Kluge and Thomas Demand," in *Thomas Demand*, exh. cat. (Serpentine Gallery, London, 2006), 90, 60.

15 Ibid., 71.

16 Ibid., 80.

17 Ibid.

18 Walter Benjamin, "The Storyteller: Observations on the works of Nikolai Leskov" (1936), in *Walter Benjamin: Selected Writings*, ed. Howard Eiland and Michael W. Jennings, vol. 3, *1935–1938* (Cambridge, MA: Belknap Press/Harvard University Press, 2002), 143.

19 Ibid., 147.

20 Ibid., 148, 149.

21 Demand, "Conversation," 90.

22 I understand Demand's use of that term "seared" as an oblique reference to Benjamin's "Little History of Photography" where the image in early photography is described as "seared" into the plate. This in turn is a reference to the effect of traumatic events, which, for Freud, force and inscribe themselves on the psyche.

23 Demand, "Conversation," 89.

24 Benjamin, "Storyteller," 148, 149.

25 Ulrich Baer, "End of the World: On Thomas Demand's Photography," in *Thomas Demand: L'esprit d'escalier*, exh. cat. (Irish Museum of Modern Art, Dublin; Verlag der Buchhandlung, Walther König, 2007), 88.

26 Benjamin, "On Some Motifs," 337.

27 Francois Quinton, "There Is No Innocent Room," in Francesco Bonami, Francois Quinton, and Régis Durand, *Thomas Demand*, exh. cat. (Paris: Fondation Cartier pour l'art contemporain; London: Thames and Hudson, 2001), 62.

28 Benjamin, "On Some Motifs," 316.

29 Benjamin, "Experience and Poverty," in *Selected Writings*, vol. 2, *1927–1934*, 732.

30 Benjamin, "Storyteller," 162.

31 Demand, "Conversation," 85.

32 André Breton, "The Surrealist Situation of the Object," in *Manifestoes of Surrealism*, trans. Richard Seaver and Helen R. Lane, 273 (Ann Arbor: University of Michigan Press, 1972). See also Breton, "The Crisis of the Object" (1936), in *Surrealism and Painting*, 275–80 (Boston: Museum of Fine Arts Publications, 2002).

33 Sigmund Freud, *The Interpretation of Dreams*, in *Standard Edition*, 4:282–84.

34 Thomas Demand, "Interview with Doug Aitken," one of a series of interviews for *The Source*, an installation at Tate Liverpool, September 2012–January 2013, http://www.tate .org.uk/context-comment/video/doug-aitken-source-thomas-demand.

35 Demand's laconic, one-word titles are explained by the fact that he wants "to leave things open and undermine any anecdotal reading of them." Demand, "Conversation," 93.

36 Thomas Demand, "Building the Scene of the Crime: Interview by Ruedi Widmer," *Camera Austria* 66 (1999): 14.

37 Fried, *Why Photography Matters*, 272, 271.

38 Hal Foster understands Warhol's project as an invitation to "mass-witnessing." He also cites Benjamin's "The Storyteller," but his reading is very different from mine. Foster, *The Return of the Real: Art at the End of the Century* (Cambridge, MA: MIT Press, 1996), 87.

39 Mark Godfrey, "Television Delivers People," in *Richard Hamilton*, ed. Mark Godfrey, Paul Schimmel, and Vicente Todoli, exh. cat. (London: Tate Publishing, 2014), 238.

40 In a provocative article, Thomas Elsaesser suggests that we might "regard our cultural store of narratives, poems and stories as 'processing programmes.'" Elsaesser, "Freud as Media Theorist: Mystic Writing-pads and the Matter of Memory," *Screen* 50, no. 1 (Spring 2009): 104.

41 Peter Brooks, *Psychoanalysis and Storytelling* (Oxford: Blackwell, 1994), 86.

42 Miriam Hansen, "Foreword," in Oskar Negt and Alexander Kluge, *Public Sphere and Experience: Toward an Analysis of the Bourgeois and Proletarian Public Sphere* (Minneapolis: University of Minnesota Press, 1993), xvi–xvii. Originally published in German in 1972, the book is part of a wave of interest in the concept of experience.

43 Miriam Hansen, "Benjamin, Cinema and Experience: 'The Blue Flower in the Land of Technology,'" *New German Critique* 40 (Winter 1987): 203. See also Diarmuid Costello, "Aura, Face, Photography," in *Walter Benjamin and Art*, ed. Andrew Benjamin, 164–84 (London: Continuum, 2005).

44 Benjamin, "On Some Motifs," 319.

Bibliography

Agamben, Giorgio. *The Open: Man and Animal.* Translated by Kevin Attell. Stanford, CA: Stanford University Press, 2004. Translation of *L'aperto: L'uomo e l'animale*, 2002.

Akerman, Chantal. *Autoportrait en cinéaste.* Exh. cat. Cahier du cinema et Centre Pompidou, Paris, 2004.

Bachelard, Gaston. *Earth and the Reverie of Will: An Essay on the Imagination of Power.* Translated by Kenneth Haltman. Dallas: Dallas Institute of Humanities and Culture, 2002. Translation of *La terre et les reveries de la volunté*, 1948.

Baer, Ulrich. "End of the World: On Thomas Demand's Photography." In *Thomas Demand: L'esprit d'escalier*, 82–112 Exh. cat. Irish Museum of Modern Art, Dublin. Cologne: Verlag der Buchhandlung; Stuttgart:Walther König, 2007.

Baker, George. "Lateness and Longing." In *50 Moons of Saturn: T2 Torino Trienniale*, edited by Daniel Birnbaum. Milan: Skira, 2008.

Bal, Mieke, Jonathan Crewe, and Leo Spitzer, eds. *Acts of Memory: Cultural Recall in the Present.* Hanover, NH: University Press of New England, 1999.

Banfield, Ann. "L'imparfait de l'objectif: The Imperfect of the Object Glass." *Camera Obscura* 24 (September 1990): 64–87.

Barriball, Anna, and Anthony Spira. "In Conversation." In *Anna Barriball*, 88–92. Exh. cat. MK Gallery, Milton Keynes; Fruitmarket Gallery, Edinburgh, 2011.

Barthes, Roland. *Camera Lucida: Reflections on Photography.* Translated by Richard Howard. New York: Hill and Wang, 1981. Translation of *La chambre claire: Note sur la photographie*, 1980.

Batchen, Geoffrey, ed. *Photography Degree Zero: Reflections on Roland Barthes's Camera Lucida.* Cambridge, MA: MIT Press, 2009.

Bazin, André. "The Ontology of the Photographic Image." In *What Is Cinema?* 1:9–16. Translated by Hugh Gray. Berkeley: University of California Press, 1967. Translation of *Qu'est-ce que le cinéma*, 1961.

Beckett, Samuel. *Proust.* London: Chatto and Windus, 1931.

Benjamin, Walter. *The Arcades Project.* Translated by Howard Eiland and Kevin

McLaughlin. Cambridge, MA: Belknap Press/Harvard University Press, 1999. Translation of *Das Passagen-Werk*, 1982.

———. "Experience and Poverty." In *Walter Benjamin: Selected Writings, 1927–1934*, vol. 2, part 2, ed. Michael W. William Jennings, Howard Eiland, and Gary Smith. Translated by Rodney Livingstone et al., 731–45. Cambridge, MA: Belknap Press/ Harvard University Press, 1999.

———. *Gesammelte Schriften*. 7 vols. Edited by Rolf Tiedemann and Hermann Schweppenhauser. Frankfurt am Main: Suhrkamp Verlag, 1972–89.

———. "Little History of Photography" (1931). In *Walter Benjamin: Selected Writings, 1927–1934*, vol. 2, part 2, ed. Michael W. William Jennings, Howard Eiland, and Gary Smith. Translated by Rodney Livingstone et al., 507–30. Cambridge, MA: Belknap Press/Harvard University Press, 1999.

———. "On the Image of Proust" (1929). In *Walter Benjamin: Selected Writings, 1927–1934*, vol. 2, part 1, ed. Michael William Jennings, Howard Eiland, and Gary Smith, 237–47. Cambridge, MA: Belknap Press/Harvard University Press, 1999.

———. "On Some Motifs in Baudelaire" (1939). In *Walter Benjamin: Selected Writings, 1938–1940*, vol. 4, ed. Howard Eiland and Michael Jennings. Translated by Edmund Jephcott et al., 313–55. Cambridge, MA: Belknap Press/Harvard University Press, 2003.

———. *The Origins of German Tragic Drama*. Translated by John Osborne. London: New Left Books, 1977. Translation of *Ursprung des Deutschen Trauerspiels*, 1928.

———. "The Storyteller: Observations on the works of Nikolai Leskov" (1936). In *Walter Benjamin: Selected Writings, 1935–1938*, vol. 3, ed. Howard Eiland and Michael W. Jennings, 143–66. Cambridge, MA: Belknap Press/Harvard University Press, 2002.

———. "The Work of Art in the Age of Its Technological Reproducibility: Second Version" (1935–36). In *The Work of Art in the Age of Its Technological Reproducibility and Other Writings on Media*, edited by Michael Jennings, Brigid Doherty, and Thomas Levin, 19–55. Cambridge, MA: Belknap Press/Harvard University Press, 2008.

Bennett, Jill. *Empathic Vision: Affect, Trauma, and Contemporary Art*. Stanford, CA: Stanford University Press, 2005.

Berger, John, and Jean Mohr. *Another Way of Seeing*. New York: Pantheon, 1982.

Biro, Matthew. "From Analogue to Digital Photography: Bernd and Hilla Becher and Andreas Gursky." *History of Photography* 36, no. 3 (2012): 353–66.

Blessing, Jennifer, and Nat Trotman. *Haunted: Contemporary Photography, Video, Performance*. Curated by Blessing and Trotman, with essays by Peggy Phelan, Lisa Saltzman, and Nancy Spector. Exh. cat. Guggenheim Museum, New York, 2010.

Boltanski, Christian. "Interview with Christian Boltanski by Irene Borger." *BOMB* 26 (Winter 1989). http://bombmagazine.org/article/1148/christian-boltanski

———. *Recherche et présentation de tout ce qui reste de mon enfance, 1944–1950* (Research and Presentation of All That Remains of My Childhood, 1944–1950). Paris: Éditions Givaudan, 1969.

Boltanski, Christian, and Catherine Grenier. *The Possible Life of Christian Boltanski*. Translated by Marc Lowenthal. Boston: Museum of Fine Art Publications, 2007.

Brady, Joan. *Theory of War*. London: Andre Deutsch, 1992; New York: Alfred Knopf, 1993.

Braun, Marta. *Picturing Time: The Work of Étienne-Jules Marey*. Chicago: University of Chicago Press, 1994.

Breton, André. "Crisis of the Object" (1936). In *Surrealism and Painting*, 313–55. Boston: Museum of Fine Arts Publications, 2002. Translation of *Le Surréalisme et la peinture*, 1965.

———. *Mad Love*. Translated by Mary Ann Caws. Lincoln: University of Nebraska Press, 1987. Translation of *L'amour fou*, 1937.

———. "Manifesto of Surrealism" (1924). In *Manifestoes of Surrealism*, edited and translated by Richard Seaver and Helen R. Lane, 1–48. Ann Arbor: University of Michigan Press, 1972. Translation of *Manifestes du Surréalisme*, 1962.

———. "Max Ernst." In *What Is Surrealism? Selected Writings*, edited by Franklin Rosemont, 7–8. London: Pluto Press, 1978.

———. "The Surrealist Situation of the Object" (1935). In *Manifestoes of Surrealism*, edited and translated by Richard Seaver and Helen R. Lane, 255–78. Ann Arbor: University of Michigan Press, 1972.

Brooks, Peter. *Psychoanalysis and Storytelling*. Oxford: Blackwell, 1994.

Buchler, Justus, ed. *The Philosophy of Peirce: Selected Writings*. New York: Harcourt Brace, 1940.

Buchloh, Benjamin. "Gerhard Richter's Atlas: The Anomic Archive." *October* 88 (Spring 1999): 117–45.

———. "Hesse's Endgame: Facing the Diagram." In *Eva Hesse Drawing*, edited by Catherine de Zegher, 98–119. New York: Drawing Center; New Haven, CT: Yale University Press, 2006.

———. "Refuse and Refuge." In *Gabriel Orozco*, edited by Yve-Alain Bois, 1–16. October Files 9. Cambridge, MA: MIT Press, 2009.

Cage, John. "On Robert Rauschenberg, Artist, and His Work" (1961). In *Silence: Lectures and Writings*, 98–108. London: Marion Boyars, 2004.

Campany, David. *A Handful of Dust: From the Cosmic to the Domestic*. Exh. cat. Le Bal, Paris. London, Mack, 2015.

———. "Man Ray and Marcel Duchamp: Dust Breeding, 1920." In *Singular Images: Essays on Remarkable Photographs*, edited by Sophie Howath, 47–53. London: Tate Publishing, 2005.

Carson, Juli, and Mary Kelly, "Mea Culpa: A Conversation with Mary Kelly." *Art Journal* 58, no. 4 (1999): 74–80.

Caruth, Cathy. *Unclaimed Experience: Trauma, Narrative, and History*. Baltimore: Johns Hopkins University Press, 1996.

Chéroux, Clément, ed. *Mémoire des camps: Photographies des camps de concentration et d'extermination nazis, 1933–1999*. Exh. cat. Hôtel de Sully, Paris, 2001.

Costello, Diarmuid. "Aura, Face, Photography." In *Walter Benjamin and Art*, edited by Andrew Benjamin, 164–84. London: Continuum, 2005.

Costello, Diarmuid, Margaret Iversen, and Joel Snyder, eds. "Agency and Automatism: Photography as Art since the Sixties." Special issue of *Critical Inquiry* 38, no. 4 (Summer 2012).

Cummings, Paul. "Oral History Interview with Robert Morris, 1968 Mar. 10." *Archives of American Art*, Smithsonian Institution. http://www.aaa.si.edu/collections /interviews/oral-history-interview-robert-morris-13065

Dagognet, Francois. *Étienne-Jules Marey: A Passion for the Trace*. Translated by Robert Galeta with Jeanine Herman. New York: Zone Books, 1992.

Davey, Moyra. "Notes on Photography and Accident." In *Long Life Cool White: Photographs and Essays*, 79–141. Cambridge, MA: Harvard University Art Museums; New Haven, CT: Yale University Press, 2008.

Dean, Tacita. "Analogue." In *Analogue: Drawings, 1991–2006*, edited by Theodora Vischer and Isabelle Friedli, 8–9. Schaulager, Basel. Göttingen: Steidl, 2006.

———. *An Aside*. National Touring Exhibitions, Hayward Gallery, London, 2005.

———. "Artist Questionnaire: 21 Responses." *October* 100 (special issue, "Obsolescence"; Spring 2002): 115–32.

———. *Disappearance at Sea II—Voyage de guérison*. In *Tacita Dean*. Exh. cat. Museu d'Art Contemporani de Barcelona, 2001.

———. *Tacita Dean: Selected Writings, Seven Books*. Paris: Musée de la Ville de Paris; Göttingen: Steidl, 2003.

———. "W. G. Sebald." *October* 106 (Fall 2003): 122–36.

de Duve, Thierry. "Time Exposure and Snapshot: The Photograph as Paradox." In *Photography Theory*, edited by James Elkins, 109–24. New York: Routledge, 2007. Original partial publication: *October* 5 (Summer 1978):113–25.

Demand, Thomas. "Building the Scene of the Crime: Interview by Ruedi Widmer." *Camera Austria* 66 (1999): 10–16.

———. "A Conversation between Alexander Kluge and Thomas Demand." In *Thomas Demand*, 85–90. Exh. cat. Serpentine Gallery, London, 2006.

———. "Interview with Doug Aitken." For *The Source*, an installation at Tate Liverpool, September 2012–January 2013. http://www.tate.org.uk/context-comment /video/doug-aitken-source-thomas-demand.

———. "Model Making: Demand in Conversation with Daniel Kehlmann." *Art Review* 88 (April 2012): 76–80.

Derrida, Jacques. *Of Grammatology*. Translated by Gayatri Chakravorty Spivak. Baltimore: Johns Hopkins University Press, 1976. Translation of *De la grammatologie*, 1967.

Didi-Huberman, Georges. *Images in Spite of All: Four Photographs from Auschwitz*. Translated by Shane B. Lillis. Chicago: University of Chicago Press, 2008. Translation of *Images malgré tout*, 2002.

———. *L'empreinte*. Exh. cat. Centre Georges Pompidou, Paris. Paris: Éditions du Centre Georges Pompidou, 1997.

———. "The Order of Material: Plasticities, Malaises, Survivals." In *Sculpture and Psychoanalysis*, edited by Brandon Taylor, 195–212. Farnham: Ashgate, 2006.

———. "Out of the Plan, Out of the Plane." In *Gerhard Richter: Pictures/Series*, edited by Hans Ulrich Obrist, with texts by Georges Didi-Huberman and Dieter Schwarz, and an interview with the artist by Obrist. Riehen/Basel: Fondation Beyeler; Berlin:Hatje Cantz Verlag, 2014.

———. *La ressemblance par contact: Archéologie, anachronisme et modernité de l'empreinte*. Paris: Éditions de Minuit, 2008

Doane, Mary Anne. *The Emergence of Cinematic Time: Modernity, Contingency, the Archive*. Cambridge, MA: Harvard University Press, 2002.

———. "The Indexical and the Concept of Medium Specificity." *Differences* 18, no. 1 (special issue, "Indexicality: Trace and Sign," edited by Doane; 2007): 128–52.

———. "Notes from the Field: Contingency." *Art Bulletin* 94, no. 3 (September 2012): 348–49.

Dungan, Beth. "An Interview with Zoe Leonard." *Discourse* 24, no. 2 (Spring 2002): 70–85.

Eleey, Peter, curator. *September 11*. Exh. cat. P.S. 1, Long Island City; MOMA, New York, September 11, 2011–January 9, 2012.

Elger, Dietmar, Andrea Rosen, Roland Waspe, et al. *Felix Gonzalez-Torres: Catalogue Raisonné*. 2 vols. Berlin: Hatje Cantz Verlag, 1997.

Elsaesser, Thomas. "Freud as Media Theorist: Mystic Writing-pads and the Matter of Memory." *Screen* 50, no. 1 (Spring 2009): 100–113.

Ernst, Max. "Beyond Painting." In *Max Ernst, Beyond Painting and Other Writings by the Artist and His Friends*, edited by Robert Motherwell. New York: Wittenborn, Schulz, 1948.

Evans, Walker. "The Direct Pitch." *Fortune*, October 1958, 139–45.

Fer, Briony. *The Infinite Line: Remaking Art after Modernism*. New Haven, CT: Yale University Press, 2004.

Foster, Hal. "Death in America," *October* 75 (Winter 1996): 37–50.

———. *The Return of the Real: The Avant-garde at the End of the Century*. Cambridge, MA: MIT Press, 1996.

———. "Trauma Culture." 1996. http://www.artnet.com/magazine_pre2000/features/foster/foster7-26-96.asp

Foster, Russell. "Take a Survey Comparing the Sleeping Habits of Germans and Britons." *Guardian* online, April 27, 2012.

Freud, Sigmund. *The Standard Edition of the Complete Psychological Works of Sigmund Freud*. Edited by James Strachey. 24 vols. London: Hogarth Press, 1956–74.

Fried, Michael. *Why Photography Matters as Art as Never Before*. New Haven, CT: Yale University Press, 2008.

Geimer, Peter. "Notes from the Field: Contingency." *Art Bulletin* 94, no. 3 (September 2012): 351–52.

Godfrey, Mark. *Abstraction and the Holocaust*. New Haven, CT: Yale University Press, 2007.

———. "Damaged Landscapes." In *Gerhard Richter: Panorama: A Retrospective*, 73–89. Exh. cat. Tate Modern, London; Nationalgalerie, Berlin; Centre Pompidou, Paris. London: Tate Publishing, 2011.

———. "Nationalgalerie." In *Thomas Demand, Nationalgalerie*, edited by Udo Kittelmann, 1–11. Exh. cat. Nationalgalerie, Berlin. Göttingen: Steidl/Mack, 2009.

———. "Photography Found and Lost: On Tacita Dean's *Floh*." *October* 114 (Fall 2005):90–119.

———. "Television Delivers People." In *Richard Hamilton*, edited by Mark Godfrey, Paul Schimmel, and Vicente Todoli, 235–48. Exh. cat. London: Tate Publishing, 2014.

Gombrich, E. H. *Aby Warburg: An Intellectual Biography*. Chicago: University of Chicago Press, 1988.

Groenenboom, Roland. "A Conversation with Tacita Dean." In *Tacita Dean*, 93–97. Exh. cat. Museu d'Art Contemporani de Barcelona, 2001.

Guillermet, Aline. "Memory, Forgetting and the Representation of History in Gerhard Richter's *18 October 1977*." In *OwnReality* (Centre Allemand d'Histoire de l'Art), Autumn 2014. www.ownreality.org

Hansen, Miriam. "Benjamin, Cinema and Experience: 'The Blue Flower in the Land of Technology.'" *New German Critique* 40 (Winter 1987): 179–224.

———. "Foreword." In *Public Sphere and Experience: Toward an Analysis of the Bourgeois and Proletarian Public Sphere* by Oskar Negt and Alexander Kluge. Translated by Peter Labanyi et al., ix–xli. Minneapolis: University of Minnesota Press, 1993.

Heiss, Alanna. *Rooms*. Exh. cat. P.S. 1, Long Island City, NY. Institute for Art and Urban Resources, 1976.

Hornstein, Shelly, and Florence Jacobwitz. *Image and Remembrance: Representation and the Holocaust*. Bloomington: Indiana University Press, 2003.

Iversen, Margaret. *Beyond Pleasure: Freud, Lacan, Barthes*. University Park: Pennsylvania State University Press, 2007.

———, ed. *Chance*. Documents of Contemporary Art. Cambridge, MA: MIT Press; London: Whitechapel Gallery, 2010.

———. "Desire and the Diagrammatic." *Oxford Art Journal* 39, no. 1 (2016): 1–17.

———. "Saussure v. Peirce: Models for a Semiotics of Visual Art." In *The New Art History*, ed. A. L. Rees and F. Borzello, 82–94. London: Camden Press, 1986.

———. "Readymade, Found Object, Photograph." *Art Journal* 63, no. 2 (special issue, "Aesthetics/Anti-aesthetics," edited by James Meyer; Summer 2004): 44–57.

———. "Susan Morris: Marking Time." In Susan Morris, *Sun Dial: Night Watch*, artist's book, 2015.

———. "What Is a Photograph?" *Art History* 15, no. 3 (September 1994): 450–63.

Iversen, Margaret, and Stephen Melville. *Writing Art History: Disciplinary Departures*. Chicago: University of Chicago Press, 2010.

Jakobson, Roman. "Quest for the Essence of Language." In *On Language: Roman Jakobson*, ed. Linda R. Waugh and Monique Monville-Burston, 407–21. Cambridge, MA: Harvard University Press, 1990. First published in *Diogenes* 13 (September 1965): 23–31.

———. "Shifters, Verbal Categories, and the Russian Verb" (1957). In *Selected Writings*, vol. 2, *Word and Language*, 130–47. The Hague: Mouton, 1979.

Johns, Jasper. *Jasper Johns: Writings, Sketchbook Notes, Interviews*. Edited by Kirk Varnedoe. New York: Museum of Modern Art, 1996.

Joselit, David. "Dada's Diagrams." In *The Dada Seminars*, edited by Leah Dickerman, 221–39. Washington: National Gallery of Art, 2005.

———. *Infinite Regress: Marcel Duchamp, 1910–1941*. Cambridge, MA: MIT Press, 1998.

Joseph, Branden W. "Preface to 'Reflections . . .'" In *Robert Rauschenberg*, edited by Branden W. Joseph, 1–5. October Files 4. Cambridge, MA: MIT Press, 2002.

Kelly, Mary. *The Ballad of Kastriot Rexhepi*. Exh. cat. Santa Monica Art Museum, December 11, 2001–January 20, 2002.

———. *Post-Partum Document*. Reprint. Vienna: Generali Foundation; Berkeley: University of California Press, 1998.

Kent, Sarah. *Michelle Stuart: Paperwork*. Exh. cat. Institute of Contemporary Art, London, 1979.

Kittler, Friedrich A. *Discourse Networks, 1800–1900*. Translated by Michael Metteer with Chris Cullens. Stanford, CA: Stanford University Press, 1990.

———. *Gramophone, Film, Typewriter*. Translated, with an introduction, by Geoffrey Winthrop-Young and Michael Wutz. Stanford, CA: Stanford University Press, 1999.

Krauss, Rosalind. "Notes on the Index: Seventies Art in America." Parts 1 and 2. *October* 3 (Spring 1977): 68–81; *October* 4 (Fall 1977): 58–67. Reprinted in *The Originality of the Avant-Garde and Other Modernist Myths*, 96–220. Cambridge, MA: MIT Press, 1985.

———. "Rauschenberg and the Materialized Image" (1974). In *Robert Rauschenberg*, edited by Branden W. Joseph, 39–56. October Files 4. Cambridge, MA: MIT Press, 2002.

Krčma, Ed. "Cinematic Drawing in the Digital Age." *Tate Papers*, no. 14 (Autumn 2010).

la Capra, Dominick. "Lanzmann's *Shoah*: 'Here there is no Why.'" *Critical Inquiry* 23, no. 2 (Winter 1997): 231–69.

Lanzmann, Claude. "Site and Speech: An Interview with Claude Lanzmann conducted by Marc Chevrie and Hervé le Roux about *Shoah*." In *Claude Lanzmann's Shoah: Key Essays*, edited by Stuart Liebman, 37–49. Oxford: Oxford University Press, 2007.

Leonard, Zoe. "Out of Time." *October* 100 (Spring 2002): 88–97.

———. "Recollection." Unpublished manuscript.

———. "Salvage." Unpublished manuscript.

———. "A Thousand Words: Zoe Leonard talks about Her Recent Work." *Artforum* 37, no. 5 (January 1999): 100–101.

———. *Zoe Leonard*. Exh. cat. Centre for Contemporary Art, Ujazdowski Castle, Warsaw, Poland, 1999.

Lingwood, James, ed. *Rachel Whiteread: House*. London: Phaidon, 1995.

Lomas, David. "Becoming Machine: Surrealist Automatism and Some Contemporary Instances." *Tate Papers*, no. 18 (Autumn 2012). http://www.tate.org.uk/research/publications/tate-papers/18/becoming-machine-surrealist-automatism-and-some-contemporary-instances

———. "'Modest Recording Instruments': Science, Surrealism and Visuality." *Art History* 27, no. 4 (September 2004): 627–51.

Lovatt, Anna. "Palimpsests: Inscription and Memory in the Work of Michelle Stuart." In *Michelle Stuart: Drawn from Nature*, edited by Anna Lovatt. Exh. cat. Djanogly Art Gallery, University of Nottingham; Berlin: Hatje Cantz Verlag, 2013.

Lyotard, Jean-François. *Discours, figure*. Paris: Éditions Klincksieck, 1971.

Malabou, Catherine. *Ontology of the Accident: An Essay on Destructive Plasticity*. Translated by Carolyn Shread. Cambridge: Polity Press, 2012.

McCollum, Allan. "Allan McCollum Interviewed by Thomas Lawson." Originally published in *Allan McCollum*. Los Angeles: A.R.T., 1996. http://allanmccollum.net/allanmcnyc/Lawson_AMc_Interview.html

Man Ray. "The Age of Light." In *Classic Essays on Photography*, edited by Alan Trachtenberg, 169–78. New Haven, CT: Leete's Island Books, 1980.

Marey, Étienne-Jules. *La méthode graphique dans les sciences experimentales, et principalement en physiologie et en médicine.* Paris, 1885.

Margulies, Ivone. *Nothing Happens: Chantal Akerman's Hyperrealist Everyday.* Durham, NC: Duke University Press, 1996.

Marrinan, Michael, and John Bender. *The Culture of the Diagram.* Stanford, CA: Stanford University Press, 2010.

Merewether, Charles, ed. *The Archive.* Documents of Contemporary Art. Boston: MIT Press; London: Whitechapel Art Gallery, 2006.

———. "A Lasting Impression." In *Trace*, 164–71. 1st Liverpool Biennial of International Contemporary Art and Tate Gallery Liverpool, curated by Anthony Bond, 1999.

Minato, Chihiro. "Is There a Future for Our Past?" In *Masao Okabe, Is There a Future for Our Past? The Dark Face of the Light*, edited by Chihiro Minato, 181–97. Tokyo: University of Tokyo Press, 2007.

Mitchell, William. "Digital Images and the Postmodern Era." In *The Reconfigured Eye: Visual Truth in the Post-Photographic Era*, 8–11. Cambridge, MA: MIT Press, 1992.

Molesworth, Helen. *Part Object Part Sculpture.* Exh. cat. Wexner Center for the Arts, Ohio State University. Philadelphia: Pennsylvania University Press, 2005.

Mulvey, Laura. "The Index and the Uncanny: Life and Death in the Photography." In *Death 24x a Second: Stillness and Moving Image*, 54–66. London: Reaktion Books, 2006.

Newman, Michael. "Salvage." In *Tacita Dean: Selected Writings, Seven Books*, 21–31. Paris: Musée de la Ville de Paris; Göttingen: Steidl, 2003.

Nietzsche, Friedrich. *The Birth of Tragedy and The Case of Wagner.* Translated by Walter Kaufmann. New York: Random House, 1967.

O'Doherty, Brian. "Taking Duchamp's Portrait." Unpublished transcript of lecture delivered at the Edgar P. Richardson Symposium on Portraiture, Donald W. Reynolds Center for American Art and Portraiture, Washington, DC, March 27, 2009.

O'Dwyer, Deirdre, ed. *Susan Morris, Sontag Montag*, London: Five Years, 2009.

Orozco, Gabriel. "In Conversation with Guillermo Santamarina." *Gabriel Orozco.* Exh. cat. Museo Nacional Centro de Arte Reina Sofia, Madrid, 2005.

———. *Photogravity.* Exh. cat. Philadelphia Museum of Art, 1999.

Pagé, Suzanne, Wenzel Jacob, Björn Springfield, Kaspar König, and Benjamin H. D. Buchloh. *Gerhard Richter: Catalogue Raisonné, 1962–1993.* Berlin: Hatje Cantz Verlag, 1993.

Patrick Ireland: The Duchamp Portrait 1966/67. Exh. cat. Corcoran Art Gallery, Washington, DC, 1974.

Peirce, Charles Sanders. *Collected Papers.* Cambridge, MA: Harvard University Press, 1960.

Phillips, David. "Photo-Logos: Photography and Deconstruction." In *The Subjects of Art History: Historical Objects in Contemporary Perspectives*, edited by Mark A. Cheetham, Michael Ann Holly, and Keith Moxey, 155–57. Cambridge: Cambridge University Press, 1999.

Pollock, Griselda. *After-affects/After-images: Trauma and Aesthetic Transformation in the Virtual Feminist Museum.* Manchester: Manchester University Press, 2013.

———. "Mary Kelly's *Ballad of Kastriot Rexhepi*: Virtual Trauma and Indexical Witness in the Age of Mediatic Spectacle." In *Digital and Other Virtualities: Renegotiating the Image*, edited by Antony Bryant and Griselda Pollock, 200–216. London: I. B. Tauris, 2012.

———. "New Encounters: Arts, Cultures, Concepts." In *Digital and Other Virtualities: Renegotiating the Image*, edited by Antony Bryant and Griselda Pollock, xiii–xviii. London: I. B. Tauris, 2010.

Porter, Fairfield. "The Education of Jasper Johns." *Artnews* 62, no. 10 (February 1964): 44–45, 61–62.

Proust, Marcel. *The Way by Swann's.* In *In Search of Lost Time*, trans. Lydia Davis. London: Penguin Books, 2002.

Quinton, Francois. "There Is No Innocent Room." In Francesco Bonami, Francois Quinton, and Régis Durand, *Thomas Demand*, 35–68. Exh. cat. Fondation Cartier pour l'art contemporain, Paris. London: Thames and Hudson, 2000.

Rancière, Jacques. *The Future of the Image.* London: Verso, 2007.

Richter, Gerhard. *Atlas.* Edited by Helmut Friedel. London: Thames and Hudson, 2006.

———. *October 18, 1977.* London: ICA and Anthony D'Offay Gallery, 1989.

———. *Text: Writings, Interviews and Letters, 1961–2007.* Edited by Dietmar Elger and Hans Ulrich Obrist. London: Thames and Hudson, 2009.

Richter, Gerhard, and Nicholas Serota. "I Have Nothing to Say and I'm Saying It." In *Gerhard Richter: Panorama, A Retrospective*, 15–27. Exh. cat. Tate Modern, London; Nationalgalerie, Berlin; Centre Pompidou, Paris. London: Tate Publishing, 2011.

Richter, Gerhard, and Robert Storr. *Gerhard Richter, October 18, 1977.* New York: Museum of Modern Art, 2002.

Rilke, Rainer Maria. *Duino Elegies.* Translated by C. F. MacIntyre. New York: Dover, 2007.

———. *Duino Elegies.* Translated by Stephen Mitchell. In *Ahead of All Parting: The Selected Poetry and Prose of Rainer Maria Rilke.* New York: Modern Library, 1995.

———. *The Notebooks of Malte Laurids Brigge.* Translated by M. D. Herter Norton. New York: W. W. Norton, 1964.

———. "Primal Sound." In *Rodin and other Prose Pieces*, translated by G. Craig Houston, 127–32. London: Quartet Books, 1986.

———. *Rilke on Love and Other Difficulties.* Translated by John J. L. Mood. New York: W. W. Norton, 1975.

Ristelhueber, Sophie. *Aftermath: Kuwait 1991.* London: Thames and Hudson, 1992.

Rodowick, D. N. *Reading the Figural; or, Philosophy after New Media.* Durham, NC: Duke University Press, 2001.

Rosen, Phillip. *Change Mummified: Cinema, Historicity, Theory.* Minneapolis: University of Minnesota Press, 2001.

Ruby, Andreas. "Thomas Demand, Memoryscapes." *Parkett* 62 (2001): 118–25.

Saltzman, Lisa. *Anselm Kiefer and Art after Auschwitz.* Cambridge: Cambridge University Press, 1999.

———. "Faraway, So Close: Mythic Origins, Contemporary Art: The Case of Kara Walker." In *Contemporary Art and Classical Myth*, edited by Isabelle Wallace and Jennie Hirsh, 19–39. Surrey: Ashgate, 2011.

———. *Making Memory Matter: Strategies of Remembrance in Contemporary Art*. Chicago: University of Chicago Press, 2006.

Saltzman, Lisa, and Eric Rosenberg, eds. *Trauma and Visuality in Modernity*. Hanover, NH: University Press of New England, 2006.

Santner, Eric L. *On Creaturely Life: Rilke, Benjamin, Sebald*. Chicago: University of Chicago Press, 2006.

Schapiro, Meyer. "On Some Problems in the Semiotics of Visual Art: Field and Vehicle in Image-Signs" (1969). In *Theory and Philosophy of Art: Style, Artist, and Society*, 1–32. New York: George Braziller, 1994.

———. *Words and Pictures: On the Literal and the Symbolic in the Illustration of a Text*. The Hague: Mouton, 1973.

Sebald, W. G. "As Day and Night, Chalk and Cheese: On the Pictures of Jan Peter Tripp." In W. G. Sebald and Jan Peter Tripp, *Unrecounted*. Translated by Michael Hamburger. London: Penguin Books, 2004.

———. *Austerlitz*. Translated by Anthea Bell. London: Penguin Books, 2001.

———. *The Immigrants* (1992). Translated by Michael Hulse. London: Harvil Press, 1996.

———. *Logis in einem Landhaus*. Frankfurt am Main: Fischer Verlag, 1989.

———. "St. Jerome Lecture 2001: W. G. Sebald in Conversation with Maya Jaggi and Anthea Bell." *In Other Words: The Journal of Literary Translators* 21 (Summer 2003): 5–18.

Semin, Didier. "From the *Impossible Life* to the *Exemplary Life*." In Didier Semin, Tamar Garb, and Donald Kuspit, *Christian Boltanski*, 46–75. London: Phaidon, 1997.

Shannon, Joshua. *The Disappearance of Objects: Art and the Rise of the Postmodern City*. New Haven, CT: Yale University Press, 2009.

Silverman, Kaja. "The Author as Receiver." *October* 96 (2001): 17–34.

Snyder, Joel. "Photography, Chemical and Numerical." Delivered to the American Society of Aesthetics, Mount Holyoke, November 6, 2008.

———. "Picturing Vision." *Critical Inquiry* 6, no. 3 (Spring 1980): 499–526.

Solakov, Nedko. "Fear." 2003. http://nedkosolakov.net/content/fear/story/index_eng .html

Solomon-Godeau, Abigail. "Mourning or Melancholia: Christian Boltanski's *Missing House*." *Oxford Art Journal* 12, no. 2 (1998): 1–20.

Spector, Nancy. *Felix Gonzalez-Torres*. Exh. cat. Guggenheim Museum, New York, March 3–May 10, 1995.

Spies, Werner, ed. *Max Ernst Frottages*. Translated by Joseph M. Bernstein. London: Thames and Hudson, 1969.

Steedman, Carolyn. *Dust: The Archive and Cultural History*. New Brunswick, NJ: Rutgers University Press, 2002.

Steinberg, Leo. "Contemporary Art and the Plight of Its Public." In *Other Criteria: Confrontations with Twentieth-Century Art*, 3–16. New York: Oxford University Press, 1972.

———. "Jasper Johns: The First Seven Years of His Art." In *Other Criteria: Confrontations with Twentieth-Century Art*, 17–54. New York: Oxford University Press, 1972.

———. "Other Criteria." In *Other Criteria: Confrontations with Twentieth-Century Art*, 55–91. New York: Oxford University Press, 1972.

———. "Reflections on the State of Criticism," *Artforum* 10, no. 7 (March 1972): 36–49.

Stokes, Adrian. *Reflections on the Nude* (1967). In *The Critical Writing of Adrian Stokes*, edited by Lawrence Gowing. Vol. 3, *1955–1967*, 301–42. London: Thames and Hudson, 1978.

———. *Stones of Rimini* (1934). In *The Critical Writing of Adrian Stokes*, edited by Lawrence Gowing. Vol. 1, *1930–1937*, 181–82. London: Thames and Hudson, 1978.

Tagg, John. *The Burden of Representation: Essays on Photographic Histories*. Amherst: University of Massachusetts Press, 1988.

Trauma. Exh. cat. National Touring Exhibitions, Hayward Gallery, London, 2001.

Vidler, Anthony. *The Architectural Uncanny: Essays in the Modern Unhomely*. Cambridge, MA: MIT Press, 1992.

Wajcman, Gérard. "De la croyance photographique." *Les temps modernes* 56, no. 613 (2001): 47–83.

Warner, Marina. "In Conversation with Tacita Dean." In Marina Warner, Jean-Christophe Royoux, and Germaine Greer, *Tacita Dean*, 7–44. London: Phaidon, 2006.

———. "Light Drawing In: The Art of Tacita Dean." In *Gehen* (Walking), edited by Theodora Vischer and Katrin Grogel, 15–28. Basel: Schaulager; Göttingen: Steidl, 2008.

Weibel, Peter. "Repression and Representation: The RAF in German Postwar Art." In *Art of Two Germanys/Cold War Cultures*, edited by Stephanie Barron and Sabine Eckmann, 256–59. New York: Abrams, 2009.

Whiteread, Rachel. "Rachel Whiteread Interviewed by Andrea Rose." In *Rachel Whiteread: British Pavilion, XLVII Venice Biennale*, edited by Ann Gallagher. Translated by Gabriella Le Grazie and Vencenzo Vergiani. Exh. cat. 1997.

Wollen, Peter. "October 18, 1977." In *Paris/Manhattan: Writings on Art*, 75–86. London: Verso, 2004.

———. *Signs and Meaning in the Cinema*. London: BFI, 1969. 5th ed., 2013.

Yacavone, Kathrin. *Benjamin, Barthes and the Singularity of Philosophy*. New York: Continuum, 2012.

Index